PERSPECTIVES

3

Hugh **DELLAR**

Andrew **WALKLEY**

Lewis **LANSFORD**

Daniel **BARBER**

Amanda **JEFFRIES**

Australia • Brazil • Mexico • Singapore • United Kingdom • United States

Perspectives 3a Combo Split
Hugh Dellar, Andrew Walkley, Lewis Lansford, Daniel Barber, Amanda Jeffries

Publisher: Sherrise Roehr

Executive Editor: Sarah Kenney

Publishing Consultant: Karen Spiller

Senior Development Editor: Lewis Thompson

Senior Development Editor: Brenden Layte

Editorial Assistant: Gabe Feldstein

Director of Global Marketing: Ian Martin

Product Marketing Manager: Anders Bylund

Director of Content and Media Production: Michael Burggren

Production Manager: Daisy Sosa

Media Researcher: Leila Hishmeh

Manufacturing Customer Account Manager: Mary Beth Hennebury

Art Director: Brenda Carmichael

Production Management, and Composition: Lumina Datamatics, Inc.

Cover Image: The Hive at Kew Gardens, London. ©Mark Hadden

For product information and technology assistance, contact us at
Cengage Learning Customer & Sales Support, cengage.com/contact
For permission to use material from this text or product, submit all requests online at **cengage.com/permissions**
Further permissions questions can be emailed to
permissionrequest@cengage.com

Student Edition: Level 3 Combo Split A
ISBN: 978-1-337-29742-4

National Geographic Learning
20 Channel Center Street
Boston, MA 02210
USA

National Geographic Learning, a Cengage Learning Company, has a mission to bring the world to the classroom and the classroom to life. With our English language programs, students learn about their world by experiencing it. Through our partnerships with National Geographic and TED Talks, they develop the language and skills they need to be successful global citizens and leaders.

Locate your local office at **international.cengage.com/region**

Visit National Geographic Learning online at **NGL.Cengage.com/ELT**
Visit our corporate website at **www.cengage.com**

4 (tl1) Lutz Jaekel/laif/Redux, (tl2) epa european pressphoto agency b.v./Alamy Stock Photo, (cl) Michael Christopher Brown/Magnum Photos, (bl1) Tasso Marcelo Leal/AFP/Getty Images, (bl2) © Bryce Duffy, **5** (tl1) © Marla Aufmuth/TED, (tl2)(cl)(bl1)(bl2) © James Duncan Davidson/TED, **6** (tl1) Christian Ziegler/National Geographic Creative, (tl2) © Hassan Hajjaj/A-WA, (cl) Yva Momatiuk and John Eastcott/National Geographic Creative, (bl1) VCG/Getty Images, (bl2) © Intuitive Surgical, **7** (tl1)(tl2)(cl) © Ryan Lash/TED, (bl1) © James Duncan Davidson/TED, (bl2) © TED, **8-9** Lutz Jaekel/laif/Redux, **10-11** Digital Vision./Getty Images, **13** Paul Darrows/Reuters, **14** Michael Christopher Brown/Magnum Photos, **15** Paul Chesley/Stone/Getty Images, **16-17** © Marla Aufmuth/TED, **18-19** Ed Norton/Lonely Planet Images/Getty Images, **20-21** epa european pressphoto agency b.v./Alamy Stock Photo, **22-23** © Rainforest Connection, www.rfcx.org, **26** (tl) Morten Falch Sortland/Moment Open/Getty Images, (cl) Ellisha Lee/EyeEm/Getty Images, (bl) wundervisuals/E+/Getty Images, **28-29** © James Duncan Davidson/TED, **30-31** © www.fairafric.com, **32-33** Michael Christopher Brown/Magnum Photos, **34-35** Mirco Lazzari gp/Getty Images Sport/Getty Images, **36** Michael Regan/Getty Images Sport/Getty Images, **38** Harry How/Getty Images Sport/Getty Images, **39** Adrian Dennis/AFP/Getty Images, **40-41** © James Duncan Davidson/TED, **42-43** Giovani Cordioli/Moment/Getty Images, **44-45** Tasso Marcelo Leal/AFP/Getty Images, **46-47** © Jeroen Koolhaas, **48** Juan Barreto/AFP/Getty Images, **50** Scott R Larsen/Moment/Getty Images, **51** David Pereiras/Shutterstock.com, **52-53** © James Duncan Davidson/TED, **54-55** James Bagshaw/Alamy Stock Photo, **56-57** © Bryce Duffy, **58-59** (spread) © National Geographic Learning, **58** (br) Maxx-Studio/Shutterstock.com, **61** Robert Clark/National Geographic Creative, **62** Puwadol Jaturawutthichai/Alamy Stock Photo, **63** © Hero Images/Getty Images, **64-65** © James Duncan Davidson/TED, **66** Sakura Photography/Moment/Getty Images, **67** © National Geographic Learning, **68-69** Christian Ziegler/National Geographic Creative, **70-71** Dietmar Temps, Cologne/Moment/Getty Images, **73** (bgd) Bryan Mullennix/Stockbyte/Getty Images, (inset) Color4260/Shutterstock.com, (t) Thaiview/Shutterstock.com, **74** Wf Sihardian/EyeEm/Getty Images, **75** Jonathan Blair/National Geographic Creative, **76-77** © Ryan Lash/TED, **78-79** Phil Moore/AFP/Getty Images, **80-81** © Hassan Hajjaj/A-WA, **82-83** © Dave Devries, **85** (bdg) tomograf/E+/Getty Images, © National Geographic Learning, **86** Troy Aossey/The Image Bank/Getty Images, **87** XiXinXing/Shutterstock.com, **88-89** © Ryan Lash/TED, **90-91** Thomas Barwick/Taxi/Getty Images, **92-93** Yva Momatiuk and John Eastcott/National Geographic Creative, **94-95** Jiro Ose/Redux, **97** AP Images/Dario Lopez-Mills, **98** Bettmann/Getty Images, **99** © Leila Dougan, **100-101** © Ryan Lash/TED, **102-103** CKN/Getty Images News/Getty Images, **104-105** VCG/Visual China Group/Getty Images, **106-107** © Patrick Meier, **108** Polina Yamshchikov/Redux, **110** Julian Broad/Contour/Getty Images, **111** © Laurie Moy, **112** © James Duncan Davidson/TED, **114** Carrie Vonderhaar/Ocean Futures Society/National Geographic Creative, **116-117** © Intuitive Surgical, **118-119** Reuters/Alamy Stock Photo, **121** Pasieka/Science Source, **122** ZUMA Press, Inc./Alamy Stock Photo, **123** Noor Khamis/Reuters, **124-125** © TED, **126-127** Media Drum World/Alamy Stock Photo.

Printed in China
Print Number: 04 Print Year: 2023

ACKNOWLEDGMENTS

Paulo Rogerio Rodrigues
Escola Móbile, São Paulo, Brazil

Claudia Colla de Amorim
Escola Móbile, São Paulo, Brazil

Antonio Oliveira
Escola Móbile, São Paulo, Brazil

Rory Ruddock
Atlantic International Language Center, Hanoi, Vietnam

Carmen Virginia Pérez Cervantes
La Salle, Mexico City, Mexico

Rossana Patricia Zuleta
CIPRODE, Guatemala City, Guatemala

Gloria Stella Quintero Riveros
Universidad Católica de Colombia, Bogotá, Colombia

Mónica Rodriguez Salvo
MAR English Services, Buenos Aires, Argentina

Itana de Almeida Lins
Grupo Educacional Anchieta, Salvador, Brazil

Alma Loya
Colegio de Chihuahua, Chihuahua, Mexico

María Trapero Dávila
Colegio Teresiano, Ciudad Obregon, Mexico

Silvia Kosaruk
Modern School, Lanús, Argentina

Florencia Adami
Dámaso Centeno, Caba, Argentina

Natan Galed Gomez Cartagena
Global English Teaching, Rionegro, Colombia

James Ubriaco
Colégio Santo Agostinho, Belo Horizonte, Brazil

Ryan Manley
The Chinese University of Hong Kong, Shenzhen, China

Silvia Teles
Colégio Cândido Portinari, Salvador, Brazil

María Camila Azuero Gutiérrez
Fundación Centro Electrónico de Idiomas, Bogotá, Colombia

Martha Ramirez
Colegio San Mateo Apostol, Bogotá, Colombia

Beata Polit
XXIII LO Warszawa, Poland

Beata Tomaszewska
V LO Toruń, Poland

Michał Szkudlarek
I LO Brzeg, Poland

Anna Buchowska
I LO Białystok, Poland

Natalia Maćkowiak
one2one, Kosakowo, Poland

Agnieszka Dończyk
one2one, Kosakowo, Poland

Perspectives teaches learners to think critically and to develop the language skills they need to find their own voice in English. The carefully-guided language lessons, real-world stories, and TED Talks motivate learners to think creatively and communicate effectively.

In *Perspectives*, learners develop:

• AN OPEN MIND

Every unit explores one idea from different perspectives, giving learners opportunities for practicing language as they look at the world in new ways.

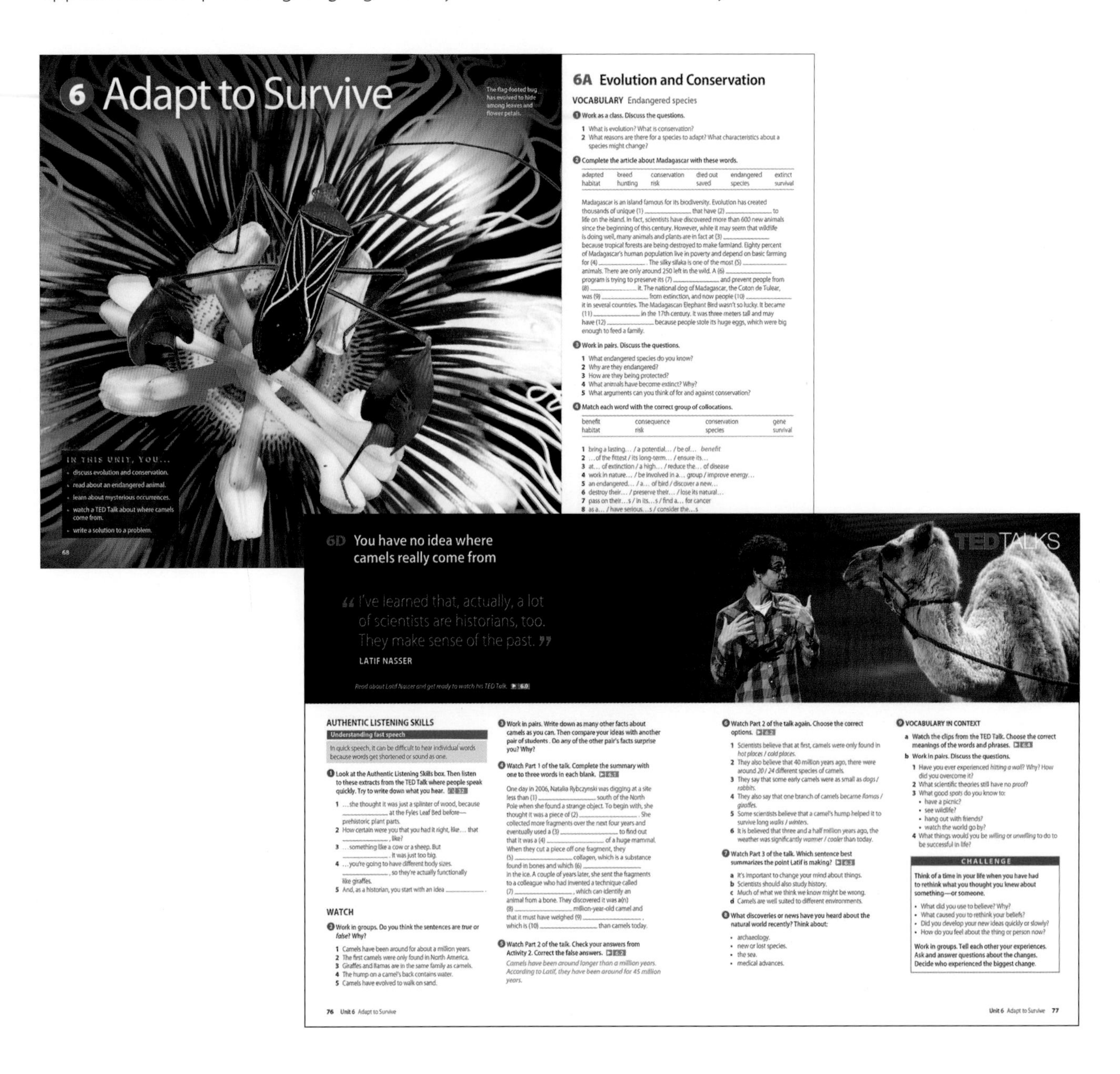

6 Adapt to Survive

The flag-footed bug has evolved to hide among leaves and flower petals.

IN THIS UNIT, YOU...
- discuss evolution and conservation.
- read about an endangered animal.
- learn about mysterious occurrences.
- watch a TED Talk about where camels come from.
- write a solution to a problem.

68

6A Evolution and Conservation

VOCABULARY Endangered species

1 Work as a class. Discuss the questions.

1 What is evolution? What is conservation?
2 What reasons are there for a species to adapt? What characteristics about a species might change?

2 Complete the article about Madagascar with these words.

adapted	breed	conservation	died out	endangered	extinct
habitat	hunting	risk	saved	species	survival

Madagascar is an island famous for its biodiversity. Evolution has created thousands of unique (1) ____ that have (2) ____ to life on the island. In fact, scientists have discovered more than 600 new animals since the beginning of this century. However, while it may seem that wildlife is doing well, many animals and plants are in fact at (3) ____ because tropical forests are being destroyed to make farmland. Eighty percent of Madagascar's human population live in poverty and depend on basic farming for (4) ____. The silky sifaka is one of the most (5) ____ animals. There are only around 250 left in the wild. A (6) ____ program is trying to preserve its (7) ____ and prevent people from (8) ____ it. The national dog of Madagascar, the Coton de Tulear, was (9) ____ from extinction, and now people (10) ____ it in several countries. The Madagascan Elephant Bird wasn't so lucky. It became (11) ____ in the 17th century. It was three meters tall and may have (12) ____ because people stole its huge eggs, which were big enough to feed a family.

3 Work in pairs. Discuss the questions.

1 What endangered species do you know?
2 Why are they endangered?
3 How are they being protected?
4 What animals have become extinct? Why?
5 What arguments can you think of for and against conservation?

4 Match each word with the correct group of collocations.

benefit	consequence	conservation	gene
habitat	risk	species	survival

1 bring a lasting... / a potential... / be of... *benefit*
2 ...of the fittest / its long-term... / ensure its...
3 at... of extinction / a high... / reduce the... of disease
4 work in nature... / be involved in a... group / improve energy...
5 an endangered... / a... of bird / discover a new...
6 destroy their... / preserve their... / lose its natural...
7 pass on their...s / in its...s / find a... for cancer
8 as a... / have serious...s / consider the...s

6D You have no idea where camels really come from

TED TALKS

“I've learned that, actually, a lot of scientists are historians, too. They make sense of the past.”
LATIF NASSER

Read about Latif Nasser and get ready to watch his TED Talk. ▶ 6.0

AUTHENTIC LISTENING SKILLS

Understanding fast speech

In quick speech, it can be difficult to hear individual words because words get shortened or sound as one.

1 Look at the Authentic Listening Skills box. Then listen to these extracts from the TED Talk where people speak quickly. Try to write down what you hear.

1 ... she thought it was just a splinter of wood, because ____ at the Fyles Leaf Bed before—prehistoric plant parts.
2 How certain were you that you had it right, like ... that ____, like?
3 ... something like a cow or a sheep. But ____. It was just too big.
4 ... you're going to have different body sizes. ____, so they're actually functionally like giraffes.
5 And, as a historian, you start with an idea ____.

WATCH

2 Work in groups. Do you think the sentences are *true* or *false*? Why?

1 Camels have been around for about a million years.
2 The first camels were only found in North America.
3 Giraffes and llamas are in the same family as camels.
4 The hump on a camel's back contains water.
5 Camels have evolved to walk on sand.

3 Work in pairs. Write down as many other facts about camels as you can. Then compare your ideas with another pair of students. Do any of the other pair's facts surprise you? Why?

4 Watch Part 1 of the talk. Complete the summary with one to three words in each blank. ▶ 6.1

One day in 2006, Natalia Rybczynski was digging at a site less than (1) ____ south of the North Pole when she found a strange object. To begin with, she thought it was a piece of (2) ____. She collected more fragments over the next four years and eventually used a (3) ____ to find out that it was a (4) ____ of a huge mammal. When they cut a piece off one fragment, they (5) ____ collagen, which is a substance found in bones and which (6) ____ in the ice. A couple of years later, she sent the fragments to a colleague who had invented a technique called (7) ____, which can identify an animal from a bone. They discovered it was a(n) (8) ____ million-year-old camel and that it must have weighed (9) ____, which is (10) ____ than camels today.

5 Watch Part 2 of the talk. Check your answers from Activity 2. Correct the false answers. ▶ 6.2

Camels have been around longer than a million years. According to Latif, they have been around for 45 million years.

6 Watch Part 2 of the talk again. Choose the correct options. ▶ 6.2

1 Scientists believe that at first, camels were only found in *hot places / cold places*.
2 They also believe that 40 million years ago, there were around *20 / 24* different species of camels.
3 They say that some early camels were as small as *dogs / rabbits*.
4 They also say that one branch of camels became *llamas / giraffes*.
5 Some scientists believe that a camel's hump helped it to survive long *walks / winters*.
6 It is believed that three and a half million years ago, the weather was significantly *warmer / cooler* than today.

7 Watch Part 3 of the talk. Which sentence best summarizes the point Latif is making? ▶ 6.3

a It's important to change your mind about things.
b Scientists should also study history.
c Much of what we think we know might be wrong.
d Camels are well suited to different environments.

8 What discoveries or news have you heard about the natural world recently? Think about:

- archaeology.
- new or lost species.
- the sea.
- medical advances.

9 VOCABULARY IN CONTEXT

a Watch the clips from the TED Talk. Choose the correct meanings of the words and phrases. ▶ 6.4

b Work in pairs. Discuss the questions.

1 Have you ever experienced *hitting a wall*? Why? How did you overcome it?
2 What scientific theories still have no *proof*?
3 What good spots do you know to:
- have a picnic?
- see wildlife?
- hang out with friends?
- watch the world go by?

4 What things would you be *willing* or *unwilling* to do to be successful in life?

CHALLENGE

Think of a time in your life when you have had to rethink what you thought you knew about something—or someone.

- What did you use to believe? Why?
- What caused you to rethink your beliefs?
- Did you develop your new ideas quickly or slowly?
- How do you feel about the thing or person now?

Work in groups. Tell each other your experiences. Ask and answer questions about the changes. Decide who experienced the biggest change.

76 Unit 6 Adapt to Survive

Unit 6 Adapt to Survive 77

• A CRITICAL EYE

Students learn the critical thinking skills and strategies they need to evaluate new information and develop their own opinions and ideas to share.

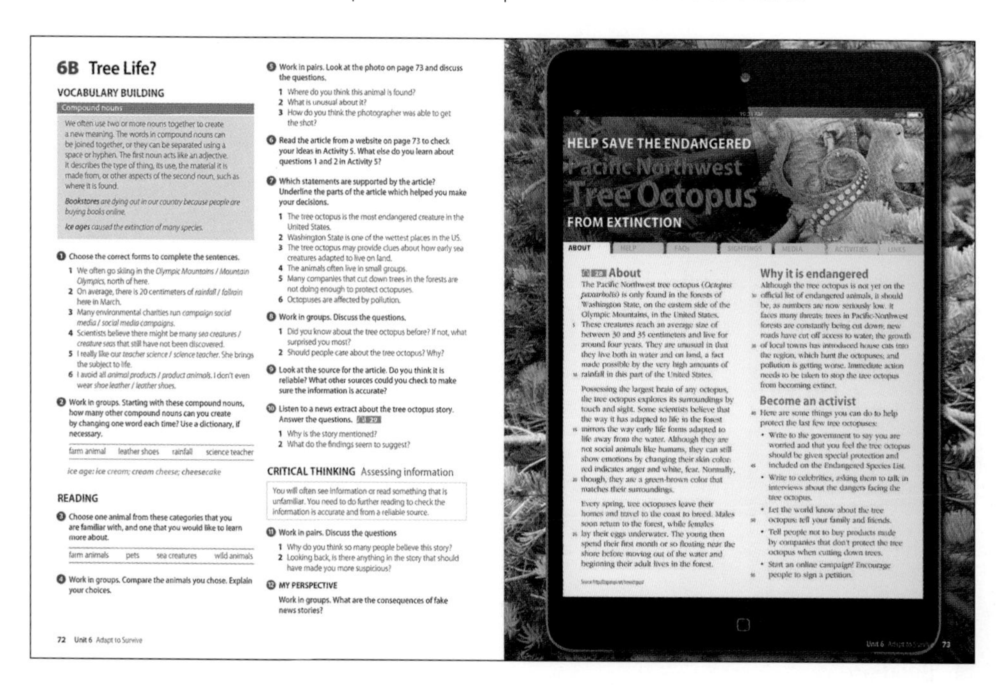

6B Tree Life?

VOCABULARY BUILDING

Compound nouns

We often use two or more nouns together to create a new meaning. The words in compound nouns can be joined together, or they can be separated using a space or hyphen. The first noun acts like an adjective. It describes the type of thing, its use, the material it is made from, or other aspects of the second noun, such as where it is found.

***Bookstores** are dying out in our country because people are buying books online.*

***Ice ages** caused the extinction of many species.*

1 Choose the correct forms to complete the sentences.

1. We often go skiing in the *Olympic Mountains / Mountain Olympics*, north of here.
2. On average, there is 20 centimeters of *rainfall / fallrain* here in March.
3. Many environmental charities run *campaign social media / social media campaigns*.
4. Scientists believe there might be many *sea creatures / creature seas* that still have not been discovered.
5. I really like our *teacher science / science teacher*. She brings the subject to life.
6. I avoid all *animal products / product animals*. I don't even wear *shoe leather / leather shoes*.

2 Work in groups. Starting with these compound nouns, how many other compound nouns can you create by changing one word each time? Use a dictionary, if necessary.

farm animal   leather shoes   rainfall   science teacher

ice age: ice cream; cream cheese; cheesecake

READING

3 Choose one animal from these categories that you are familiar with, and one that you would like to learn more about.

farm animals   pets   sea creatures   wild animals

4 Work in groups. Compare the animals you chose. Explain your choices.

5 Work in pairs. Look at the photo on page 73 and discuss the questions.

1. Where do you think this animal is found?
2. What is unusual about it?
3. How do you think the photographer was able to get the shot?

6 Read the article from a website on page 73 to check your ideas in Activity 5. What else do you learn about questions 1 and 2 in Activity 5?

7 Which statements are supported by the article? Underline the parts of the article which helped you make your decisions.

1. The tree octopus is the most endangered creature in the United States.
2. Washington State is one of the wettest places in the US.
3. The tree octopus may provide clues about how early sea creatures adapted to live on land.
4. The animals often live in small groups.
5. Many companies that cut down trees in the forests are not doing enough to protect octopuses.
6. Octopuses are affected by pollution.

8 Work in groups. Discuss the questions.

1. Did you know about the tree octopus before? If not, what surprised you most?
2. Should people care about the tree octopus? Why?

9 Look at the source for the article. Do you think it is reliable? What other sources could you check to make sure the information is accurate?

10 Listen to a news extract about the tree octopus story. Answer the questions.

1. Why is the story mentioned?
2. What do the findings seem to suggest?

CRITICAL THINKING Assessing information

You will often see information or read something that is unfamiliar. You need to do further reading to check the information is accurate and from a reliable source.

11 Work in pairs. Discuss the questions

1. Why do you think so many people believe this story?
2. Looking back, is there anything in the story that should have made you more suspicious?

12 MY PERSPECTIVE

Work in groups. What are the consequences of fake news stories?

72 Unit 6 Adapt to Survive

HELP SAVE THE ENDANGERED
Pacific Northwest
Tree Octopus
FROM EXTINCTION

ABOUT | HELP | FAQs | SIGHTINGS | MEDIA | ACTIVITIES | LINKS

About

The Pacific Northwest tree octopus (*Octopus paxarbolis*) is only found in the forests of Washington State, on the eastern side of the Olympic Mountains, in the United States. These creatures reach an average size of between 30 and 35 centimeters and live for around four years. They are unusual in that they live both in water and on land, a fact made possible by the very high amounts of rainfall in this part of the United States.

Possessing the largest brain of any octopus, the tree octopus explores its surroundings by touch and sight. Some scientists believe that the way it has adapted to life in the forest mirrors the way early life forms adapted to life away from the water. Although they are not social animals like humans, they can still show emotions by changing their skin color: red indicates anger and white, fear. Normally, though, they are a green-brown color that matches their surroundings.

Every spring, tree octopuses leave their homes and travel to the coast to breed. Males soon return to the forest, while females lay their eggs underwater. The young then spend their first month or so floating near the shore before moving out of the water and beginning their adult lives in the forest.

Why it is endangered

Although the tree octopus is not yet on the official list of endangered animals, it should be, as numbers are now seriously low. It faces many threats: trees in Pacific Northwest forests are constantly being cut down; new roads have cut off access to water; the growth of local towns has introduced house cats into the region, which hunt the octopuses; and pollution is getting worse. Immediate action needs to be taken to stop the tree octopus from becoming extinct.

Become an activist

Here are some things you can do to help protect the last few tree octopuses:

- Write to the government to say you are worried and that you feel the tree octopus should be given special protection and included on the Endangered Species List.
- Write to celebrities, asking them to talk in interviews about the dangers facing the tree octopus.
- Let the world know about the tree octopus: tell your family and friends.
- Tell people not to buy products made by companies that don't protect the tree octopus when cutting down trees.
- Start an online campaign! Encourage people to sign a petition.

Unit 6 Adapt to Survive 73

• A CLEAR VOICE

Students respond to the unit theme and express their own ideas confidently in English.

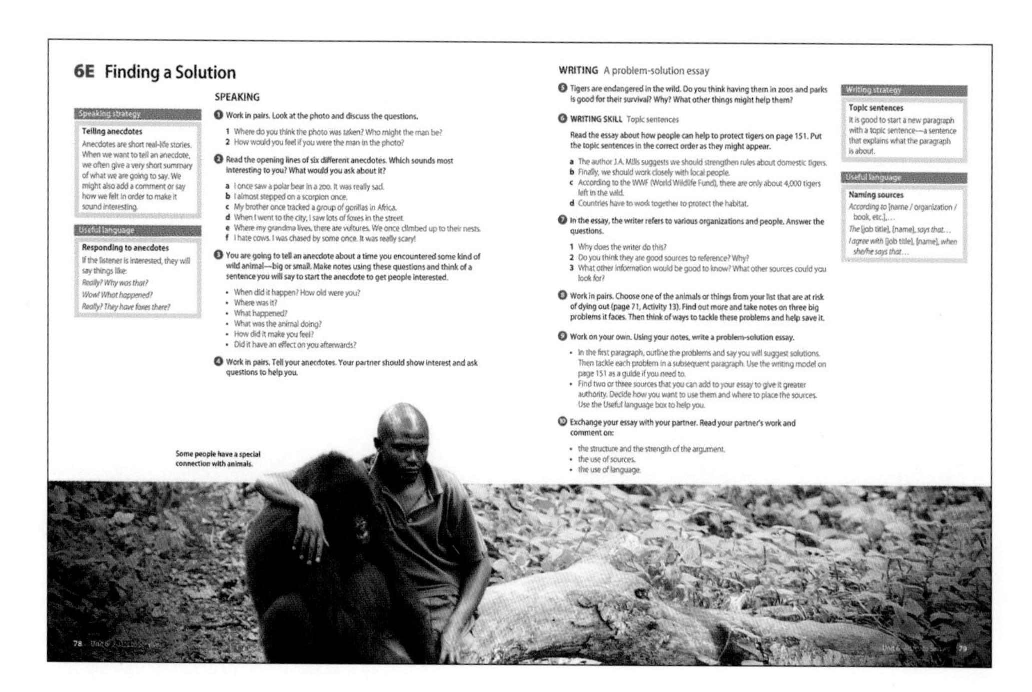

6E Finding a Solution

Speaking strategy

Telling anecdotes

Anecdotes are short real-life stories. When we want to tell an anecdote, we often give a very short summary of what we are going to say. We might also add a comment or say how we felt in order to make it sound interesting.

Useful language

Responding to anecdotes

If the listener is interested, they will say things like:

Really? Why was that?

Wow! What happened?

Really? They have foxes there?

SPEAKING

1 Work in pairs. Look at the photo and discuss the questions.

1. Where do you think the photo was taken? Who might the man be?
2. How would you feel if you were the man in the photo?

2 Read the opening lines of six different anecdotes. Which sounds most interesting to you? What would you ask about it?

a. I once saw a polar bear in a zoo. It was really sad.
b. I almost stepped on a scorpion once.
c. My brother once tracked a group of gorillas in Africa.
d. When I went to the city, I saw lots of foxes in the street.
e. Where my grandma lives, there are vultures. We once climbed up to their nests.
f. I hate cows. I was chased by some once. It was really scary!

3 You are going to tell an anecdote about a time you encountered some kind of wild animal—big or small. Make notes using these questions and think of a sentence you will say to start the anecdote to get people interested.

- When did it happen? How old were you?
- Where was it?
- What happened?
- What was the animal doing?
- How did it make you feel?
- Did it have an effect on you afterwards?

4 Work in pairs. Tell your anecdotes. Your partner should show interest and ask questions to help you.

Some people have a special connection with animals.

WRITING A problem-solution essay

5 Tigers are endangered in the wild. Do you think having them in zoos and parks is good for their survival? Why? What other things might help them?

6 WRITING SKILL Topic sentences

Read the essay about how people can help to protect tigers on page 151. Put the topic sentences in the correct order as they might appear.

a. The author J.A. Mills suggests we should strengthen rules about domestic tigers.
b. Finally, we should work closely with local people.
c. According to the WWF (World Wildlife Fund), there are only about 4,000 tigers left in the wild.
d. Countries have to work together to protect the habitat.

7 In the essay, the writer refers to various organizations and people. Answer the questions.

1. Why does the writer do this?
2. Do you think they are good sources to reference? Why?
3. What other information would be good to know? What other sources could you look for?

8 Work in pairs. Choose one of the animals or things from your list that are at risk of dying out (page 71, Activity 13). Find out more and take notes on three big problems it faces. Then think of ways to tackle these problems and help save it.

9 Work on your own. Using your notes, write a problem-solution essay.

- In the first paragraph, outline the problems and say you will suggest solutions. Then tackle each problem in a subsequent paragraph. Use the writing model on page 151 as a guide if you need to.
- Find two or three sources that you can add to your essay to give it greater authority. Decide how you want to use them and where to place the sources. Use the Useful language box to help you.

10 Exchange your essay with your partner. Read your partner's work and comment on:

- the structure and the strength of the argument.
- the use of sources.
- the use of language.

Writing strategy

Topic sentences

It is good to start a new paragraph with a topic sentence—a sentence that explains what the paragraph is about.

Useful language

Naming sources

According to [name / organization / book, etc.],…

The [job title], [name], *says that…*

I agree with [job title], [name], *when she/he says that…*

CONTENTS

GRAMMAR	TED TALKS		SPEAKING	WRITING
Used to and *would* **Pronunciation** *To* in natural speech	How Airbnb designs for trust	**JOE GEBBIA** Joe Gebbia's idea worth spreading is that we can design products, services, and experiences that feel more local, authentic, and that strengthen human connections. **Authentic Listening Skills** Reporting	Advice / Making recom-mendations	A review **Writing Skill** Adding comments
Verb patterns (*-ing* or infinitive with *to*)	This is what happens when you reply to spam email	**JAMES VEITCH** James Veitch's idea worth spreading is that spam email can lead us to some surprising, bizarre, and often hilarious exchanges with others. **Authentic Listening Skills** Intonation and pitch	Persuading	A persuasive article **Writing Skill** Getting people's attention **Pronunciation** Intonation for persuasion
Comparatives and superlatives **Pronunciation** Linking words together in fast speech	Are athletes really getting faster, better, stronger?	**DAVID EPSTEIN** David Epstein's idea worth spreading is that the amazing achievements of many modern-day athletes are thanks to a complex set of factors, not just natural ability. **Authentic Listening Skills** Slowing down and stressing words	Reporting findings	A survey **Writing Skill** Describing statistics
Future forms 2 **Pronunciation** Contrastive stress	Building a Park in the Sky	**ROBERT HAMMOND** Robert Hammond's idea worth spreading is that we can work together to turn abandoned and neglected parts of our cities into vibrant community spaces. **Authentic Listening Skills** Recognizing words you know	Making suggestions	A *for* and *against* essay **Writing Skill** Introducing arguments
Passives 2	Science is for everyone, kids included	**BEAU LOTTO AND AMY O'TOOLE** Beau Lotto and Amy O'Toole's idea worth spreading is that all of us can be scientists if we approach the world with the curiosity, interest, innocence, and zeal of children. **Authentic Listening Skills** Fillers	Staging and hypothesizing	A scientific method **Writing Skill** Describing a process

1 Travel, Trust, and Tourism

IN THIS UNIT, YOU...

- talk about student exchanges and study-abroad programs.
- read about a disappearing way of traveling for free.
- learn about the Grand Tours that were popular in the past.
- watch a TED Talk about how design can build trust between strangers.
- write a review of a place you have visited.

Jemaa el-Fnaa is a square and a marketplace in Marrakesh, Morocco. Every evening, food stalls and entertainers attract local people and tourists to the main square of the city.

1A Cultural Exchange

VOCABULARY Experiences abroad

1 Work in pairs. Discuss the questions.

1. What do you normally do on vacation?
2. Have you been abroad? If yes, where? If no, would you like to? Why?
3. What do you know about student exchanges and study-abroad programs?

2 Check that you understand the words and phrases in bold. Use a dictionary, if necessary. Then tell your partner which experiences you think are good and which are bad. Give your reasons.

1. be **left to your own devices**
2. experience **culture shock**
3. find people very **welcoming**
4. **get a real feel for** the place
5. get **food poisoning**
6. get **robbed**
7. go **hiking** in the mountains
8. **hang out** with local people
9. **lie around** a house all day
10. see all **the sights**
11. stay in **a B&B**
12. stay with **a host family**
13. take a while to **get used to the food**
14. travel **off the beaten path**

3 Work in groups. Look at the words and phrases in Activity 2. Discuss the questions.

1. Which are the most connected to visitors to your country? The least?
2. Which have you done, or which have happened to you? When?
3. Which three do you most want to remember and use? Why?

4 Work in pairs. Look at the photo and discuss the questions.

1. How is the market different from markets near where you live? How would visiting this place make you feel? Why?
2. Which words and phrases from Activity 2 can you use to describe what is happening? Make a list. Then explain your choices to a partner.

5 Complete the description with words or phrases from Activity 2.

In the past, it was very common for teenagers to do student exchanges, where they would go abroad and stay in each other's homes. The idea was not only to learn a new language, but also to (1) _______________ with the local teenagers, go to their school, and get a (2) _______________ the place and culture. Sometimes the (3) _______________ was very welcoming and students got along well with the people in the home; other times the (4) _______________ was too much. The students couldn't (5) _______________ the food and ended up being left to their (6) _______________. Maybe that's why these days it is more common for teenagers to go on a group trip abroad, where everyone stays in a (7) _______________ or hostel together. During the trip, students go and see (8) _______________ and only briefly meet up with a group from a local school. This way teenagers don't (9) _______________ a foreign house all day, and there is no awkwardness. The worst that could happen might be a case of (10) _______________ from a bad clam and some sore feet from walking around the town.

6 Work in pairs. Do you think that the old or new way of doing student exchanges is better? Why?

LISTENING

7 Listen to the first part of a podcast about study-abroad programs. Find out: 1

1 who can do these programs.
2 how long people can go abroad and study for.
3 when the system started.
4 what the possible benefits are.

8 Listen to Kenji and Catalina. Answer the questions. 2

1 Where did they do their study-abroad programs?
2 How long did they stay for?
3 Did the trip increase their understanding of other cultures and develop their language skills? If yes, how do you know?

9 Work in pairs. Are the sentences *true* or *false*? Listen again to check your answers. 2

1 Kenji had visited several countries before studying abroad in Munich.
2 He was really excited about studying abroad.
3 His host family helped him develop a better understanding of the German language.
4 He's still in touch with his host family.
5 Catalina has family roots* in Italy.
6 She felt at home as soon as she arrived.
7 After a few weeks, she spoke enough Italian to do what she needed to do.
8 She's glad she went to Italy, but has no plans to go back.

family roots *original place where a family is from*

10 MY PERSPECTIVE

Work in pairs. Think of two more benefits and three possible issues students might face when doing a study-abroad program. Then discuss the questions.

1 What do you think the biggest benefit is? Why?
2 What do you think the biggest issue is? Why?

GRAMMAR Present and past forms

11 Look at the sentences in the Grammar box. Then answer the questions.

1 Which two are about the present?
2 Which four are about the past?
3 Which two describe actions that happened before something else in the past?
4 Which three use simple forms?
5 Which three use continuous forms?

Present and past forms

a *I was actually thinking about canceling my trip.*
b *I'd been wanting to go there for ages.*
c *We're talking about study-abroad programs.*
d *I'd never left Argentina!*
e *I spent six months in Germany last year.*
f *I miss my host family.*

Check the Grammar Reference for more information and practice.

Some study-abroad programs allow students to visit countries like China, where they can go to places like the Great Wall.

12 **Match the rules (1–6) with the examples (a–f) in the Grammar box.**

1 We use **the simple present** to talk about habits, permanent states, and things that are generally true.
2 We use **the present continuous** to talk about actions we see as temporary, in progress, and unfinished.
3 We use **the simple past** to describe finished actions in the past, especially when there is one finished action after another.
4 We use **the past continuous** to emphasize an action in progress around a time in the past.
5 We use **the simple past perfect** to emphasize that one thing happened before a particular point in the past.
6 We use **the past perfect continuous** to talk about an action that was in progress over a period of time *up to* or *before* a particular point in the past.

13 **Complete the text with the correct form of each verb.**

I really (1) ___________ (love) traveling. It's probably the most important thing in my life. I'm 17, and I (2) ___________ (plan) to spend the summer on a National Geographic Student Expedition! I actually (3) ___________ (go) on my first adventure trip a few years ago when I (4) ___________ (spend) two months in China. It was the first time I (5) ___________ (ever / go) abroad, and I (6) ___________ (love) every minute of it! While we (7) ___________ (stay) in Beijing, we (8) ___________ (visit) the Great Wall of China, which was something I (9) ___________ (dream) of doing ever since I was a child. It was amazing! I (10) ___________ (hope) to do an expedition to Iceland next year and stay somewhere really off the beaten path.

14 **Complete the pairs of sentences with the correct simple form of one of the verbs and the correct continuous form of the other.**

1a We usually ___________ (spend) the summers with my grandparents at their house on the coast.
1b This summer, though, my brother is in Costa Rica. He ___________ (stay) with a host family there.
2a This weekend I ___________ (go) hiking in the mountains with some friends.
2b The bus ___________ (leave) at six every morning, so we should be at the station 15 minutes before.
3a I ___________ (get) really bad food poisoning while I was in Scotland. I have no idea why!
3b Things got worse when somebody stole my suitcase while I ___________ (wait) in line to buy train tickets to Glasgow.
4a I spoke good French by the time I left Quebec because I ___________ (hang out) with the locals for the last few months of the ski season.
4b It was a great trip, but it was scary, because I ___________ never ___________ (try) skiing before.

15 **Choose one of the situations below. Then plan what you want to say about where you were, when you went, and what happened. Think about how to use all four past forms at least once.**

a Something that happened while you were on vacation
b A time you stayed with other people
c A place you have visited

16 **Work in pairs. Tell each other your stories.**

1B Ask for a Ride

VOCABULARY BUILDING

Phrasal verbs

Phrasal verbs are often used in conversation instead of more formal words. They are very common in English. The meaning of a verb often changes when it is used in a phrasal verb.

1 **Rewrite the words in italics using the correct forms of these phrasal verbs.**

break down	come down to	line up
pick up	pull over	turn out

1. They offered to give me a ride to the airport and *got me* from the hotel at eight o'clock.
2. The bus *stopped working* on the way there, so we were five hours late.
3. It was New Year's Day, so I had to *wait in line* for hours to get a train ticket.
4. I think the changes *are basically because of* two things: wealth and technology.
5. A car *stopped by the side of the road* and the driver asked us for directions.
6. I was worried because I'd never been abroad before, but everything *was* great in the end.

2 **Write sentences using these phrasal verbs.**

hang out	lie around	look after	step out

3 **Work in pairs. Look at the photo on page 13 and discuss the questions.**

1. What is happening?
2. Which of the phrasal verbs from Activity 1 can you connect to the photo? Explain your choices.

READING

4 **Read the article about hitchhiking. Match these headings with the numbered paragraphs.**

a Fear
b More wealth
c New needs and opportunities
d Legal restrictions
e Low-cost flights
f Greater access to cars

5 **Work in pairs. Which of these ideas does the author present? What evidence is given?**

1. There used to be far more hitchhikers.
2. There was a high number of robberies involving hitchhikers.
3. It's difficult to find a place to hitchhike these days.
4. More people drive now than in the past.
5. Air travel is safer than driving or hitchhiking.
6. We are wasting a lot of energy by driving alone.
7. People only hitchhike now if they are poor.
8. Hitchhiking brings benefits to communities and individuals.

6 **Work in pairs. Imagine you are standing at the side of a road, trying to hitchhike. Tell your story. Before you do, talk and make notes about:**

- where you are going.
- why you are hitchhiking.
- how you are feeling.
- what happens next.
- how the story ends.

7 **Tell your stories to other people in your class. Vote on the best one. Explain why it is the best story.**

CRITICAL THINKING Evaluating ideas

Evaluating ideas and judging them against other perspectives helps to form a basis for developing your own point of view.

8 **Work in groups. Discuss the questions.**

1. Which is the most important reason the author gives for the decline in hitchhiking? Do you agree? How important are the other reasons?
2. What comparison does the author provide from the website Wand'rly? Is it a fair comparison? Why?
3. How is the example of hitchhiking in Virginia different from other kinds? Does this make it safer? Why?
4. Why do you think the author says he gained a different perspective from other tourists? Do you think that is true? Do you think his perspective was better? Why?

9 **MY PERSPECTIVE**

Work in pairs. Discuss the questions.

1. Do you think hitchhiking is a good idea? What other reasons could there be for doing it?
2. How could you make hitchhiking safer?

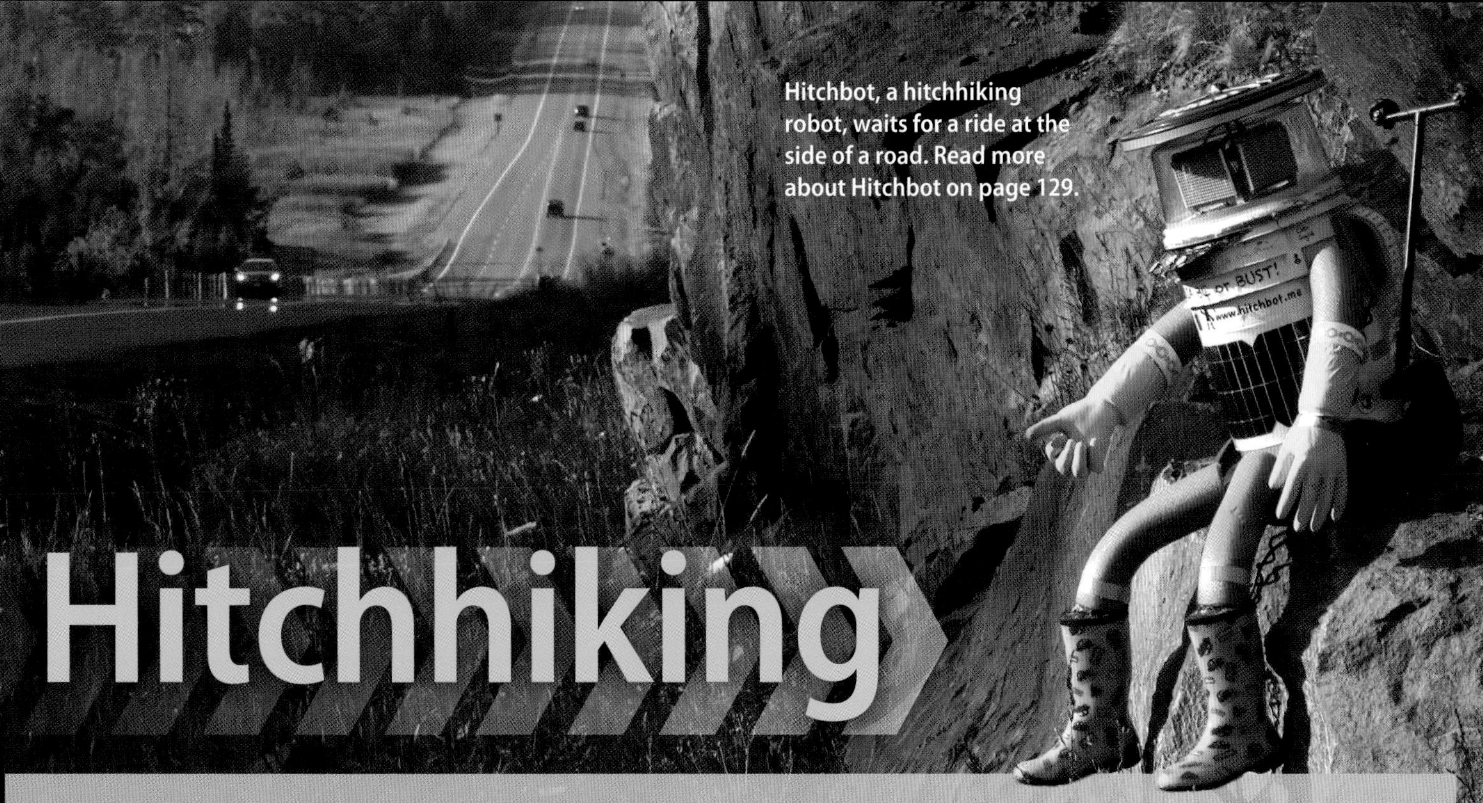

Hitchbot, a hitchhiking robot, waits for a ride at the side of a road. Read more about Hitchbot on page 129.

Hitchhiking

Where did all the hitchhikers go?

3 I was driving along the other day, and I passed a man sticking his thumb out. He was asking for a ride. When we had gone past, my daughter, who is 15, asked me, "What was that man doing?" The question surprised me, because hitchhiking used to be so common. I used to do it all the time when I was a student going home to visit friends, and I also spent one summer hitchhiking around South America. Often when you went to some hitching spots, you'd have to line up behind several others already waiting for a ride—it was so popular. So what happened? Why is it so rare now? The authors of *Freakonomics*, Stephen Dubner and Steve Levitt, have also asked this question in one of their regular podcasts. They suggest that it probably comes down to five main reasons.

(1) ______________________

Several horror movies have shown psychotic drivers who kidnap and murder the hitchhiker they pick up (or vice versa). This has been reinforced by certain stories in the media of people getting robbed and being left in the middle of nowhere. Unsurprisingly, this has caused trust to break down. Some people believe that the chances of these things happening are small. The website Wand'rly, for example, suggests that people are far more likely to die by tripping and falling than by hitchhiking.

(2) ______________________

There are more major roads now than there used to be, and hitching is either banned or drivers are not allowed to pull over on these roads.

(3) ______________________

Alan Piskarsi, a transportation expert, points to the fact that cars last longer, so there are more of them available at a cheaper price. What's more, many more people have driver's licenses than they used to.

(4) ______________________

In the past, young people simply couldn't afford to fly long distances, and traveling by train wasn't necessarily much quicker than traveling by car. Now, however, we have budget airlines, making air travel more accessible.

(5) ______________________

Along the same lines, people's standard of living has increased. Perhaps people opt for higher levels of comfort, privacy, or reliability when they travel.

(6) ______________________

The trouble is that privacy comes at a cost. Levitt and Dubner state that in the United States, 80 percent of passenger space in cars is unused, which makes them more costly to operate and creates unnecessary traffic and pollution. The solution could be more hitchhiking! They give the example of a city in Virginia, where commuters have organized a spot where they meet to hitch a ride so drivers with no passengers can use carpool lanes on the highway that are reserved for cars that contain more than one person.

Fresh Fears

But what about general travel? I often argued with my parents about the dangers of hitchhiking, and I would tell them about all the amazing experiences I'd had and the generous, interesting people I'd met. I think it genuinely gave me a different perspective on other travelers and tourists. But now, I look at my daughter and think about her going on a trip. Would I want her to go hitchhiking?

Andrew Skurka's longest "Grand Tour" was 7,775 miles.

1C The Grand Tour

GRAMMAR *Used to* and *would*

1 Look at the Grammar box. Match the structures with the uses, based on the examples in bold.

1 simple past
2 *used to, would,* simple past
3 *used to* or simple past

a to describe a past state over a period of time
b to describe individual past events and situations
c to describe a habit or regular action in the past

Used to* and *would

*Hitchhiking **used to be** so common. I **used to do it** all the time when I **was** a student going home to visit friends, and I also **spent** one summer hitching around South America. Often when you went to some hitching spots, **you'd have to line up** behind several others already waiting for a ride—it was so popular. **I often argued** with my parents about the dangers of hitching, and **I would tell them about** all the amazing experiences I'd had.*

Check the Grammar Reference for more information and practice.

2 Read about Grand Tours. Find out what they were and why people did them.

Humans have always been travelers, moving out of Africa to all parts of the world in search of space, food, and resources. But the idea of guided tourism for leisure and education (1) **didn't really start** until the 17th century, when the Grand Tour (2) **began** to be established. Young aristocrats* from different parts of the world (3) **spent** several months traveling around important sights in Europe after they had finished their schooling. The Tour often (4) **started** in the Netherlands, where the tourists (5) **hired** a horse and carriage, servants, and a tutor to show them the sights and teach them about what they saw.

From the Netherlands, they went to Paris, where they (6) **did** a French language course, before moving on to Switzerland and then crossing the Alps to Italy. After an extensive tour of Italy, they (7) **went** home directly, (8) **traveled** back to the Netherlands via Austria and Germany, or (9) **continued** south to Greece.

The Grand Tour (10) **played** an important part in education and in spreading culture. The tourists would often bring back paintings and books, which influenced artists in their own country. The Venezuelan Francisco de Miranda even (11) **saw** the beginnings of the French Revolution on his Grand Tour, which (12) **led** him to fight for independence for his country.

aristocrat *person belonging to a high class*

3 Change the words in bold in Activity 2 from the simple past to *used to* or *would* + verb, where possible.

4 **MY PERSPECTIVE**

Work in pairs. Discuss the questions.

1 Do you think anyone does Grand Tours today? Why?
2 Where would you go on a Grand Tour? Why? Think about:

- the sights you would visit.
- the food you would eat.
- the people you would meet.

5 PRONUNCIATION *To* in natural speech

> When unstressed, the word *to* is usually pronounced "tuh."
> *I was a student going home to visit friends.*
>
> It can also be reduced and joined with the previous word.
> *Hitchhiking used to be so common.*
> *You'd have to line up behind several others.*

a Listen to the sentences from the Pronunciation box. Notice the differences between unstressed *to* and the sentences with reductions. 4

b Listen and repeat. 4

6 Read about Andrew Skurka. Decide if *used to*, *would*, and the simple past are used correctly or incorrectly. Change the ones which are incorrect.

Andrew Skurka is an ultra-hiker. Every year, he (1) *used to go* on hikes that are thousands of miles long, walking between 25 and 40 miles a day. One of his most amazing tours was circling the Arctic in 176 days. His boots (2) *got very wet* for 156 of those days and they (3) *used to froze* overnight. He (4) *would then have to* force his feet into the icy boots each morning. Unsurprisingly, he (5) *didn't use to see* many people during his tours and once, he (6) *would spend* 24 days completely on his own. He'd sometimes (7) *get depressed* and (8) *cried,* but one day he came across a herd of caribou and it (9) *used to change* his perspective. He (10) *realized* he was very similar to them—just one more creature on Earth, like them.

7 CHOOSE

Choose one of the following activities.

- What did your parents or grandparents do on vacation when they were growing up? Write any similarities and differences to what you do.
- Work in groups. Share what you know about tourism in your country in the past compared to now. Talk about:
  - resorts.
  - the kinds of people who visit or visited.
  - the kinds of vacations.
  - the number and length of vacations.
  - destinations people from your country visit or visited.
- Work in pairs. Tell your partner about two of the following.
  - Something you used to believe and why you changed your mind.
  - Something you used to like doing and why you don't like it or do it now.
  - Something you do now that you never used to do and why.
  - Someone you used to spend a lot of time with and what you would do.

In the past, only young aristocrats were able to visit classical sites such as the Pantheon in Rome, Italy.

AUTHENTIC LISTENING SKILLS

Reporting

When people tell stories, they often use present tenses to make events sound more immediate. They also often report what people said or what was going through their mind at the time, as if they were speaking.

1 Look at the Authentic Listening Skills box. Listen and complete the extracts. 5

1 I make the mistake of asking him,
"______________________________?"
2 And I'm thinking,
"______________________________?"
3 And the voice in my head goes,
"______________________________?"
4 I'm staring at the ceiling, I'm thinking,
"______________________________?"

2 Look at your completed extracts in Activity 1. What do you think happened before? What do you think will happen next?

3 Work in pairs. Read the sentences below. Discuss what may have happened before somebody said each one.

1 So I'm thinking to myself, "What do I do now?"
2 She looks at me and goes, "I've met you somewhere before."
3 The voice in my head says, "Don't do it!"

WATCH

4 Work in groups. Discuss the questions.

1 Have you or your family ever asked for help from a stranger while on vacation? What happened?
2 Have you or someone in your family ever helped a stranger while on vacation? What happened?
3 Why might you trust or not trust a stranger? How do you decide who to trust for help or advice?

5 Watch Part 1 of the talk. Choose the correct options. ▶ 1.1

1 From his meeting with the "Peace Corps guy," Joe learns
a he should always have an airbed.
b he should start a hosting business.
c we should be less fearful of strangers.

2 He decided to start his business because
a there weren't many hotels in the city.
b he really needed somewhere to stay.
c it offered him an opportunity as a designer.

3 The business wasn't immediately successful because
a people didn't trust Joe and his co-founder.
b the website wasn't very well designed.
c it didn't get any additional investment.

6 MY PERSPECTIVE

How can you make people feel that they can trust each other more? Think of three ideas. Then share them with the class. Does anyone have the same ideas as you?

7 Watch Part 2 of the talk. Complete these notes. ▶ 1.2

- Experiment—shows how host can feel ____________ but guest can feel ____________ = how business works. Well-designed reputation (review) system—key to ____________ .
- ____________ must leave reviews before they are revealed.
- ____________ = people stop worrying about differences (reputation beats similarity).
- ____________ and prompts = right amount of honesty and sharing (disclosure).

8 Watch Part 3 of the talk. Then work in groups and summarize what Joe said using these ideas. What did you like about these ideas? ▶ 1.3

- when trust works
- a man having a heart attack
- the sharing economy
- human connection
- Seoul, South Korea
- students and empty-nesters*

empty-nesters *parents whose children have left home*

9 Look back at your ideas in Activity 6. Did Joe mention any of your ideas? Have any of them changed?

10 **VOCABULARY IN CONTEXT**

a Watch the clips from the TED Talk. Choose the correct meanings of the words and phrases. ▶ 1.4

b Work in groups. Discuss these questions.

1. What things can increase or reduce *anxiety* when traveling?
2. Have you ever met someone on vacation you got along with? Have you *kept in touch*? Why?
3. Would you be *up for* doing any of these things on vacation? Why?
   - rafting or bungee jumping
   - going to a nightclub
   - doing a guided tour of a museum
   - going camping
4. When did you last *rush* somewhere? Why?
5. Have you ever experienced anything that *tripped you up*? What?

CHALLENGE

Work in groups. Make a list of things you have which you could share with others in your area or with people visiting you on vacation. Think about:

- skills and abilities.
- knowledge.
- possessions that you do not use all the time.

How could you share the things in your list in a way that people could trust and avoid danger?

1E Trip Advice

SPEAKING

Useful language

Making suggestions

If sightseeing is their thing, then the best place to go is…

If they want to experience a genuine local night out, I'd suggest trying…

If they're only staying here for a little while, they should probably…

If you ask me, the one place they really have to go to is…

Reacting to suggestions

If they'd rather try something different, …might be worth a shot.

I wouldn't bother going to…, personally.

They'd be better (off) going to…

1 Work in pairs. Make a list of three places close to where you live that you would recommend to each of these groups of people. Think about places to stay, eat, shop, and visit.

a couple in their 50s or 60s	a father with a young teenage son
a group of teenage friends	a young married couple with a child

2 Compare your list with another pair. Make suggestions for the best places for each group of people. Use the Useful language box to help you.

3 Put the sentences in the correct order to make a conversation between a local person and a guest. Then listen and check your answers. 6

a Well, there's a great steak place down by the river.
b I'm thinking of seeing some sights today. Can you recommend anywhere?
c In that case, you'd be best off going to Madragora—a nice little vegetarian place near the park.
d OK. Well, I'll check that out this morning, then. And do you know anywhere good to have lunch?
e Great. Thanks for the tip.
f Oh, right. Well, actually, I don't eat meat, so…
g Well, the Old Town is well worth a visit. There are some amazing buildings there.

4 Roleplay two conversations similar to the one in Activity 3, using places you know. Underline phrases from Activity 3 that you want to use. Then have the conversations. Take turns being the local person and the guest.

Tourists walk across the Perito Moreno Glacier in Santa Cruz Province, Argentina.

WRITING A review

5 Look at page 149 and read the four short online reviews. What kind of place is each review about?

6 Work in pairs. Which reviewer:

1 does not feel that he or she got a good value?
2 managed to negotiate a deal?
3 strongly recommends a place?
4 had to entertain himself or herself quite a lot?
5 complained?
6 had to wait far longer than he or she had been expecting to?
7 felt very comfortable where he or she was?
8 mentions local sights?

7 Look at page 149 again. Underline the sentences in the reviews that helped you answer the questions in Activity 6.

8 **WRITING SKILL** Adding comments

Match the first half of each excerpt (1-4) with the second half (a-d).

1 Our room had a great view of the ocean, but the hotel restaurant closed at nine,
2 We had an amazing time, but terrible weather on the day we left,
3 We complained about the room, so they offered us two full days at the spa,
4 The beach was a five-minute walk from the hotel, but so was the snake market,

a which meant we were delayed for several hours.
b which was rather disappointing.
c which was a bit of a culture shock, to say the least.
d which was kind of them.

9 Choose one of these places and write a review. Use the Useful language box to help you.

- vacation destination
- local tourist attraction
- local cafe or restaurant
- place you have stayed

Writing strategy

Writing reviews

In reviews, it's quite common to use a relative clause starting with *which* to add a comment about a whole sentence.

I was far from my school, ***which wasn't ideal****.*

It serves great breakfasts, lunches, and snacks, ***which is perfect if you're feeling hungry****.*

Useful language

Introducing follow-up comments

On top of that,…

What's more,…

One other thing was the fact that…

Recommending and not recommending

I can't recommend it enough.

It's well worth a visit.

It's just not worth it.

I'd skip it (if I were you).

2 The Business of Technology

IN THIS UNIT, YOU...

- discuss young entrepreneurs.
- read about online scams.
- learn how to be a responsible user of social media.
- watch a TED Talk about responding to email scams.
- persuade people to invest in a product.

A man stands inside a virtual cave at the Gdansk University of Technology in Poland. Virtual caves can be used by architects, doctors, and firefighters to simulate real-world scenarios.

2A Young Business

VOCABULARY Setting up a new business

1 Look at the photo and read the caption. How do you think the virtual cave works? How can it help people? In what other jobs might the virtual cave be useful?

2 Work as a class. Discuss the questions.

1 What is the difference between an **entrepreneur** and a **businessperson**?
2 What qualities and skills do you think you need to be an entrepreneur?
3 How easy is it for young people to become businesspeople or entrepreneurs?
4 Can you think of any young entrepreneurs? Who was the youngest? What was his or her business?

3 Work in pairs. Discuss the questions.

1 How do people **raise money** for a business or a charity?
2 Who might businesspeople **negotiate with**? What about?
3 In what ways do businesses **market products**?
4 What might a business or a person **recover from**?
5 What are good and bad ways of **handling pressure**?

4 What skills do you need to start a new business? Choose the correct option to complete each skill.

1 ______________ something new
a negotiate **b** invent **c** redesign

2 ______________ money from investors
a raise **b** lend **c** ask

3 ______________ with suppliers to get the best deal
a handle **b** manage **c** negotiate

4 find partners to ______________ the product in different countries
a send **b** distribute **c** deal

5 have the confidence to ______________ from failure
a recover **b** repair **c** accept

6 be good at ______________ your product to increase sales
a meeting **b** networking **c** marketing

7 be capable of ______________ stress and pressure
a preparing **b** holding **c** handling

8 be able to ______________ a diverse range of people
a deal with **b** talk **c** get on

9 ______________ a team of people
a apply for **b** figure **c** put together

10 ______________ in an impressive office
a live **b** be based **c** show

5 **MY PERSPECTIVE**

Work in pairs. What are the three most important skills from Activity 4 that make a new business a success? Can you think of any other skills?

6 Explain your choices from Activity 5 to another pair. Do they agree? Why?

LISTENING

7 Listen to a woman talking about entrepreneurs. Think about the questions and take notes. 7

1. How is being an entrepreneur changing?
2. According to the speaker, what is the most important aspect of being an entrepreneur?

8 Work in pairs. Discuss the sentences. Are they *true* or *false*? Listen again to check. 7

1. Nick D'Aloisio became a millionaire when he was eighteen.
2. Amanda Hocking didn't go through a traditional publisher to market her books.
3. The speaker suggests that most investments from banks in the past went to older, wealthy businessmen.
4. D'Aloisio's first investor chose him because he was young and had potential.
5. Kickstarter investors buy a share of the company.
6. Projects advertised on Kickstarter aim to make a profit.
7. The majority of Kickstarter projects get no investments.
8. Hocking is an example of recovering from failure.

9 Work in pairs. Discuss the questions.

1. How has the internet changed entrepreneurship?
2. Do you think Kickstarter is a good idea? What are the benefits and risks of raising money this way?
3. What do you think might be good or bad about being an entrepreneur?

GRAMMAR Present perfect forms and the simple past

10 Look at the Grammar box. Read the sentences. Then answer the questions.

1. Which tense is each of the verb forms in bold?
2. Why do you think the different forms are used?

Present perfect forms and the simple past

a *D'Aloisio's first investor* ***contacted*** *him by email from Hong Kong.*
b *Kickstarter* ***has been running*** *for several years now.*
c *Most successful entrepreneurs* ***have failed*** *at least once.*

Check the Grammar Reference for more information and practice.

11 Based on your ideas from Activity 10, complete the summary. Use each form once.

The number of entrepreneurs (1) ________________ (grow) ever since the arrival of new technology and online services. This new technology (2) ________________ (reduce) the barriers that previously (3) ________________ (discourage) people from setting up a business.

12 Do the underlined verbs use the correct forms? Change the ones you think are incorrect.

Topher White is a young entrepreneur. In college, he (1) trained as a physicist, but since 2012 he (2) ran a non-profit company, Rainforest Connection, to help prevent the illegal practice of logging.* He (3) has invented a system using old cell phones and solar power to hear the sound of saws and vehicles that illegal loggers use. The phones then send a warning to guards so they can stop the activity before it does too much damage. Topher first (4) has tested the system in Borneo, and in 2014, his Kickstarter campaign (5) has raised almost $170,000 to expand the company. Since then he's (6) been working with groups such as the Tembe tribe in South America, as well as with people in Africa and Indonesia to adapt the system to meet local needs. They successfully (7) detected a lot of illegal activity. The work Topher is doing is important because in some parts of the world they (8) have been losing ten percent of forest cover this century, and deforestation is one of the biggest contributors to climate change.

logging *cutting down trees*

13 Complete the sentences so they are true for you.

1 I haven't ______________ since ______________ .
2 ______________ has been doing a lot better since ______________ .
3 I ______________ over the last five years.
4 I ______________ for the first time last year.
5 The number of ______________ has grown a lot over the last few years.

14 **MY PERSPECTIVE**

Look again at the three most important skills you listed in Activity 5. Give examples of when you have demonstrated these skills. List any other qualities or ideas you have that show that you would be a good entrepreneur.

15 Work in groups. Try to convince other students that you would make the best entrepreneur. Use the present perfect and simple past forms.

I've been running our school debate team for the last two years, so I believe that I can negotiate well with other people.

I took nine exams last year, so I think I'm capable of handling stress and pressure.

Topher White attaches a Rainforest Connection listening device to a tree in the Amazon Rainforest in Brazil to help stop illegal logging.

2B Risky Business

READING

1 Complete the sentences with these pairs of words.

confirm + scam	deleted + permission
emails + filter	inbox + attached
infected + backups	profile + edit
social media + posting	store + flash drive

1. Some of my posts were ____________ without my ____________. I have no idea why!
2. I can't believe how many ____________ manage to get through my spam ____________.
3. He's very active on ____________. He's always ____________ new updates and adding photos.
4. I keep my ____________ very private, and I often go back and ____________ things I've written.
5. This strange email just arrived in my ____________ with a file ____________ to it, so I deleted it.
6. When they asked me to ____________ my bank details, I started to think it must be a ____________.
7. I ____________ all my documents in the cloud now, rather than using a ____________.
8. My computer got a virus that ____________ a lot of my files and I didn't have any ____________.

2 Work in pairs. How do you think the things in Activity 1 can happen? Why would people do them?

3 Look at the infographic and read the stories. Then answer the questions.

1. What mistake did each person make?
2. What was the result of each mistake?

4 Work in pairs. Answer the questions.

1. Who didn't realize they'd made a mistake for a long time?
2. Who received several emails from the same person?
3. Who thought they had found a bargain?
4. Who was scared into responding too quickly?
5. Who accepted the blame for what happened?
6. Who didn't read a product description carefully enough?

5 Read the stories again to check your ideas in Activity 4. Underline the parts that helped you decide.

6 **MY PERSPECTIVE**

Make a list of the different ways you could protect yourself from the same kinds of online crimes that Laura, Bruno, and Janella encountered.

VOCABULARY BUILDING

Adjective and noun collocations 1

When you learn adjectives, it is a good idea to remember the nouns that they describe. Sometimes the adjective is next to the noun; however, sometimes it appears later in the sentence.

It's a very user-friendly website with lots of functions and it is also very secure.

7 Match the adjectives with the nouns they are used with in the stories on page 25.

1 the normal	**a** hotels
2 a secondhand	**b** relative
3 my personal	**c** PlayStation
4 luxury	**d** documents
5 common	**e** fees
6 a distant	**f** price
7 official	**g** sense
8 legal	**h** details

CRITICAL THINKING Interpreting data

You will often see visuals and charts in newspapers, books, and articles online to add information and support the text. You need to check that these statistics are from a reliable source and interpret the data for yourself before you read.

8 Work in groups. Look at the cybercrime graphs on page 25. Discuss the questions.

1. Where does the data come from? Do you think this is a reliable source?
2. What crimes do the graphs focus on? What do you know about them?
3. What's the most common crime? Why do you think that is?
4. Which age groups are the least affected? Which are the most affected? Why do you think that is?
5. Do you think the statistics would be different for your country? Why? Do you know where to find this data?

9 Work in groups. Discuss the questions.

1. Which of the three mistakes do you think is the most serious? Which is the least serious? Why?
2. Why do you think each person acted as they did?
3. What do you think each person did after realizing their mistake?
4. Have you heard any stories about similar mistakes? If so, what happened?

Online Crime

8 The world becomes more connected every day. It's now easier than ever to keep in touch with friends and family around the world. Online banking allows people to access their accounts from anywhere that has an internet connection. People don't even have to leave the house to go shopping! However, with greater connectivity comes greater risk. Every year, hundreds of thousands of people become victims of online crime. We asked our readers to share some of their terrible tech tales while we examine where the crimes originate.

Laura One day last year, I got a call from what I thought was my bank. They said someone was trying to take money from my account without my permission, and that they needed to confirm my personal details to stop it. I'll be honest—I didn't really understand what was going on and wanted to stop anything bad from happening, so I gave them my name and address and date of birth. I didn't hear back, but a month later I got my credit card statement and found someone had spent over 11,000 pounds on flights and luxury hotels!

Origin of crime: The United States

Romania

The United States

West Africa

Bruno I was surfing the web one day when I found a site selling Xboxes and PlayStations. I couldn't believe how cheap they were. They had stuff on there for half the normal price! I clicked on one item and bought what was advertised as a "PlayStation 4 original box and receipt." I assumed it was secondhand and, since it was only 150 euros, I bought it without checking the details. You can imagine how I felt a few days later when the postman brought me just the box and the receipt!

Origin of crime: Romania

Janella Looking back, it was my own fault, but when I got an email saying a distant relative had died and left me millions of dollars, common sense went out of the window! It was from someone claiming to be a lawyer in West Africa. I know my dad's side of the family had connections there, so I thought it must be true. They attached documents that looked official and kept writing, so eventually I sent them 8,000 dollars to pay the legal fees. Of course, it was a scam and I never heard from them again… or got my money back!

Origin of crime: West Africa

Cybercrime by age (US)

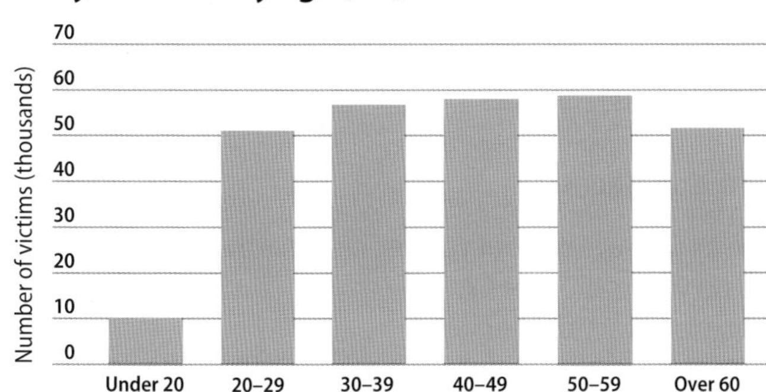

Cybercrime by type (US)

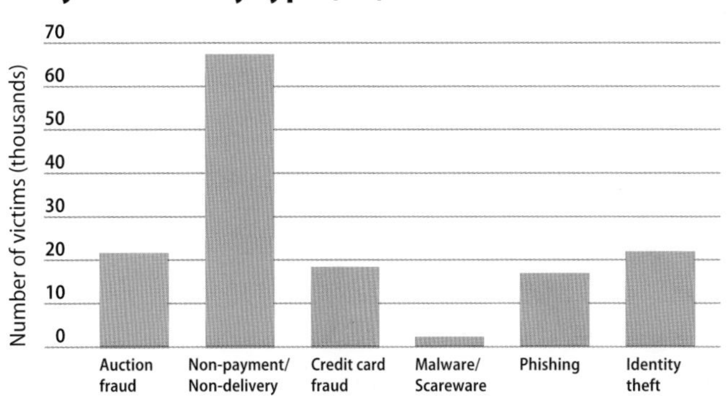

Source: U.S. Department of Justice / Federal Bureau of Investigation Statistics shown are for 2015.

Do you enjoy posting on social media?

2C What's in a post?

GRAMMAR Verb patterns (*-ing* or infinitive with *to*)

1 Work in pairs. Look at the Grammar box. Which verbs below can be followed by the *-ing* form? Which can be followed by the infinitive with *to*?

admit	agree	arrange	can't stand	consider
decide	delay	enjoy	expect	finish
hope	intend	mind	miss	offer
plan	practice	promise	recommend	refuse

Verb patterns (*-ing* or infinitive with *to*)

When two verbs are used together, the second one often takes the *-ing* form or the infinitive with *to.*

They attached documents that looked official and ***kept writing to me****.*

Websites such as Kickstarter allow entrepreneurs to ***avoid selling*** *part of their business to an investor.*

They ***needed to confirm*** *my personal details.*

Over half of the campaigns on Kickstarter don't receive any funding because they ***fail to reach*** *their set target.*

Check the Grammar Reference for more information and practice.

2 Choose the correct options to complete the blog post.

If you're anything like most people, you probably enjoy (1) *posting / to post* on social media. Maybe you hope (2) *creating / to create* a particular kind of image of yourself, or intend (3) *showing / to show* others what good taste you have. You're probably not planning (4) *providing / to provide* information that could be used against you in the future, but every time you post online or "like" something, you're agreeing (5) *sharing / to share* that personal information with the world!

Most of us avoid (6) *revealing / to reveal* too much about ourselves face-to-face, but for some reason, we don't mind (7) *doing / to do* this online. Everything you decide (8) *making / to make* public on the internet helps to build a very detailed picture of who you are and what you believe—and we're failing (9) *understanding / to understand* that this helps companies guess your age, gender, education, political views... and much more.

Of course, most social media companies refuse (10) *guaranteeing / to guarantee* privacy for users. After all, we are their product. What they sell is the information we give them! Given this, I recommend (11) *using / to use* science to help us gain control over our data! Sites could warn us of the risks we are taking when we post certain kinds of information, for example. Failing that, of course, we could all just consider (12) *posting / to post* less.

3 Work in pairs. Discuss the questions.

1 How much do you think you reveal about yourself on social media? Why?
2 What kinds of things do you post online? Why?
3 Are you concerned about privacy online? Why?
4 What do you think social media sites do with the personal information they gather? How does this make you feel?

4 Complete the comments with the correct form of these verbs.

be	feel	have	hear
post	protect	quit	spend

Eric Wong **Posted 3 hours ago**

I can't stand (1) ________ like everything I do online is being used by someone. Really, we should all promise (2) ________ social media! The only reason we don't is because we're too scared we'd miss (3) ________ from friends!

Luisa Hernandez **Posted 2 weeks ago**

If you use social media, you should expect (4) ________ these experiences. Why should companies offer (5) ________ our privacy? They already provide us with free services. That should be enough.

Back to the Future **Posted a month ago**

The secret of being happy is to practice (6) ________ more patient! Delay (7) ________ until you're sure you really want the world to have access to what you write—and try (8) ________ as much time offline as you can!

5 Work in groups. Do you agree with the comments in Activity 4? Why?

6 Write your own short response to the blog post in Activity 2. Include two or more verbs from Activity 1. Then share your comments in groups.

Objects before *-ing* and *to*

Some verbs always have an object before an *-ing* form or an infinitive with *to*.

When they ***asked me to confirm*** *my bank details, I started to think it must be a scam.*

Check the Grammar Reference for more information and practice.

7 Look at the Grammar box. Complete the sentences so that they are true for you. Then explain your ideas to a partner.

1 My parents always expected me ________ .
2 In a few years' time, I can see myself ________ .
3 If I could, I'd hire someone ________ .
4 We should do more to prevent ________ .
5 I can still remember begging my parents ________ .

Verbs with two objects

Some verbs can be followed by two objects.

The indirect object is usually a person and the second, direct object is usually a thing.

Can you ***email me your essays****, please, instead of* ***handing them to me*** *in class?*

Check the Grammar Reference for more information and practice.

8 Look at the Grammar box. Complete the sentences with these direct objects. You will also have to add an indirect object. The first one has been done for you.

anything	a loan	a new tablet
a special dinner	permission	~~the remote control~~

1 This show is terrible. Let's see what else is on. Pass *me the remote control* .
2 My dad bought ________ for my birthday.
3 If you're under twenty, it's difficult to find a bank that'll give ________ to start a business.
4 By posting on their website, you're basically giving ________ to use your data.
5 If I were you, I wouldn't tell ________ . He can't keep a secret!
6 My sister and I cooked ________ for their wedding anniversary.

9 **CHOOSE**

Choose one of the following activities.

- Work in pairs. Write a blog post explaining best practices when it comes to using social media. Use as many of the phrases below as you can.

  If I were you, I'd avoid...
  I'd strongly recommend...
  It's best not to agree / try...
  Lots of people fail...
  You may want to prevent people from...
  It's sometimes good to ask friends...
  Don't allow everyone...
  Think carefully before you tell...

- Write a short story about someone who started a new business. Use at least five verbs from pages 21–27.
- Work in groups. Search online for a story about someone who was a victim of cybercrime. Report what happened to another group. Use at least five verbs from pages 21–27.

2D This is what happens when you reply to spam email

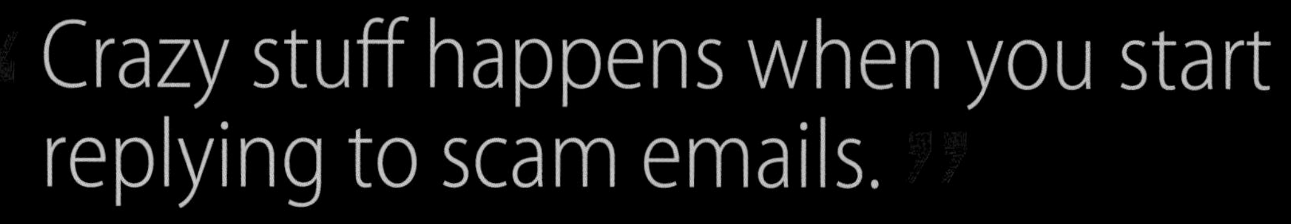

“Crazy stuff happens when you start replying to scam emails.”

JAMES VEITCH

Read about James Veitch and get ready to watch his TED Talk. ▶ 2.0

AUTHENTIC LISTENING SKILLS

Intonation and pitch

When we are surprised or shocked by what someone says, we often repeat a key word, phrase, or short sentence with a high pitch and a questioning intonation. We may then add a comment with a falling tone.

1 Look at the Authentic Listening Skills box. Then work in pairs. Practice the exchange.

A We can start with 50 kilograms as a trial shipment.
B Fifty kilograms? There's no point doing this at all unless you're shipping at least a metric ton.

2 Listen to James Veitch. Compare your intonation with his. 🎧 9

3 Work in pairs. Take turns responding to the comments using the same intonation pattern as James.

1 I got an email offering to distribute gold.
2 He's sixteen years old.
3 It cost ten dollars.
4 I've never watched *Star Wars*.
5 Her dad is the mayor of our city.
6 My bank called me and asked for my address.

WATCH

4 Work in groups. Guess what this email means and why it was written.

From: Solomon Odonkoh
To: James Veitch
(No Subject)

The business is on. I am trying to raise the balance for the Gummy Bear so he can submit all the needed Fizzy Cola Bottle Jelly Beans to the Creme Egg for the Peanut M&Ms process to start. Send £1,500.00 via a Giant Gummy Lizard.

5 Watch Part 1 of the talk. Answer the questions. ▶ 2.1

1 How was "Solomon Odonkoh" trying to make money?
2 Do you still have the same answer to Activity 4?

6 Work in pairs. Put the sentences in the correct order.

a I figured I had to knock it on the head.
b On real estate, what about you?
c Dude, you have to use the code!
d I'm a hedge fund executive bank manager.
e I have to go to bed now.
f I could do what I think we've all always wanted to do.
g If we're going to do it, let's go big.
h I didn't hear back. I thought, "I've gone too far."

7 Watch Part 1 of the talk again to check your ideas in Activity 6.
▶ 2.1

8 Work in groups. Discuss why you think James Veitch replies to spam. Which of these points is he trying to make?

1. He replies to spam email when he is bored.
2. He suggests it is a good way to spend any spare time.
3. He replies to spam email to take up the time of the spammer. He suggests that this stops them from contacting other people.
4. He replies to spam email because he is interested in the financial benefits. He suggests that people can make money by doing business online.

9 Watch Part 2 of the talk. Check your ideas in Activity 8. How effective do you think James's approach is? Why?
▶ 2.2

10 Watch Part 3 of the talk. How are the emails James receives from "Solomon Odonkoh" and the emails he receives this time similar? ▶ 2.3

11 **VOCABULARY IN CONTEXT**

a Watch the clips from the TED Talk. Choose the correct meanings of the words and phrases. ▶ 2.4

b Work in pairs. Tell your partner about:
- something or someone who *turned up* unexpectedly.
- a situation that *got out of hand / went too far*.
- something or someone that / who *intrigues* you.

12 **MY PERSPECTIVE**

Work in pairs. Come up with five different ways to deal with internet scams. Then discuss which ones are most relevant to these groups of people. Explain your reasons.

- elderly people
- people who enjoy playing video games
- people who do a lot of online shopping

CHALLENGE

Work in groups. Design a questionnaire to find out about people's experiences with internet scams. You should find out how much is already known and what, if anything, people are doing to reduce the risks. You will need at least ten questions.

2E Investment Opportunity

SPEAKING

Speaking strategy

Persuading

When we are persuading people, we sometimes turn our own experiences and opinions into a negative question to challenge the other person's ideas.

I think it will lose money.
Don't you think it'll lose money?
I'd find it really useful.
Wouldn't you find it really useful?
I have sometimes had that problem.
Haven't you ever had that problem?

1 Work in groups. Discuss the questions.

1. Are there any TV shows about business or selling products in your country? Do you watch them? Why?
2. Would you be good at selling a product? Why?
3. Have you ever had to present something in front of people? What did you present? Was the presentation successful? Why?

2 Work in pairs. Read about the Kickstarter project. One person should think of reasons to invest and one person should think of reasons not to invest. Then discuss your reasons and try to persuade each other.

mXers was set up by high school student Bharat Pulgam. He has invented a new kind of earbuds that allow you to easily replace the different parts that can break, so you don't have to buy a whole new set. They also allow you to customize your earbuds for an individual look. mXers needs money to develop the product and start production.

3 Make negative questions from these sentences. Which negative questions could you use to support your reasons from Activity 2? Why?

1. It'd be good to have something like that.
2. I think it's a bad idea to give money to strangers online.
3. There's something similar to that already.
4. Sometimes I've wished that I could do that.
5. I would be happy to pay a little more to help.

4 PRONUNCIATION Intonation for persuasion

a Listen to the negative questions and notice the intonation. 10

b Practice saying the negative questions.

1. Wouldn't it be good to have something like that?
2. Don't you think it's a bad idea to give money to strangers online?
3. Isn't there something similar to that already?
4. Haven't you ever wished that you could do that?
5. Wouldn't you be happy to pay a little more to help?

An woman harvests cocoa in Ghana for Fairafric.

5 Work in pairs. Read about two other Kickstarter projects. Choose one each and try to persuade each other to invest.

The Possible Project is an after-school program that teaches teenagers, mainly from low-income families, the skills to be entrepreneurs. The project has been running for several years and has trained over 250 students. The team wants to raise money for a laser cutter so that students can make a variety of products quickly.

Hendrik Reimers is a German chocolate maker. He has set up a chocolate-making company, Fairafric, in Ghana. By producing the chocolate bars in their own country, rather than only exporting cocoa beans, people in Ghana can earn over 25 percent more—even compared to fair-trade chocolate. The money raised will help fund production, packaging, shipping, and distribution.

WRITING A persuasive article

6 Read the short article on page 149 and find out:

1 what the aim of the article is.
2 what the nightmare is.
3 what the business is.

7 **WRITING SKILL** Getting people's attention

Work in pairs. Look at the article again and answer the questions.

1 How does the article grab your attention?
2 How does the article try to persuade you to continue reading?
3 Where does the factual information come from?
4 What is the purpose of the final paragraph?

8 Would you invest in the *i-save*? Why? Discuss with a partner.

9 Using the product you chose in Activity 5, a product you have heard about recently, or something you invented yourself, write an article to explain the product and encourage people to invest or find out more about it.

10 Work in groups. Share your article. People in your group should ask you questions or share comments about your article.

Useful language

Getting people's attention

- *Have you ever wanted to...? Well, now you could have the opportunity.*
- *Have you ever wondered...? Well, now scientists have discovered the answer.*
- *Have you ever dreamed of...? Well, that's exactly what happened to...!*
- *Have you ever...? Well, all that could be a thing of the past, thanks to....*
- *Do you think...? Well, think again!*

3 Faster, Higher, Stronger

IN THIS UNIT, YOU...

- describe athletes.
- read about the lengths countries will go to in order to host the Olympics and do well.
- learn about small changes that can make big differences.
- watch a TED Talk about how athletes are improving.
- write and carry out a survey.

Sports fans experience a range of emotions as they watch an event.

3A Incredible Achievements

VOCABULARY Describing athletes

1 Work in groups. Look at the photo and discuss the questions.

1. Would you like to be in a crowd like this? Why?
2. Which sport do you think they are watching? Is it popular in your country?
3. Which are the most popular sports in your country? Do you like them? Why? Do you know any famous people who take part in them?

2 Work in pairs. Choose the option which cannot complete the sentence.

1. He has... *incredible awareness / very energetic / great technique / a real passion for the game.*
2. She's... *a very skillful player / a really great attitude / a forward / a positive role model.*
3. She won... *a great goal / silver at the Olympics / the world championship / a gold medal.*
4. He scored... *an average of 20 points a game / 300 goals in his career / the most last season / the race.*
5. *He set a new / He won the / He holds the / He smashed the old...* world record.
6. *She captained / She was the star of / She competed / She played a key role on...* the team.

3 Complete the sentences with words from Activity 2.

1. Everyone on the team has a really great ____________. They always fight right to the end of the game.
2. She still ____________ the world record she set 30 years ago.
3. When I was younger, I won a gold ____________ in the 400 meters.
4. He has incredible ____________. He can anticipate the other players' moves and create opportunities for scoring.
5. He was a key player in their success, but he never ____________ the team.
6. I've always had a real passion ____________ wrestling.
7. She's ____________ in four Olympics and won two golds, one ____________, and one bronze.
8. He scored the winning ____________ in the last World Cup final.

4 Choose five phrases from Activity 2 to describe an athlete, a friend, and a family member. Then tell your partner about the people you thought of.

My favorite soccer player is Pierre-Emerick Aubameyang. He has incredible awareness and scores some amazing goals.

I think my big sister is a positive role model for me. She has a great attitude and never gives up.

5 **MY PERSPECTIVE**

How do you think sports and athletes have changed in your lifetime? With a partner, discuss changes in these categories.

- fame / celebrity status
- equipment
- achievements

LISTENING

6 Listen to four people explain why they admire certain athletes. As you listen: 11

1 find out where each athlete is or was from.
2 find an example of something each athlete won.

7 Listen to the four people again. What does each person say about the following? 11

1	275 times	
	over 150	
	eight or nine out of ten	
2	popular	
	Italian	
	celebrations	
3	videos	
	personal problems	
	a great lesson	
4	her future husband	
	introduced	
	fought	

8 Work in groups. Discuss which of the four athletes you think achieved the most. Explain your ideas.

GRAMMAR Determiners

9 Complete the information about the functions of determiners using these words.

articles demonstratives possessives quantifiers

Determiners are words used before nouns. They have two main functions:

- They show which noun we mean, using (1) ________ (*the*, *a*[*n*]), (2) ________ (*this*, *that*, *these*, *those*), and (3) ________ (*my*, *your*, *his*, *her*, *its*, *our*, *their*).
- They show how much or how many of something there is, using (4) ________ .

10 Look at the Grammar box. Underline the determiners in the sentences.

Determiners

a *That year, Susi won the women's singles.*
b *Ask any Indonesian of his generation.*
c *He won many medals, including one gold.*
d *Without him, fewer people would watch motorcycle road racing.*
e *We'd never won any gold medals.*

Check the Grammar Reference for more information and practice.

Valentino Rossi (left) attempts to overtake Maverick Vinales during a race at the Motorland Aragón Circuit in Alcañiz, Spain.

11 **Work in pairs. Complete the sentences with determiners. Then discuss.**

1 She used to be ________ forward on ________ US women's soccer team and she's one of the most successful soccer players ever.
2 She played for ________ country 275 times and scored 150 goals. ________ man has ever managed that!
3 Not ________ people can claim to have made a sport popular more or less on ________ own.
4 He has ________ ego problems and ________ great personality.
5 ________ coach has shown me some videos of Joaquín when he was at ________ best.
6 She always fought right to ________ end, even when it seemed there was ________ hope.

12 **Work in pairs. Look at the corrected sentences. Discuss why you think the original sentences were wrong.**

1 I don't like ~~no~~ *any* sports.
2 Hardly any ~~athlete~~ *athletes* from my country ~~has~~ *have* ever won an Olympic medal.
3 I think I'm pretty healthy. I eat very ~~few~~ *little* junk food.
4 There aren't ~~much~~ *many* places near here where you can exercise outside.
5 A ~~little~~ *few* people I know are crazy about sports.
6 I don't think it's right that some athletes earn so ~~many~~ *much* money.
7 Most ~~of~~ people I know have no interest in soccer.
8 I try to exercise every ~~weekends~~ *weekend* if I can.

13 **Decide which sentences you agree with in Activity 12. Change the sentences that you do not agree with. Share your ideas in groups.**

Number 1 isn't true for me. I like some sports. I'm really into basketball and baseball.
Number 2 isn't true. Lots of athletes from my country have won medals!

14 **Complete the biography with one word in each blank.**

Yao Ming is (1) ________ retired professional basketball player. He stopped playing a (2) ________ years ago, but he's still one of (3) ________ most famous athletes in China. I have a (4) ________ of great memories of watching him play. He spent (5) ________ years playing in the NBA in North America, which was amazing because (6) ________ Chinese player had ever done that before—and (7) hardly ________ have done it since. (8) ________, if not all, Chinese people know him and are very proud of what he achieved. He's instantly recognizable because he's 7 feet 6 inches tall. He made (9) ________ other player in the NBA look small in comparison! In the end, though, he had a (10) ________ of injuries that ended his career.

15 **Think again about the people you chose in Activity 4. Make notes about their lives, achievements, and why you admire them.**

16 **Work in groups. Tell each other about the people you wrote about in Activity 15. Ask each other more questions.**

3B Is the cost of coming in first too high?

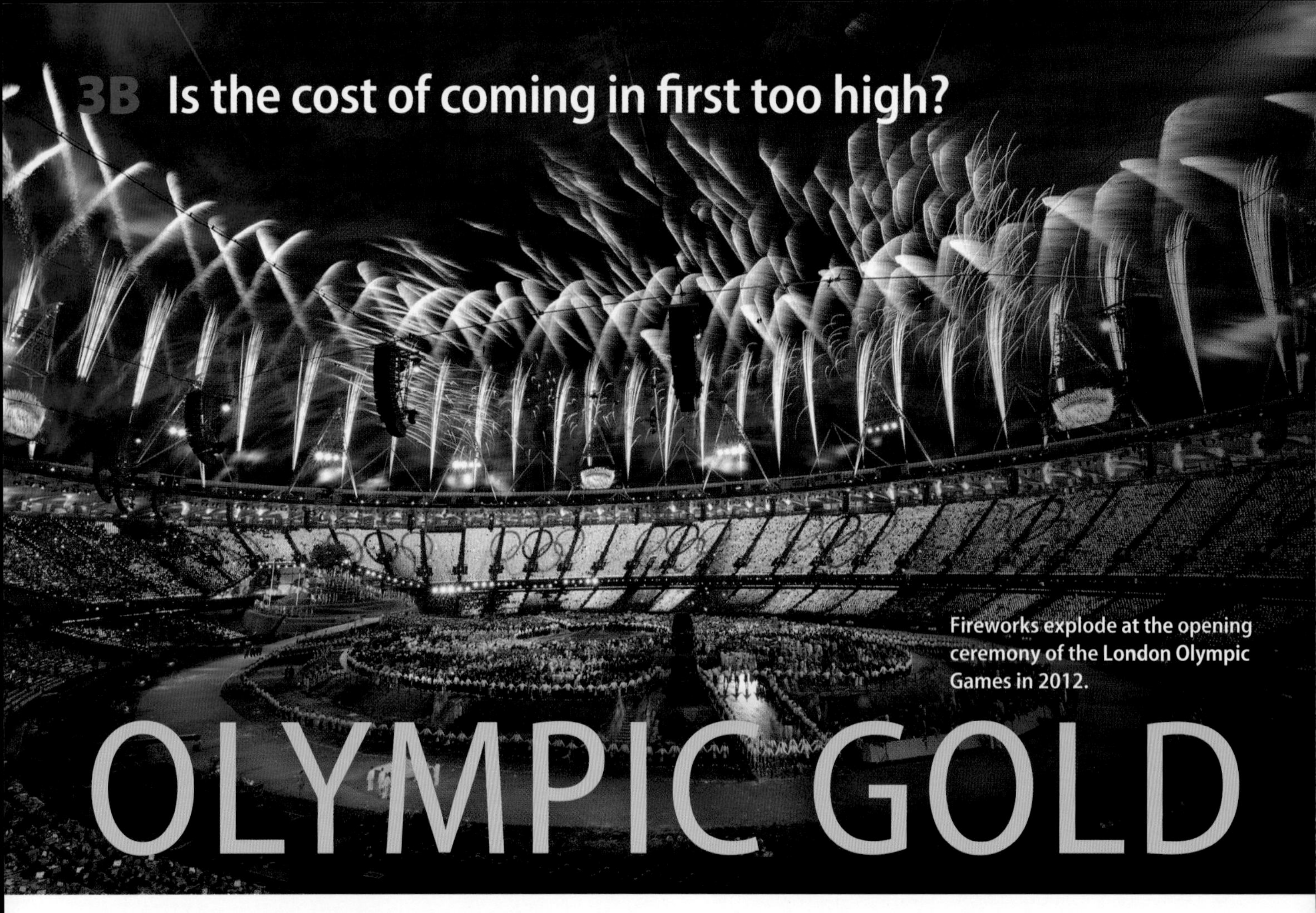

Fireworks explode at the opening ceremony of the London Olympic Games in 2012.

OLYMPIC GOLD

VOCABULARY BUILDING

Synonyms in texts

Writers often use words or phrases with similar meanings to make their work more interesting and to avoid repetition.

Countries competing to ***host the Olympics*** *will often spend huge amounts to* ***hold the 16-day event.***

1 **Complete the sentences with these synonyms. Use a dictionary, if necessary.**

establish	funding	hold
selected	sums	top

1 Countries compete to **host** the Olympics.
Countries spend huge amounts to ______________ the 16-day event.
2 Hosts spend huge **amounts**.
Hosts invest large ______________ of money.
3 They have programs for **elite** athletes.
They support ______________ competitors.
4 There is **money** to help develop successful athletes.
This ______________ is directly linked to success.
5 They helped to **set up** a program that promotes excellence in sports.
They helped to ______________ a system that promotes excellence in sports.
6 Children are **chosen** as potential stars.
Children hope to be ______________ as potential stars.

2 **Work in pairs. Rewrite the phrases using synonyms.**

prove to have talent—*prove to have a natural ability*

1 achieve their targets
2 core principle
3 got its highest ranking
4 linked to success
5 tackle the challenges you face

READING

3 **Work in groups. Which of these statements do you agree with?**

1 The most important thing is not winning, but taking part.
2 Hosting the Olympics is a waste of money.
3 In sports and in life, you get what you pay for.
4 Increasing participation in sports at low levels could help tackle health and social challenges.

12 When Baron Pierre de Coubertin set up the first modern Olympics in Athens in 1896, he declared that "The most important thing in the Olympic Games is not winning, but taking part; the essential thing in life is not conquering, but fighting well." These days, it can seem that this core principle has been forgotten, (1) ______________ .

The hosting countries spend huge amounts of money to hold the 16-day event. Many of the countries taking part invest huge sums in programs for elite athletes. And that money is not spent to come in fourth; the only thing that matters is having "the best Games" and winning medals—preferably gold.

The figures are enormous! Depending on who you ask, China spent 40 billion dollars on the Beijing Olympics and Russia invested 50 billion in Sochi; the Rio and London Games each cost between 14 and 18 billion dollars. In terms of money for athletes, the UK spent over 400 million dollars supporting 1,300 top competitors. This funding is directly linked to success: those who fail to achieve their targets will have their funding cut and, in some cases, completely removed. (2) ______________!

Similarly, several years ago, China established a system known as *Juguo Tizhi* ("whole country support for the elite sport system") for developing athletes. Children are identified as potential sports stars between the ages of six and nine, and are sent to special sports schools run by the local government, (3) ______________ . Those who prove to have talent move on to a semi-professional schedule of four to six hours a day, five or six days a week. Later, the top performers move on to provincial training centers. Students there live and breathe their sport and hope to be selected for their provincial team (4) ______________ . There are around 400,000 young people in this system, whose main purpose is to win glory for their nation. In the years before Beijing, it accounted for a very large percentage of all sports funding.

In both sports and life, you tend to get what you pay for; (5) ______________ . China came in first in Beijing, and Great Britain got its highest ranking in over 100 years in 2016. The question is whether this search for success at all costs comes at the expense of investing in something which is arguably more valuable: (6) ______________ . Seeing your team win can obviously lift your spirits. However, this feeling is only temporary, while taking part in regular exercise and sports has been shown to have long-term physical and psychological benefits. Given this, surely spending more money on increasing sports participation from the lowest levels up would be a better way of tackling some of the health and social challenges that many countries face.

4 Read about what some countries will do to host the Olympics and do well. Complete the text with the phrases (a–f).

a the more money you spend, the better the results
b overtaken by the other motto de Coubertin is known for: "faster, higher, stronger"
c local clubs and competitions; facilities for people to stay healthy and play for fun
d and then to be full-time professional athletes representing their country
e where they train for up to 15 hours a week
f So much for the value of just "taking part"

5 **MY PERSPECTIVE**

Work in pairs. Discuss the questions.

1. Would you like to participate in a system like *Juguo Tizhi*? Why?
2. Do you know any schools that specialize in sports? Do you think they are a good idea? Why?
3. Do you have to play sports at school? How much importance is given to winning?
4. Have you seen any great sporting events? How did they make you feel? Why?

CRITICAL THINKING Supporting arguments

Sometimes writers select information to support their point of view.

6 Work in pairs. Read the facts below. Do they support an argument for spending money on the Olympics? Why?

1. Six million dollars of the Beijing Olympics' costs went toward sports. The rest included new subway lines, an airport terminal, a light railway, and roads.
2. The majority of *Juguo Tizhi* athletes retire from their sport without a formal education.
3. According to the Chinese National Audit Office, the Beijing Olympics made a profit of 146 million dollars.
4. Montreal took over 30 years to pay off its debts from holding the Olympics.

7 A city in your country wants to host the Olympics. Divide into two teams—one for and one against. In your teams, discuss the arguments you would give. Then debate the issue as a class. Think about:

- the impact on the local community.
- what would happen after the Olympics.
- alternatives to hosting the Olympics.

Swimmers wear caps and body suits to help them move through the water faster than other competitors.

3C Getting Better All the Time

GRAMMAR Comparatives and superlatives

1 How much do you agree with this quote? Give examples to show how things are better or worse now than they were in the past.

"This is the best time to be alive—ever." —TED Speaker Gareth Cliff

Comparatives and superlatives

a *Bicycles have improved and become* ***far*** *more aerodynamic.*
b *There are* ***many*** *more people training today.*
c *Athletes are training harder and more intelligently than before.*
d *The running tracks used in the 1930s were not as fast as the ones today.*
e *The soft surface of old running tracks stole* ***much*** *more energy from athletes' legs compared to modern tracks.*
f *Usain Bolt is the fastest man in history.*
g *On average, elite shot-putters now are* ***two and a half inches*** *taller and* ***130 pounds*** *heavier than they were in the 1920s.*
h *The current hour record in cycling is* ***only slightly*** *better than it was over 40 years ago.*
i *The more money governments spend on athletes, the better the results.*

Check the Grammar Reference for more information and practice.

2 Look at the Grammar box. Read the sentences about how sports and athletes have changed. Answer the questions.

1 Which sentences use a comparative form with:
   - an adjective?
   - an adverb?
   - a noun?
2 Which sentence uses a superlative adjective?
3 Which sentence emphasizes that something is "less than"?
4 Which of the words in bold show a small difference and which show a big difference?
5 Why do we say *many more people*, but *much more energy*? What is the opposite of each of them?
6 Which sentence shows how one change causes another change to happen at the same time?

3 **PRONUNCIATION** Linking words together in fast speech

When one word ends in a consonant sound and the next begins with a vowel sound, we often link the two words together when speaking.
I don't do it as much… may sound like: *I don't do it as* (tas) *much…*

If one word ends with a consonant sound and the next word starts with the same consonant sound, we often leave out the first consonant sound.
…than it did last season may sound like: *…than it did last season*

a Read about linking words together in fast speech. Then listen to the sentences. Underline where you hear the links. 13

1 I'm better at it than I used to be.
2 It's the best thing I've experienced in my life.
3 I don't do it as much as I used to.
4 It's a lot more popular than it used to be.
5 It's a bit more difficult than it was in the past.
6 It's far easier than it was in the past.
7 I'm not as good at it as I'd like to be.
8 They're doing worse than they did last season.

b **Work in groups. Replace *it* in each sentence to make sentences that are true for you.**

I'm better at speaking English than I used to be!

4 **Read about how small changes made a big difference for the British cycling team. How can small changes make big differences in your life?**

Between the Olympics in 1908 and 2004, the British cycling team won just three gold medals. No British cyclist had even come close to winning (1) ______________ world's greatest cycle race, the Tour de France. Yet over the next twelve years, the British team won more than 25 gold medals and had two winners of the Tour. How could the team perform so (2) ______________ better?

The first thing was that cycling received a (3) ______________ more funding (4) ______________ it had before and, thanks also to a new Olympic track in Manchester, the team could train (5) ______________ intensively. The coaches also began to focus on making small improvements in lots of areas. This was not just about training better and eating (6) ______________ healthily, but also included things like teaching the cyclists to wash their hands properly and finding the (7) ______________ comfortable pillow for them to use at night! (8) ______________ cleaner their hands, the (9) ______________ colds and viruses the cyclists pick up, and the more training they can do. If they do not get as much sleep (10) ______________ they need, they may ride one percent (11) ______________ the next day. The more of these small improvements you can make, the (12) ______________ the difference compared (13) ______________ your competitors.

With the recent successes in British cycling, there are (14) ______________ more people cycling in the country than there used to be. Having a much bigger pool of riders improves the chances of finding talented cyclists to continue that success.

There is a lesson here for all of us. We often set big goals which aren't so easy to achieve when perhaps we should focus on all the things we can do (15) ______________ better. Small changes can add up to a big difference.

5 **Complete the summary in Activity 4 with one word in each blank. Compare your ideas with a partner.**

6 **CHOOSE**

Choose one of the following activities.

- Write a short essay on the question in Activity 1. Use comparatives in your response.
- What is better now than in the past? What is worse? Make lists of five things that are better and five things that are worse. Use comparatives to explain the differences.
- Work in pairs. How many small changes can you think of which would contribute to these big improvements? Explain how the changes will affect the final result.
  - Improving the performance of a school's sports team
  - Getting better grades at school
  - Increasing people's life expectancy in your country
  - Stopping global warming

On average, elite shot-putters now are two and a half inches taller and 130 pounds heavier than they were in the 1920s.

3D Are athletes really getting faster, better, stronger?

“We all have this feeling that we’re somehow just getting better as a human race… but it’s not like we’ve evolved into a new species in a century.”

DAVID EPSTEIN

Read about David Epstein and get ready to watch his talk. ▶ 3.0

AUTHENTIC LISTENING SKILLS

Slowing down and stressing words

Speakers will often slow down and stress words when they are contrasting two ideas. The surrounding language can sound very fast.

1 **Look at the Authentic Listening Skills box. Listen to an extract from the TED Talk. Underline where David slows down and stresses words.** 14

The winner of the 2012 Olympic marathon ran two hours and eight minutes. Had he been racing against the winner of the 1904 Olympic marathon, he would have won by nearly an hour and a half.

2 **Work in pairs. Underline the contrasts in the extracts. Then practice saying them aloud.**

1. Usain Bolt started by propelling himself out of blocks down a specially fabricated carpet designed to allow him to travel as fast as humanly possible. Jesse Owens, on the other hand, ran on cinders.
2. Rather than blocks, Jesse Owens had a gardening trowel that he had to use to dig holes in the cinders to start from.
3. …had he been running on the same surface as Bolt, he wouldn’t have been fourteen feet behind—he would have been within one stride.
4. Rather than the last beep, Owens would have been the second beep. Listen to it again.
5. Rather than the average body type, you want highly-specialized bodies that fit into certain athletic niches.

WATCH

3 **Work in pairs. Which of these sports do you do or watch? What equipment, skills, and physical attributes do you need for each one?**

basketball	cycling	gymnastics	soccer
swimming	tennis	track and field	water polo

4 **Watch Part 1 of the talk. Guess what David is going to argue.** ▶ 3.1

a The human body has evolved to be better at sports.
b New records in sports are largely due to technology and professionalism.
c Sport is a natural part of human development.

5 **Watch Part 2 of the talk. Complete the summary with a number, year, or measurement in each blank.** ▶ 3.2

In (1) ______________, Jesse Owens held the world record in the (2) ______________ meters. If he had run more recently against Usain Bolt, he would’ve finished (3) ______________ feet behind him. However, Owens was competing in very different times, and modern runners are greatly helped by technological advances. Given the same conditions, Owens would have been within (4) ______________ stride of Bolt!

Technology also helped to improve the hour record that cyclist Eddy Merckx set in (5) ______________ by almost (6) ______________ miles, but after the rules were changed in (7) ______________, cyclists had to use the same equipment. Subsequently, they were only able to go (8) ______________ feet farther than Merckx.

6 Watch Part 3 of the talk. Match what David mentions (1–6) with the points he is making (a–f). ▶ 3.3

1 high-jumpers and shot-putters
2 digital technology
3 financial incentives, fame and glory
4 Michael Phelps and Hicham El Guerrouj
5 the Kalenjin tribe
6 a radiator

a The move towards specialized types of bodies for particular sports accelerated.
b Kenyans are the best marathon runners.
c It made elite sports more available to a wider group of people.
d Some people might have long, thin legs because of evolution.
e Swimmers have long torsos, and runners require proportionately longer legs.
f Specific groups of people have advantages for some sports.

7 Watch Part 4 of the talk. Are the statements *true*, *false*, or *not stated*? ▶ 3.4

1 When a person gets an electric shock, it activates their muscles.
2 We only use a small percentage of our brain power at any one time.
3 We can train our brains to accept more pain.
4 Primates are more suited to endurance than humans.
5 Kílian Jornet was the first person to ever run up the Matterhorn.
6 David does not expect Kílian's record to be broken.

8 **VOCABULARY IN CONTEXT**

a Watch the clips from the TED Talk. Choose the correct meanings of the words and phrases. ▶ 3.5

b Work in pairs and think of at least one example of:

1 a recent change or event that has affected people *throughout* the world.
2 someone or something that *changed the face of* your country.
3 two brands which are *essentially* the same.
4 an activity that has *shrunk* in popularity.

9 Work in pairs. Discuss the questions.

1 How much of David's talk was new to you? Was there anything he said you already knew?
2 What were the three most interesting facts for you?
3 What do you think is the most important factor in improving results that David mentions? Why?
4 Do you think all sports are better than they were in the past? Why?

CHALLENGE

Choose a sport you are interested in. Find out:

- if it has changed in the ways David Epstein describes.
- if there have been any other changes.
- how the records today compare to 50 years ago.
- why any changes have occurred.

3E Surveys

Useful language

Introducing main findings

The most surprising / interesting thing we found was that…

You won't be surprised to hear that… but one thing that was interesting was…

The main thing we discovered was…

(By far) the most popular… was…

Introducing other points

Another thing that was interesting was…

Apart from that, we found that…

Some other things worth mentioning are…

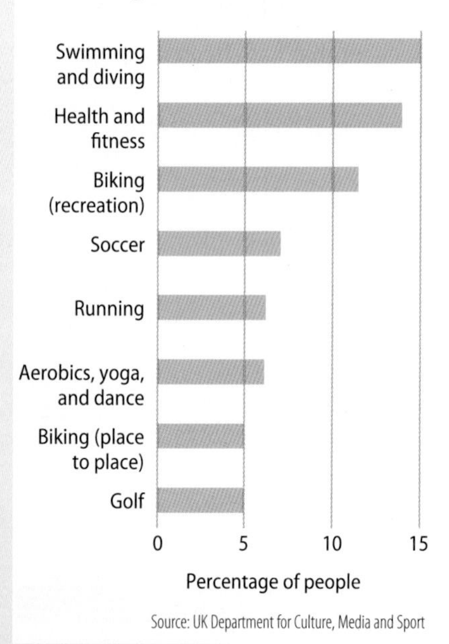

SPEAKING

1 **Work in groups. The bar graph on this page shows the results of a survey into which sports people had done during the previous month. Discuss:**

- whether anything shown surprises you. If so, why?
- why you think certain activities were more or less popular.
- which results you would expect to be similar and different where you live.

2 **Work in pairs. Discuss which claims are supported (S) and not supported (NS) by the data in the graph.**

1. One fifth of those surveyed used a gym in the month before the survey.
2. Swimming and diving are the most popular sports.
3. One in twenty of those surveyed played golf in the month before the survey.
4. Just under five percent of those surveyed bike to and from work.
5. The popularity of certain sports may change depending on the season.

3 **Work in pairs. You are going to conduct a survey. Choose a question from below or think of one that interests you. Your survey should have at least six options.**

1. What activities have you done in your free time in the past two weeks?
2. What is your favorite type of movie to watch?
3. What subjects do you want to study in college?

4 **Interview as many students as you can and take notes. Discuss your notes with your partner. Then present the findings to the whole class.**

WRITING A survey

5 **Work in pairs. Read the description on page 150 of the bar graph on this page. Answer the questions.**

1. What extra information is included which was not shown in the bar graph?
2. Which part of the description expresses opinion rather than fact?

6 **Passive forms are often used in reports. Complete the sentences using the past participles of the verbs in parentheses. You will learn more about passives in Unit 5.**

1. The graph shows the result of a survey ______________ (conduct) at our school last month.

Beach soccer is popular on Ipanema Beach in Rio de Janeiro.

2 Fifty students ______________ (age) thirteen to fifteen were ______________ (interview) about their reading habits.
3 As can be ______________ (see), only 20 percent of those ______________ (survey) said they had read a novel in the previous six months.
4 The most popular author was J.R.R. Tolkien, ______________ (follow) by Anthony Horowitz.
5 We might expect a higher response if the survey were ______________ (repeat) with a younger age group.

7 **WRITING SKILL** Describing statistics

Replace the percentages in italics with these phrases.

Almost half	A significant majority	A tiny percentage
Just under three quarters	Roughly a third	The vast majority

1 *2%* of those surveyed spend more than an hour a day exercising.
2 *35%* of those who responded play a team sport at least once a month.
3 *48%* of those who responded prefer exercising alone.
4 *65%* of those surveyed would do more sports if they had more free time.
5 *74%* of respondents play fewer sports now than they did five years ago.
6 *96%* of the people I spoke to recognize the importance of exercise.

Writing strategy

Describing statistics

When we describe statistics, we sometimes use phrases or estimates instead of specific percentages. Instead of *10.3 percent cycled*, we might say ***one in ten** biked*. We do this for variety or to emphasize a point. For example, ***over half*** may sound bigger than *52 percent*.

8 **Work in pairs. Refer to the Writing strategy and use the passive forms in Activity 6 to describe the statistics in this bar graph.**

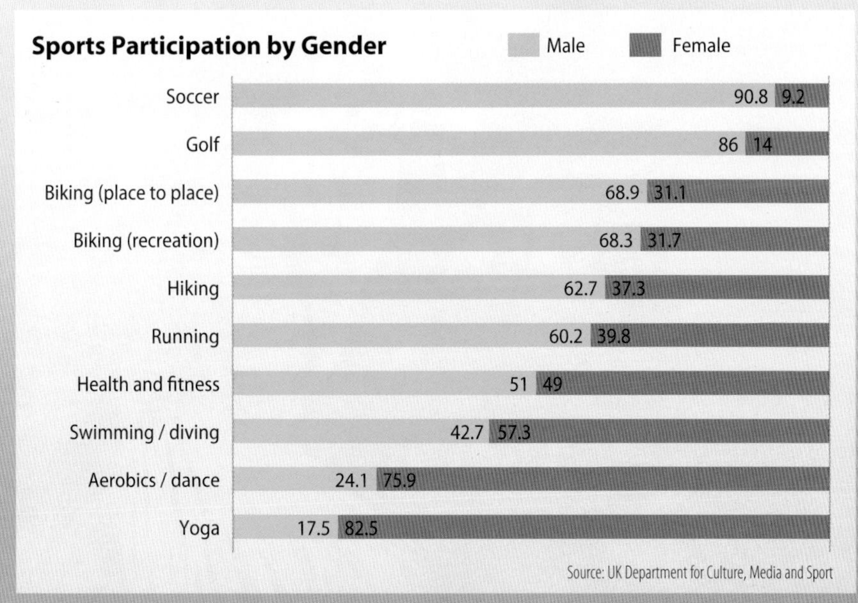

4 Cultural Transformation

IN THIS UNIT, YOU...

- discuss how art and cultural events can benefit people and places.
- read about an innovative program for teaching music.
- learn about a Spanish city that was transformed by art and architecture.
- watch a TED Talk about how a park was created on an old railroad line.
- write a *for* and *against* essay.

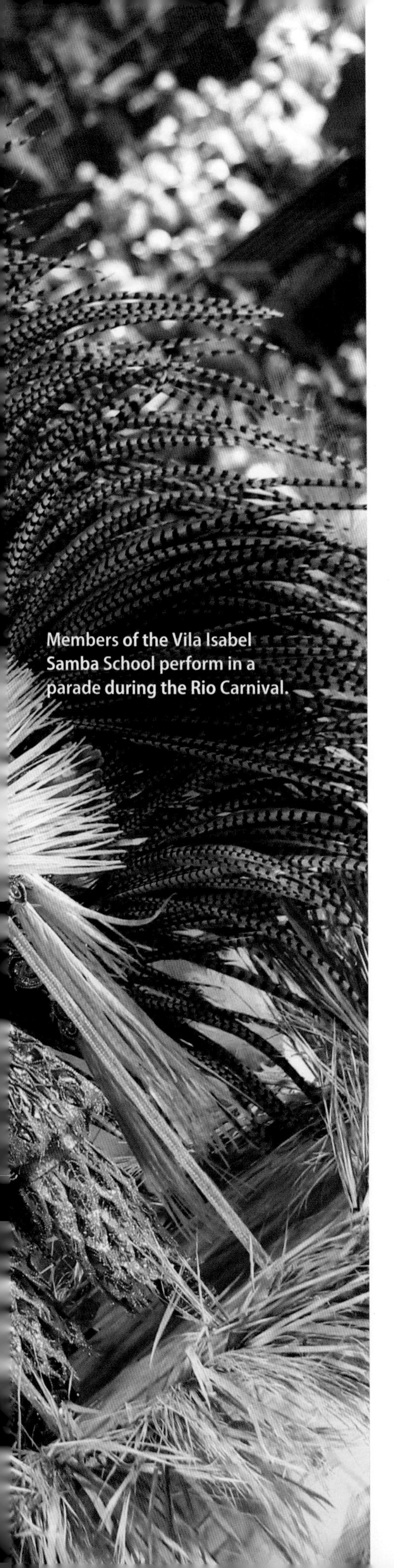

Members of the Vila Isabel Samba School perform in a parade during the Rio Carnival.

4A Putting the Town on the Map

VOCABULARY Cultural events

1 **Work in groups. Look at these cultural attractions and discuss the questions.**

art gallery / museum	art / music festival
comedy club	food festival
movie theater	music venue
public art	theater

1 Which of these cultural attractions do you have near where you live?
2 Do you go to any of them? Why?
3 Would you like to have any of them near where you live? Why?

2 **Complete the summary by putting the words in bold in the correct order.**

The Rio Carnival, one of the world's leading festivals, (1) **every held is February** in Rio de Janeiro, Brazil. During the festival, organizers (2) **huge put on a of parades number** and parties all over the city, which (3) **million tourists almost a attract**. The festival (4) **on impact has a the city big** and on people's cultural lives. The carnival involves around 200 Samba schools which compete to have the best costumes, dance routines, and musical bands. It (5) **million over income $750 in generates** locally in Rio, which comes from tourists who (6) **four-day attend event the** and the Samba schools, which can sometimes spend over 3 million dollars on costumes and preparations. The festival also (7) **Brazil's economy boosts broader**. But it's not just about money. There's (8) **wide for support festival the** because (9) **it together people brings** and helps (10) **create a of pride sense** in the country. Many of the Samba schools are from the poorest neighborhoods in the city, and the festival (11) **opportunities to offers young people part take** in cultural activities and learn new skills. In many ways, the festival has (12) **put map on the Rio** as a world city and cultural hotspot.

3 **Listen to the summary. Check your answers in Activity 2.** 15

4 **Complete the sentences with six different cultural attractions you know of. Then work in pairs and share your ideas.**

1 ____________________ is held every year.
2 ____________________ attracts a lot of tourists to our area.
3 ____________________ has had a big impact on our country.
4 ____________________ brings people together.
5 ____________________ has very wide support.
6 I'd like to get involved in ____________________ .

5 **Work as a class. Use the words and phrases in bold from Activity 2 to talk about the places and events you thought of in Activity 1.**

We have a music venue near where we live. The promoters put on a lot of small concerts and parties.

6 **MY PERSPECTIVE**

Work in pairs. Discuss the question.

What other benefits can you think of that are related to cultural attractions and events? Think about the benefits to you, your town, and your country.

LISTENING

7 Work in groups. Look at the photo and discuss the questions.

1. Where do you think the photo was taken?
2. What has been done to the building? Why?
3. Do you like it? Why?
4. Have you ever seen anything similar? Where?

8 Listen to a podcast about two big art projects aiming to make a difference. What are the plans for these places? 16

1. Port-au-Prince, Haiti
2. Birmingham, UK

9 Work in pairs. Do the speakers mention these points in reference to *Port-au-Prince*, *Birmingham*, or *both*. Listen again and check your answers. 16

1. The project is based on previous work.
2. The project aims to improve the local economy.
3. The project is initially expensive.
4. Local people are involved in creating the work of art.
5. Other things are being built as well.
6. It will bring people together.
7. It may be difficult to keep the art in good condition.
8. There might be an alternative that costs less.

10 **MY PERSPECTIVE**

Think about your community. What would you choose if you had to decide between the two public art projects and Mark's suggestion of putting on a local festival? Why?

GRAMMAR Future forms 1

11 Look at the Grammar box. Why do you think the forms in bold are used in each sentence?

Future forms

- **a** *And in Haiti, the project* ***is certainly going to create*** *jobs, and it'll be employing local artists.*
- **b** *I guess that work* ***won't last****, but I think the locals are hoping the project* ***will attract*** *interest in the area.*
- **c** *The piece should be low maintenance, so they* ***won't be spending*** *thousands of pounds every year to keep it in good condition.*
- **d** *What about once it****'s been completed****?*
- **e** *What'll happen when the paint* ***fades****?*
- **f** *We****'re about to put on*** *a community arts festival.*
- **g** *We****'re holding*** *various shows and events over a week.*
- **h** *You can continue the discussion on the Arts Spot website and get information on Mark's festival, which* ***starts*** *soon.*

Check the Grammar Reference for more information and practice.

12 Match each explanation of how to create future forms with an extract in the Grammar box. There are two extracts for one of the explanations.

1. The simple present is used to refer to a scheduled or regular event.
2. The simple present or present perfect is used because it follows a time word.
3. The present continuous is used because they are talking about an arrangement they have made with other people.

With the help of Haas and Hahn, members of a Caribbean community came together to transform a part of their community.

4 *Will* + infinitive is used because they are making predictions about the future they are certain about.
5 The future continuous is used because they are talking about an ongoing or unfinished future action.
6 *Be about to* + verb is used to talk about something which is going to happen in the very near future but has not started yet.
7 *Be going to* + verb is used because they are making a prediction. *Going to* can also be used to talk about arrangements and scheduled events.

13 Choose the correct options.

Our town (1) *holds / is going to hold* a festival next year for the total solar eclipse. There (2) *will be being / are going to be* some small events in the week before the eclipse (3) *takes / is taking* place, like talks and music. On the actual day, the eclipse is expected early in the morning, so we (4) *are about to put on / are putting on* a concert with some local bands as the sun (5) *rises / will rise*. After the concert (6) *has ended / will end*, we're going to have a huge breakfast barbecue to prepare for the big event. It should be great! A lot of people (7) *will be coming to / come to* the area next year to catch the eclipse, so we (8) *will hopefully get / are hopefully getting* a few visitors here, although that's not the main reason for putting on the event. We're really doing it because we want to bring people together, and it's not like we (9) *will be spending / spend* thousands of dollars on it. If (10) *it's going to be / it will be* a success, we'll need lots of volunteers.

14 How many times can you complete the sentences so that they are correct and true? Compare with a partner and see who got the most.

1 I'm ______________ next weekend.
2 I'm going to ______________ after ______________ .
3 There's about to be ______________ in our town.
4 I will be ______________ , so I can ______________ .
5 Next semester, ______________ .
6 In five years' time, ______________ .

15 Work in pairs. Make a list of at least four ideas for pieces of art, cultural events, or festivals for your community.

16 Work with another pair of students. Compare the ideas you came up with in Activity 15. Discuss which you think would:

- be the most fun.
- be best at bringing the whole community together.
- do most to boost the local economy.
- have the longest lasting impact.
- be the most difficult to organize.

17 Work in the same groups. Choose one of your ideas. Discuss more about the details of the project. Use future forms. Think about:

- the venue.
- how long it will take to set up and how long it will last.
- who will take part.
- who will organize it (professionals / volunteers).
- how much it will cost.
- how you will raise the money.
- any permission you will need.
- how to get people to support the project.
- anything else you think might be important.

18 Present your ideas to the class. Vote for your favorite.

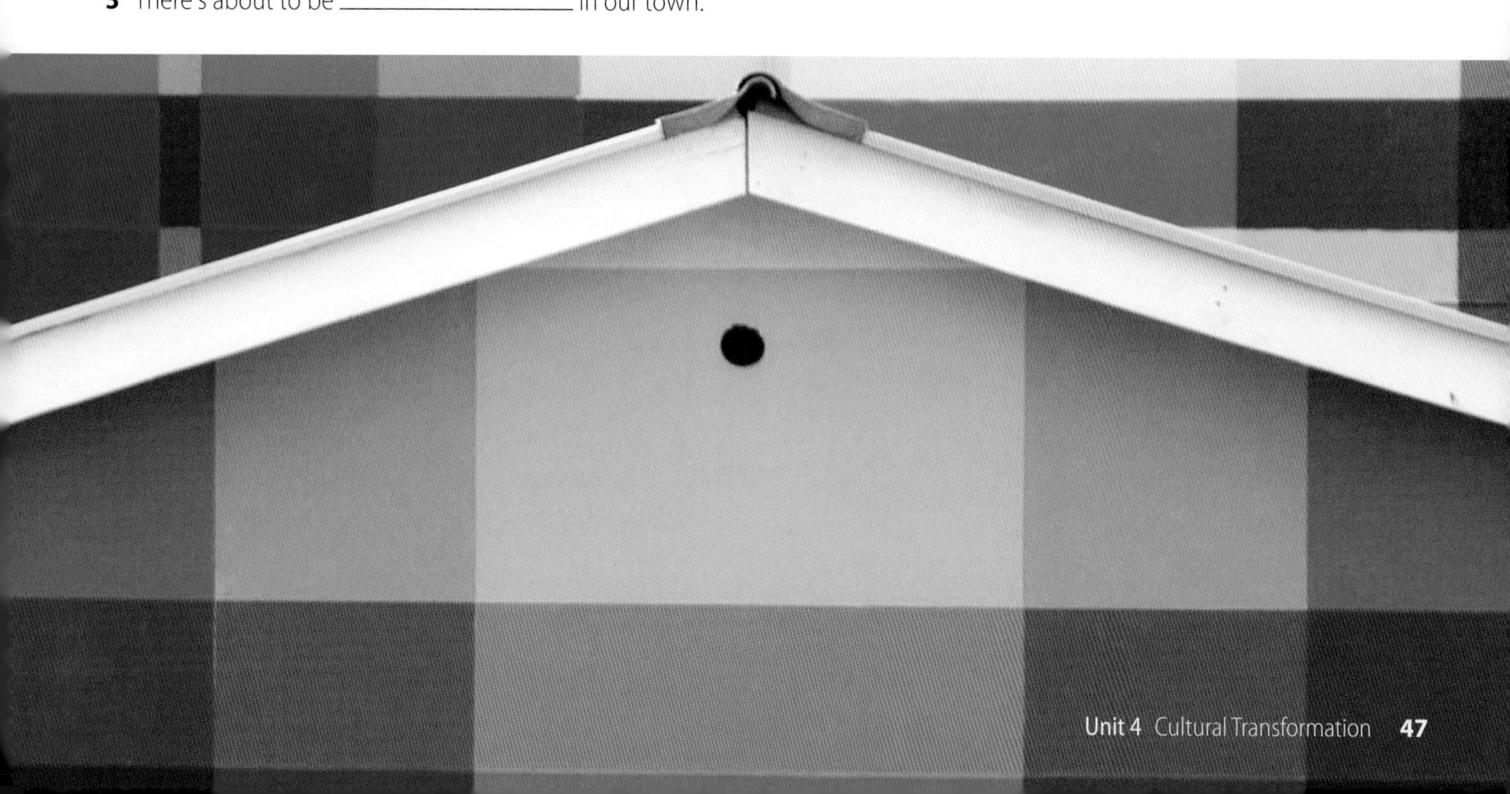

4B Music to Their Ears

A SYSTEM THAT'S LEADING THE WAY

Gustavo Dudamel is the musical director of the Venezuelan Youth Orchestra.

VOCABULARY BUILDING

Adjective and noun collocations 2

It is a good idea to notice and learn adjective-noun collocations. When you learn them, consider how they might be used. Think about:

- what verbs or phrases go with the collocation.

*give an **individual performance** / get a mark for your **individual performance***

- examples from real life.

*We have to work in groups, but we get a mark for our **individual performance**.*

1 Work in pairs. Look at these adjective-noun collocations. Take turns explaining what each one means. Use a dictionary, if necessary.

diverse social backgrounds
hard work
leading orchestra
mixed results
straightforward process
fierce ambition
innovative program
low income
private companies
strict set of rules

2 Work in pairs. Put the collocations in Activity 1 in pairs and say how they might be linked together.

fierce ambition / private companies

To get to the top of a private company, you need fierce ambition.

READING

3 Read about *El Sistema*, a program for teaching music. Put the sentences in the correct places in the article. There is one extra sentence that you do not need to use.

a It has also been credited with improving relations between different communities and saving many children from getting involved in gangs and violence.
b Obviously, the resources that the Venezuelan government puts into *El Sistema* are important.
c Central to *El Sistema* is a focus on discipline and commitment.
d Abreu was also a politician and a minister in the government.
e However, it seems that there are always individuals whose lives are changed.

17 **JOSE ANTONIO ABREU** trained and worked as an economist for many years, but his dream was to have a life in music. He fulfilled that dream, first through individual performance, but later, and more importantly, by founding *El Sistema. El Sistema* is an innovative program for teaching music to children from diverse social backgrounds. It has been so successful that an orchestra that is part of the program, the Venezuelan National Youth Orchestra, has been named among the five leading orchestras in the world. (1) ________ .

When he first started the orchestra, Abreu had managed to get 50 music stands for the 100 children he was expecting to come and rehearse. In the end, only 11 showed up. What was he going to do? Give up? Try to get more children involved? In fact, he went several steps further, and promised those 11 students that he would turn the orchestra into a world leader! So apart from this fierce ambition, how did it happen?

(2) ________ . It pays for instruments and teaching for over 500,000 young musicians who are involved in the program and also provides monthly grants to older students as a reward for their hard work. It also pays for performances and teaching younger children in the program. Private companies often sponsor local groups and parents also raise funds for tours.

However, money is not the only factor in its success. (3) ________ . New students can start from as young as three, but students and their parents must agree to a strict set of rules and attend classes and rehearsals for between one and four hours a day, up to six days a week. Teachers may visit parents to help them understand the hours required to improve and how to support their children.

While discipline is important, the musical training also emphasizes fun, team spirit, physical expression, and the value of performance. Students start in a choir and work on rhythm and percussion, before moving on to playing the recorder, and then finally choosing their instrument at the age of seven. (4) ________ .

El Sistema is seen by many people from low-income families as a way to stay in education and escape poverty. It can present opportunities to travel via tours within Venezuela and abroad. (5) ________ . No wonder many other countries have looked to copy the program.

Setting up a "sistema" is not a straightforward process, and there have been mixed results. (6) ________ . As one parent from the Scottish Sistema put it, "My son was struggling, and I was worried he was going to drop out of school and end up hanging out with the wrong kids. *El Sistema* has made a huge difference. He's gained confidence, learned discipline, and he's definitely back on track."

f Yet, 40 years ago, such an idea seemed a long way off.
g Lessons are mainly conducted as a group, with all the class working towards performing a piece in front of an audience.

4 **Read about *El Sistema* again. Answer the questions.**

1. How many children went to Abreu's first rehearsal? How many participate now?
2. How old are children when they choose a musical instrument?
3. How much do they practice?
4. Why do other countries like *El Sistema*?

5 **Work in pairs. Discuss the questions.**

1. Have you ever learned how to play a musical instrument? How good were / are you?
2. If you gave up playing a musical instrument, why?
3. If you still play a musical instrument, how much do you practice? Do you ever perform?
4. What kind of music do you listen to? What do you like about it?

6 **Work in pairs. Look at the adjective-noun collocations in Activity 1 again. Tell each other what was said about them in the article. Check your answers.**

CRITICAL THINKING Understanding and evaluating ideas

If you want to copy a successful idea or make use of what you have learned in a new context, you need to understand all the factors that made the idea a success and evaluate how far they can be applied in a new context.

7 **Work in groups. Discuss the different factors you read about that help make *El Sistema* a success.**

8 **Work as a class. Discuss:**

1. Are all the factors you discussed in Activity 7 possible in your country? Why?
2. Are there any factors that you think are not necessary? Why?
3. Would *El Sistema* work in your country? Why?

9 **MY PERSPECTIVE**

Would you like to participate in a program like *El Sistema*? Why?

The Guggenheim Museum contributed to the "Bilbao Effect."

4C High Hopes

GRAMMAR Future forms 2

1 Look at the Grammar box. Then look at the sentences in each set. Which sentence in each set does not show the future in the past?

a ***was / were going to***
1. Before the election, the mayor said he **was going to** make changes.
2. I **was going to** enter a painting competition but didn't finish in time.
3. I fell asleep in the car when we **were going to** the gallery.

b ***would***
1. I **would** really like to go to the Edinburgh Festival next year.
2. They thought it **would** bring a lot of investments into the city.
3. If we did more cultural activities here, I'm sure we **would** attract more tourists.

c ***was / were* + present participle**
1. The show **was starting** in a matter of minutes, so we had to rush.
2. I couldn't hear the movie because the people behind me **were talking**.
3. I only bought two tickets because I thought your brother **wasn't coming**.

The future in the past

a *My son was struggling, and I was worried he* ***was going to*** *drop out of school and end up hanging out with the wrong kids.*

b *He went several steps further and promised those 11 students that he* ***would*** *turn the orchestra into a world leader!*

c *Abreu had managed to get 50 music stands for the 100 children he thought* ***were coming*** *to rehearse.*

Check the Grammar Reference for more information and practice.

2 Complete the first parts of the sentences using *was / were going to* and these verbs. Then match them with the second parts of the sentences.

be	cost	get	hold	play	rain

1. They said the building ____________ something like $35 million,
2. The forecast did say it ____________ a bit,
3. We ____________ tickets for the concert next month,
4. They told us the band ____________ on stage around nine,
5. I thought they ____________ all their hits,
6. When they announced they ____________ the World Cup here,

a but they just played loads of new stuff. They were absolutely terrible.
b but it literally sold out in seconds. I couldn't believe it.
c loads of people were actually against it.
d but it cost way more than that.
e but we had to wait for hours. It must've been midnight before they came on.
f but it just poured all day.

3 **PRONUNCIATION** Contrastive stress

a Listen to how the quantity words in the second part of the sentences are stressed to emphasize the contrast with previous plans or predictions. 18
b Practice saying the complete sentences from Activity 2.

4 Read about the Bilbao Effect. What is it? Which of the italicized parts are grammatically incorrect? Correct them.

By the 1990s, the city of Bilbao in northern Spain was no longer the industrial center it once was and the future (1) *was looking* bleak. It was hard to see how new jobs (2) *was going to be* created or what could be done to ensure things (3) *improve*. Local authorities decided to invest over $1 billion in the hope that a new focus on culture (4) *would attract* visitors. The money (5) *was going to be spent* on transportation, bridges, parks, libraries, and the remarkable Guggenheim Museum, designed by Frank Gehry. Once people saw what the building (6) *was looking like*, excitement grew. When it opened, the authorities (7) *were expecting* around 300,000 visitors in the first year, but by the end of that year it had attracted a million! The impact on the city has been even more dramatic than people hoped it (8) *was*, so it's no wonder other cities are now desperate to copy what has become known as the "Bilbao Effect"!

5 **MY PERSPECTIVE**

Think of three possible reasons why the "Bilbao Effect" might not work in another city.

6 Listen to three people describing cultural events they went to. Answer the questions. 19

1 What event did each person go to?
2 How did they feel about it? Why?

7 Think of places or cultural events you have been to. Plan what you want to say, using the language below. Then share your experiences in groups.

It was much / way... than I thought it would be.

I wasn't expecting it to be very..., but it was actually...

It was nowhere near as good as I was expecting.

I was expecting it to be pretty... but it was actually very...

8 Work in pairs. Look at the Grammar box. Answer the questions.

1 What is the form of the future perfect? What is the form of the future perfect continuous?
2 Which form do we use to emphasize the duration of an activity before a certain point in the future?
3 Which form do we use to emphasize completed actions by a certain point?
4 Which word shows a point in the future?

The future perfect

Use the future perfect to show the time in the future by which something will be complete.

*It **will** soon **have been running** for 70 years, and over 10 million people **will have seen** it.*

Check the Grammar Reference for more information and practice.

9 Complete the sentences with the future perfect or future perfect continuous form of the verb.

1 By the end of next year, the band __________ (play) together for 30 years!
2 By the end of this course, I __________ (study) English for ten whole years!
3 I can't talk now. I'll call you after five. I __________ (finish) school by then.
4 He's originally from Peru, but by June he __________ (live) in Canada for ten years.
5 This museum __________ soon __________ (be) open for a whole century.

10 **CHOOSE** Choose one of the following activities.

- Find out about a new development in your town or country. Why was it built? Has it been a success?
- List ten things that will have happened in your life by the time you are 30. Then work in pairs. Which are the most or least likely to happen?

The Zubizuri (Basque for "white bridge") stretches across the Nervion River in Bilbao.

can have to transform how people experience their city and interact with each other. ”

ROBERT HAMMOND

Read about Robert Hammond and get ready to watch his TED Talk. ▶ 4.0

AUTHENTIC LISTENING SKILLS

Recognizing words you know

Sometimes you may not recognize words in fast speech because you expect to hear the full form. For example, in a dictionary *with* is shown as /wɪθ/, but in fast speech it may sound more like /wɪ/.

1 **Look at the Authentic Listening Skills box. Then listen and complete the extracts from the TED Talk.** 🎧 20

1 And by 1980, the last train rode. It was a train __________________ .
2 I first read about it in the *New York Times*, in an article __________________ demolished.
3 And __________________ we were the only two people that were sort of interested in the project.
4 And that's really where we started… the idea coalesced around… let's make this a park, and __________________ this wildscape.

2 **Listen to the extracts again. Which of the words were the most difficult to hear?** 🎧 20

3 **Say each sentence twice, slowly the first time—with a gap between each word—then faster, linking the words in each part of the sentences together.**

WATCH

4 **Work in pairs. Discuss the questions.**

1 Where you live, are there any old buildings, industrial places, or pieces of land that are no longer used? Do you know when or why they stopped being used?
2 Do you know of any old buildings or places that used to be used for one purpose, but are now used for a different purpose? Do you like the change?
3 What's your favorite public space? Why? How often do you go there?

5 **Watch Part 1 of the talk. Choose the correct options.** ▶ 4.1

1 In the old days, the freight line trains:
   a used cowboys to protect the goods they were carrying.
   b were pulled by horses.
   c caused several fatal accidents.
2 As time went by:
   a more freight started being transported by road.
   b the line was mainly used to transport meat.
   c people in the neighborhood wanted it demolished.
3 At the community board meeting, Robert:
   a offered to volunteer to help preserve the High Line.
   b realized he was in a small minority.
   c knew a writer from the *New York Times*.
4 The main inspiration for the project came from:
   a the spectacular views of Manhattan.
   b the industrial architecture of the line.
   c the way nature had started reclaiming the abandoned space.

6 **Watch Part 2 of the talk. Why were the following mentioned?** ▶ 4.2

1 9/11
2 100 million
3 20 years and 250 million
4 half a billion
5 three

7 Work in groups. Robert Hammond explains that a special study was designed to show whether the High Line would add value to the city. Discuss:

- how the creation of a park on the High Line might add value to the local area.
- how demolishing the High Line might add value to the area.
- who you think would benefit most in each case—and which plan of action is better.

8 Watch Part 3. Are the sentences *true* or *false*? ▶ 4.3

1. Twice as many people as expected used the High Line last year.
2. Architects have taken inspiration from the High Line.
3. Some parts of the High Line have been elevated to a higher level.
4. Robert Hammond doesn't really like the design.
5. He believes the space encourages people to behave in ways they wouldn't normally.

9 **VOCABULARY IN CONTEXT**

a Watch the clips from the TED Talk. Choose the correct meanings of the words and phrases. ▶ 4.4

b Work in pairs. Discuss the questions.

1. What different ways of reducing the number of people who get *run over* can you think of?
2. What problems might arise if ancient *relics* are found in a construction area?
3. Who do you usually talk to if you need to *figure out* what to do about a problem? Why?
4. Which ideas do you think your town or city would really *get behind*? Why?
   - Free art gallery and museum entrance for everyone
   - Spending more money on public art
   - Official areas for young people to put up street art
   - Free art materials for all schoolchildren
   - Displaying work by local poets on public transportation

CHALLENGE

Work in pairs. Make a list of all the activities you think Friends of the High Line had to do at each stage to transform the abandoned rail line into a park. Think about:

- events and meetings.
- money.
- people.
- the law.

Work with another pair of students. Then use some of the phrases below to discuss:

- what personal qualities are needed to help change a neighborhood in this way.
- which of these qualities you think you have.
- how you could develop these kinds of qualities and skills.

I think you'd need to be very… if you were going to…

You'd have to be a very… kind of person if you wanted to…

I'd like to think I'm fairly…

I'd be lying if I said I was…

The best way to get better at… would be to…

4E What's the plan?

SPEAKING

Useful language

Making suggestions

Do you feel like going to...?

I was wondering if you'd like to go to...?

Rejecting suggestions

To be honest, it's not really my kind of thing.

Doesn't really sound like my kind of thing, I'm afraid.

Suggesting alternatives

OK. Well, in that case, how about going to...?

OK. Well, if you'd rather, we could always go to...

1 **Choose the options that are true for you. Then work in pairs and explain your choices.**

1. I usually go out to meet friends *four or five times a week / two or three times a week / maybe once a week.*
2. I *hardly ever / sometimes / often* go out with my parents.
3. I prefer going out *alone / with one or two close friends / with a big group.*
4. When it comes to deciding where and when to meet, *I let other people decide / we generally try to reach a group decision / I basically like to take charge.*
5. I mostly like going to *the same place / different kinds of places.*
6. When I go out with friends, *I like to plan everything in advance / I'm happy to just go with the flow and see what happens.*
7. I *often / rarely / never* go to cultural events like concerts, exhibits, and plays.

2 **Listen to two friends making plans. Answer the questions.** 21

1. What different cultural events do they mention?
2. What do they decide to do in the end?
3. Why are the other ideas rejected?
4. Where and when do they arrange to meet? Why?

3 **Listen to the two friends again. Complete the sentences by adding two or three words in each blank.** 21

1. I was wondering. Do you ______________ somewhere with me tomorrow?
2. Where did you have ______________ ? Anywhere in particular?
3. OK. What ______________ is it? I'm not really into art, so...
4. How about ______________ this band that are playing in the park tomorrow night?
5. What about just going to see a film? Would you be ______________ that?
6. Let's ______________ the later one—but meet a little bit earlier.
7. I'll book tickets ______________—just to ______________ .

4 **Work in pairs. Make plans to go to a cultural event. Make sure you:**

- use real places or events that are local to you.
- reject at least one suggestion and explain why.
- arrange where and when to meet.
- use language from Activity 3 and the Useful language box.

Some festivals and events that attract a lot of people like this color run sometimes require a large cleanup operation.

WRITING A *for* and *against* essay

5 Work in pairs. Look at this essay title. Think of two reasons why you might agree with the statement in the title, and two reasons why you might disagree.

Building a new museum would boost tourism in the area and benefit the whole community

6 Read the essay on page 150. Does the writer agree with the statement in the essay title? Why?

7 **WRITING SKILL** Introducing arguments

Work in pairs. Look at the essay on page 150 again. Use the Writing strategy box to identify each of the three stages of the introduction. Answer the questions.

1. How does the writer stress the importance of the subject?
2. What phrase is used to introduce an opposing point of view?
3. How does the writer signal a disagreement?

8 Complete the sentences, which give a weak argument, with these words.

believed	claimed	common	seen	sometimes	supposedly

1. It is ______________ said that art is a mirror of society. In fact,…
2. Creativity ______________ belongs to the world of the arts. In reality, though,…
3. It is widely ______________ that music can help to connect young people from different backgrounds. However,…
4. It is often ______________ that comedy works best when it's cruel. However,…
5. Museums are sometimes ______________ as being of no interest to young people. However,…
6. One ______________ argument against more focus on the arts in schools is that they do not make students more employable. In reality,…

9 Work in pairs. Complete the second sentences in Activity 8 to show how each of the arguments could be seen as weak.

10 Choose one of the options and write a *for* and *against* essay of 250 words.

a Argue the opposite point of view to the student essay you read on page 150.
b Write an essay on one of these titles:
What our city needs is a big new concert hall
We should not host a festival because the cleanup is too expensive
New technologies have had a very negative effect on our cultural lives

Writing strategy

Opening paragraph

When writing the opening paragraph of a *for* and *against* essay:

- show the reader you know why the subject is relevant.
- give what you feel is a weak argument or point of view.
- say why you disagree and give your own opinion.

Useful language

Showing relevance

Over recent years,… has become increasingly important.

…is getting better and better / worse and worse at the moment.

Over the last few years, there has been a dramatic increase / drop in…

Introduce an opposing view

It is sometimes said that…

It is often claimed that…

Say why we disagree

…but, in fact,…

In reality, though,…

However,…

5 It's Not Rocket Science

IN THIS UNIT, YOU...

- learn about and discuss different life hacks.
- read about why humans are curious.
- learn about brain research.
- watch a TED Talk about science being for everyone.
- design and write about an experiment.

Taylor Wilson is the youngest person ever to produce a type of energy called *nuclear fusion*. He did it by building a reactor in his parents' garage.

5A Life Hacks

VOCABULARY Science in action

1 Work in groups. Discuss the questions.

1 In what ways has science made life easier or better in your lifetime?
2 Can you think of two mysteries science has yet to solve?
3 Which scientists have you heard of? Why are they famous?
4 What personal qualities are most important if you want to be a scientist? Why?

2 Work in pairs. Do you understand the words in bold? Use a dictionary, if necessary.

1 **design** an experiment
2 **conduct** research
3 **form** a hypothesis and **prove** it
4 **put** a substance in water and **heat** it **up** to help it **dissolve**
5 **create** a chemical reaction that **releases** a gas
6 **track** students' progress
7 **record** the results of an experiment and **analyze** them
8 **write** a report and **add** references at the end
9 **place** something under a microscope
10 **reward** hard work
11 **get rid of** a chemical
12 **submit** an assignment

3 Work in pairs. Do the actions in Activity 2 happen in your science classes at school? Who does each activity? Give examples.

We don't really design experiments at school. We just follow the ones in the textbook or do what the teacher tells us to do.

4 Complete the phrases. Add verbs from Activity 2 that are commonly used with each set of words.

1 ...a theory / ...an opinion
2 ...samples / ...the results
3 ...an operation / ...a survey
4 ...chemicals into the atmosphere / ...an animal
5 ...an essay / ...it before the deadline
6 ...their effort / ...her for her work
7 ...the movement of birds / ...your progress

5 Work in pairs. Compare your answers in Activity 4. Then think of one more word or phrase to go with each verb. Use a dictionary, if necessary.

6 Look again at your completed phrases in Activity 4. Who might perform each action? Why?

7 MY PERSPECTIVE

Work in groups. Discuss the questions.

1 What science experiments have you done at school that you enjoyed?
2 Have you ever designed an experiment yourself? If yes, what for? If no, why not? What experiment would you like to design?

LISTENING

8 Work in pairs. Read the definition. Then tell each other any life hacks you know for:

1 smartphones.
2 computers / computer games.
3 the home.
4 food and drink.

Life hack /laɪf hæk/ *noun* [countable]
A simple solution or a piece of advice that helps you solve a problem, save time, or improve how something works.

9 Listen to an extract from a radio show called *Life Hacks*. Answer the questions. 22

1 What four life hacks are mentioned?
2 What problems do the life hacks help solve?

10 Correct the false information in each sentence. Then listen again to check your ideas. 22

1 Marie bought herself a phone for her birthday.
2 Marie's a morning person.
3 It's best to put the paper cup right next to your bed.
4 The cup throws the sound around the room.
5 The app alters your sleep patterns.
6 Phones can be charged faster on airplanes.
7 Spicy food increases the temperature in your mouth.
8 The chemical in chilies is easily dissolved with water.

11 Complete the extracts with three words in each blank. Then listen again to check. 22

1 Well, I ________________ this lovely new smartphone.
2 And of course it works better as an alarm if the cup ________________ far away from your bed, as then ________________ to get up to turn it off.
3 The cup channels the sound in one direction, whereas normally ________________ around all over the place.
4 ________________ to track your sleep patterns and wake you up during light sleep rather than deep.
5 If your ________________ and you need it done ASAP, then what you need to do is put it in airplane mode.
6 An email has ________________ to me by Maxine, who's suggested a hack for anyone out there who likes a spicy curry from time to time.

12 **MY PERSPECTIVE**

Which of the four life hacks do you think is:

- the most useful? the least? Why?
- the easiest to understand from a scientific point of view? the hardest? Why?

GRAMMAR Passives 1

13 Work in groups. Look at the Grammar box. Then answer the questions.

1 What tense are each of the passive forms in Activity 11?
2 Why is the passive used in each case?
3 Identify the object(s) in the sentences in the Grammar box. Are the objects direct or indirect? What do they refer to?

The passive

The passive is made by using a form of the verb *be* + past participle.

a *I was recently given this lovely new smartphone.*
b *An email has just been sent to me by Maxine.*

Check the Grammar Reference for more information and practice.

14 Complete the blog entry with the correct passive forms.

If you're making a list of the most important inventions ever, the internet should (1) ________________ (place) right at the top! Our lives (2) ________________ completely ________________ (transform) since the first web page (3) ________________ (create) in 1990. It could even (4) ________________ (say) that the internet is the ultimate life hack! Of course, various linked systems of computers (5) ________________ (use) for some time before the birth of the world wide web, and early versions of what was to become the web (6) ________________ regularly ________________ (test) throughout the 1970s and 80s. Today, though, it's rare to meet someone who has no interest in (7) ________________ (connect). For many young people, that means more than 20 hours a week online! Indeed, the internet has become so essential to our lives that some argue it is like air, and that everyone should (8) ________________ (give) free access to it.

15 **PRONUNCIATION** Stress in passives

When using the passive, greater stress is placed on the main verb and less stress is placed on the auxiliary verb.

a Look at the completed blog entry in Activity 14. Which word is stressed in each passive construction?
b Work in pairs. Practice reading the blog entry in Activity 14 with the correct stress.

16 Work in pairs. Discuss the questions.

1 Do you agree that the internet is the most important invention ever? Why?
2 What other inventions would you put near the top of the list? Why?

17 Underline the passives in the descriptions. Can you name the things described?

1 The name is taken from Tagalog, a language that's spoken in the Philippines, where it was used as a weapon for hundreds of years. It was first produced as a toy in California in the 1920s.
2 It is thought that it was first produced in Mocha, Yemen, over a thousand years ago. It's now consumed all over the world—particularly in the morning.
3 It was first invented in Ancient China over 2,000 years ago for use in government, but wasn't introduced into Europe until the 11th century.
4 You've probably been asked to type letters into one of these when using the web. They're used to prevent spam and were invented by TED speaker Luis Von Ahn from Guatemala.

18 Work in pairs. Write a description of something like in Activity 17. Use the passive. Then work with another pair of students. Can they correctly guess what is being described?

People have created more original ways to use cups as loudspeakers.

5B Curiosity, Cats, and Kids

VOCABULARY BUILDING

Adjective endings

Adjectives can sometimes be recognized by their endings. Common adjective endings include:

-ous: curious, tremendous, previous
-able: reliable, treatable, adaptable
-ive: effective, innovative, imaginative
-ful: beautiful, hopeful, helpful
-al: practical, electrical, social

1 Work in pairs. Think of a noun that each adjective in the Vocabulary Building box often goes with. Use a dictionary, if necessary.

2 Choose four pairs of words from Activity 1. Write a sentence for each pair.

*Research needs to have **practical applications**.*

3 Choose the correct options.

It is often thought that (1) *innovation / innovative* in science comes from the labor of (2) *curiosity / curious* geniuses: the kinds of individuals who work in isolation, find (3) *pleasure / pleasurable* in exploration, and who don't worry too much about the (4) *practicality / practical* applications of their findings. While it is true that the (5) *use / useful* of many new discoveries is not always immediately clear, you only have to look at the results of scientific work conducted by teams to see that it is a (6) *social / society* process and involves far more (7) *cooperation / cooperative* than is often imagined. (8) *Collaborative / Collaboration* can not only help to speed up scientific work; it can also enhance the quality of the work and help share knowledge amongst a wider group of individuals.

4 **MY PERSPECTIVE**

Work in pairs. Answer the questions.

1 What are the advantages and disadvantages for scientists or researchers working on their own, as part of a small team, and in a much bigger team?
2 How do you prefer to work? Why?

READING

5 Read the article about curiosity. Which sentence is the best summary of the main point?

a Technology can help us become more curious, but it can also kill our curiosity.
b It's more important than ever to make sure kids learn to be curious.
c Social media doesn't help us know people better.
d We run the risk of becoming less curious if we're not careful.

6 Work in pairs. Which statements do you think the writer would likely agree and disagree with? Refer to the article to explain why.

1 Parents should make sure kids don't experiment too much.
2 You can't create anything new unless you recognize the limits of your understanding.
3 The people funding scientific research should demand clear outcomes.
4 Humans are basically programmed to ask why.
5 You don't get a full picture of people from the way they present themselves online.
6 We need to share ideas with like-minded people if we are to develop our curiosity.

7 Work in groups. Do you agree with the statements in Activity 6? Why?

CRITICAL THINKING Asking critical questions

To check ideas and deepen understanding, ask questions about statements or research. For example:

Research has shown that curiosity is just as important as intelligence in determining how well students do at school.

The starting points for thinking critically about this statement might be:

How is student success measured? In what subjects?

How are curiosity and intelligence measured? How different are they?

Can you be intelligent without being curious, and vice versa?

Can you be successful at school without one of these characteristics?

Is curiosity important for doing well in a job? What kind of jobs?

8 Work in pairs. What are two questions you would ask if you wanted to think critically about each statement?

1 Hard work is more important for success than either curiosity or intelligence.
2 There is some evidence that bees can think like humans.
3 It has been shown that you can only learn seven words in a language lesson.

9 Compare your ideas in Activity 8. How many of the questions can you already answer? What is the best question to explore each statement?

Back to the future?

Curiosity allows us to embrace unfamiliar circumstances, brings excitement into our lives, and opens up new possibilities. But how curious are we in the 21st century?

Curious explorers make their way through Rising Star Cave in South Africa.

23 Perhaps you've heard the old saying "curiosity killed the cat." It's a phrase that's often used to warn people—especially children—not to ask too many questions. Yet it's widely agreed that curiosity actually makes learning more enjoyable and effective. In fact, research has shown that curiosity is just as important as intelligence in determining how well students do in school.

Curiosity also allows us to embrace unfamiliar circumstances, brings excitement into our lives, and opens up new possibilities. Being curious requires us to be both humble enough to know we don't have all the answers, and confident enough to admit it. Asking the questions that help us bridge the gap between what we already know and what we'd like to know can lead us to make unexpected discoveries.

In science, basic curiosity-driven research—conducted without pressure to produce immediate practical results—can have unexpected and incredibly important benefits. For example, one day in 1831, Michael Faraday was playing around with a coil and a magnet when he suddenly saw how he could generate an electrical current. At first, it wasn't clear what use this would have, but it actually made electricity available for use in technology, and so changed the world.

Unsurprisingly, there are chemical and evolutionary theories to explain why humans are such curious creatures. When we become curious, our brains release a chemical called dopamine, which makes the process of learning more pleasurable and improves memory. It is still not known why learning gives us such pleasure, but one theory is that we may have developed a basic need to fight uncertainty—the more we understand about the world around us, the more likely we are to survive its many dangers!

However, curiosity is currently under threat like never before—and perhaps the biggest threat comes from technology. On one level, this is because technology has become so sophisticated that many of us are unable to think too deeply about how exactly things work anymore. While it may be possible for a curious teenager to take a toaster apart and get some sense of how it works, how much do you understand about what happens when you type a website address into a browser? Where does your grasp of technology end and the magic begin for you?

In addition to this, there's the fact that we all now connect so deeply with technology, particularly with our phones. The more we stare at our screens, the less we talk to other people directly. To make matters worse, all too often we accept the images of people that social media provides us with, and then feel we know enough about a person not to need to engage further with them.

The final—and perhaps most worrying—way in which technology stops us from asking more has to do with algorithms, the processes followed by computers. As we increasingly get our news via social media, algorithms find out what we like and push more of the same back to us, meaning that we end up inside our own little bubbles, no longer coming across ideas that challenge our pre-existing beliefs. Perhaps the real key to developing curiosity in the 21st century, then, is to rely less on the tech tools of our age.

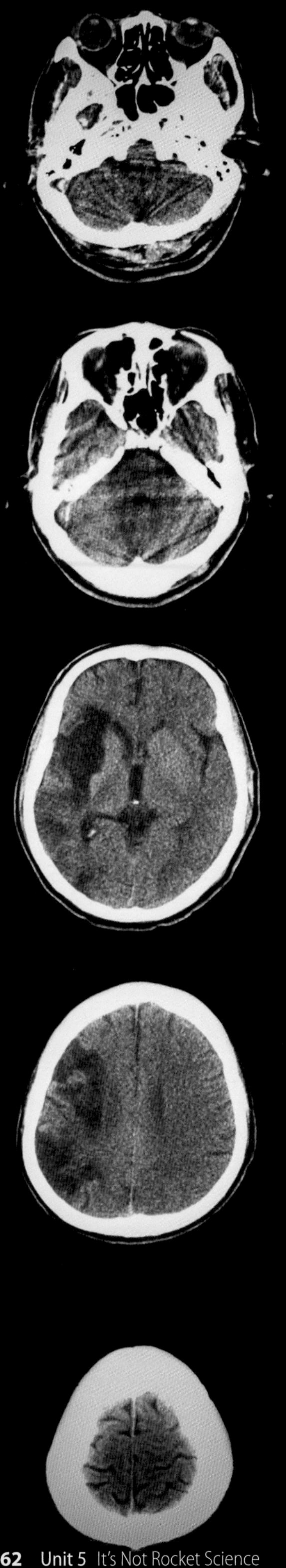

5C Mind-blowing!

GRAMMAR Passives 2

1 Work in groups. Look at the Grammar box. Do you believe the sentences are true? Explain why using these phrases.

I'm absolutely sure.
I'm not sure but, if I had to guess, I'd say…
I read about it recently. / We did it in class.
I remember hearing about it.
I've got a feeling it's a myth / it's a trick question.

Passive reporting verbs

a *The heart was believed to be the center of intelligence until the Middle Ages.*
b *It is claimed that computer training programs can limit the effects of aging on the brain.*
c *Einstein's brain was said to be bigger than average, which explains his intelligence.*
d *It is estimated that the human brain is about 75 percent water.*
e *It is well known that most of the time we only use ten percent of our brain capacity.*
f *Exercising is thought to create chemicals that reduce your ability to think.*
g *The part of the brain called the hippocampus is known to be connected with our sense of direction.*
h *It has been generally accepted that creative people have a dominant right brain.*

Check the Grammar Reference for more information and practice.

2 Listen and find out which sentences in the Grammar box are true. How many did you get right? 24

3 Work in pairs. Look at the Grammar box again and:

1 identify the whole passive reporting pattern in the sentences that begin with *It*.
2 identify the form of the verb that follows the passive forms in sentences that do not begin with *It*.
3 discuss what you notice about the different patterns.

4 Write sentences about the brain using these notes and the passive.

1 The brain / estimate / contain…around 12 percent fat.

The brain is estimated to contain around 12 percent fat.

2 It / once / think / the brain / become…fully mature by the time children were six.
3 The brain / now / know / develop…most during the teenage years.
4 It / once / believe / the brain's networks / become…fixed as we aged.
5 Brain training activities / claim / improve…listening skills and memory.
6 It / sometimes / say / brain size / affect…intelligence.
7 It / still / not really know…why we dream while we sleep.
8 Brain transplants / generally accept / be…impossible.

5 Work as a class. Discuss how you think research into the brain is carried out.

6 Choose the correct options to complete the article about brain research. Does the article cover the ideas you thought of in Activity 5?

Our understanding of the brain has changed with developments in science, surgery, and medical technology. For example, as new technologies were invented, the brain was thought (1) *to be / that it is* like a mechanical watch or telephone communication. More recently, it (2) *has been described / describes* as a computer.

After Galen proved that the brain was the center of intelligence, it was generally assumed that different parts of the brain (3) *to control / controlled* certain senses and functions of the body. However, the brain could only really (4) *understand / be understood* from the outside by studying animal brains and dissecting human bodies. Knowledge increased as a result of surgery where a patient had a tumor removed from their brain and the resulting physical change meant that functions could be mapped to the part of the brain that had been operated on. This mapping came about as much through failed operations as successful ones. Now, operations (5) *sometimes conduct / are sometimes conducted* while the patient is awake and talking. If a part of the brain (6) *touched / is touched* and it affects one of the patient's senses, he or she can tell the surgeon!

Since the late 1970s, medical technology, such as MRI scanning, (7) *has allowed / has been allowed* safe research into the brain without the need for surgery or X-rays. MRI uses powerful magnets and computer imaging to see high blood flows in different parts of the brain that (8) *believe / are believed* to show brain activity. If people (9) *have / is* their brains scanned while doing various thinking activities, researchers think they can (10) *identify / be identified* more accurately how the brain works. One result of this research is to show the limits of the brain-computer comparison. For example, it is now understood that memories are not stored in one place, but are the result of activity in many parts of the brain.

Causative *have* and *get*

a *Scientists can do research into the brain by using scanners.*
b *Research into the brain can be done (by scientists) by using scanners.*
c *To get the research done, scientists used a brain scan.*

Check the Grammar Reference for more information and practice.

7 Look at the Grammar box. Then complete the explanation.

- In the first sentence, __________ is the object of the verb *do*.
- In the second sentence, *research* becomes the __________ of the passive structure *can be done*.
- In the third sentence, we use the structure *get* + something + __________ so we can make the person affected by an action (scientists) the subject of the sentence.

8 Write normal sentences in the passive, based on these sentences.

1 They had their brains scanned while they were singing.
2 The hospital is having a new MRI scanner installed.
3 The scientists had their research evaluated.
4 I'm going to have my examination later.
5 My dad had his head examined when we were in the hospital.

9 Work in pairs. Complete the sentences in as many different ways as you can. Use a dictionary, if necessary.

1 The patient had __________ scanned.
2 I had __________ examined.
3 They should have __________ tested.
4 The scientists are having the laboratory __________.
5 I'm going to have my injury __________.
6 The research center is going to have __________.

10 **CHOOSE**

Choose one of the following activities.

- Write a set of sentences like the ones in the first Grammar box. Share your facts.
- Discuss ways in which the brain could be compared to:
  - a city.
  - a computer.
  - an orchestra.
  - a spider's web.
- Write about one of these experiences.
  - a time you had to have something scanned or tested
  - a time something in the news proved to be wrong

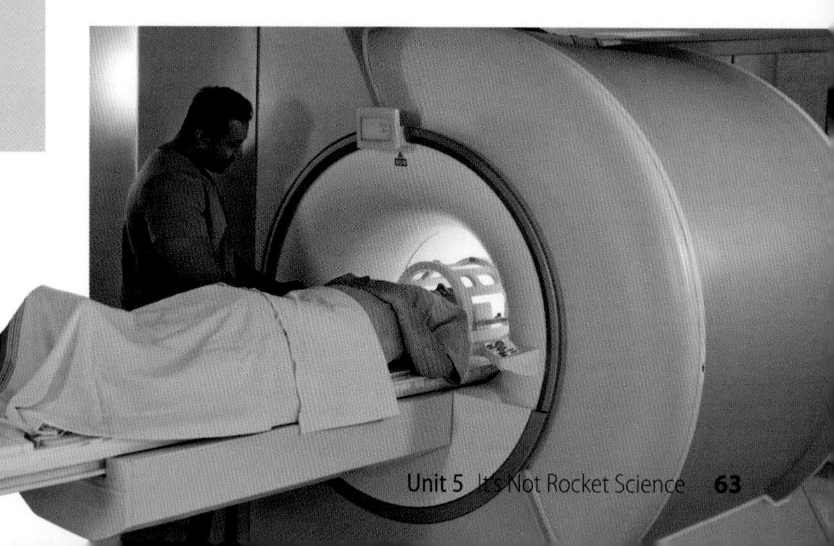

Since the late 1970s, medical technology, such as MRI scanning, has allowed safe research into the brain without the need for surgery or X-rays.

AUTHENTIC LISTENING SKILLS

Fillers

You can use words and phrases like *right, all right,* and *you know* to ask for agreement, to check that people are understanding, or as a filler while we pause or move on to the next point.

So, this game is very simple. All you have to do is read what you see. ***Right?***

1 Look at the Authentic Listening Skills box. Listen to the extract. Identify where Beau adds *right* or *all right*. 25

What are you reading? There are no words there. I said, read what you're seeing. It literally says, "Wat ar ou rea in?" That's what you should have said. Why is this? It's because perception is grounded in our experience. The brain takes meaningless information and makes meaning out of it, which means we never see what's there, we never see information, we only ever see what was useful to see in the past. Which means, when it comes to perception, we're all like this frog. It's getting information. It's generating behavior that's useful.

2 Practice reading aloud the extract in Activity 1 in a similar style to Beau.

WATCH

3 Work in groups. Discuss the questions.

1. Are you good at science? Why?
2. In what ways do you think science is similar to play?
3. Have you ever asked someone a question about science that they could not answer? What was it?

4 Put the sentences (a–h) in order. The first and last are given.

1 Perception is grounded in our experience.

- **a** These are the exact same ways of being you need in order to be a good scientist.
- **b** If perception is grounded in our history, it means we're only ever responding according to what we've done before.
- **c** Uncertainty is what makes play fun. It opens possibility and it's cooperative.
- **d** The question "why?" is one of the most dangerous things you can ask, because it takes you into uncertainty.
- **e** But actually, it's a tremendous problem, because how can we ever see differently?
- **f** So what is evolution's answer to the problem of uncertainty? It's play.
- **g** So if you add rules to play, you have a game. That's actually what an experiment is.
- **h** Now… all new perceptions begin in the same way. They begin with a question.

10 So armed with these two ideas—that science is a way of being and experiments are play—we asked, can anyone become a scientist?

5 Watch Part 1 of the talk. Check your order of the sentences in Activity 4. ▶ 5.1

6 What does Beau not mention when he talks about uncertainty making play fun?

- **a** Play is adaptable to change.
- **b** Play is cooperative.
- **c** Play opens up possibility.
- **d** Play is unrewarding.

7 Watch Part 2 of the talk. Are the sentences *true*, *false*, or *not stated*? ▶ 5.2

1 None of the questions the children thought of had ever been studied before.
2 The children wanted to research if bees adapt their behavior to solve problems like humans do.
3 Bees are one of the most intelligent insects.
4 The experiment required bees to recognize the correct color to get a reward.
5 There were several ways for the bees to solve the puzzle the children set up.
6 The results of the experiment were surprising.
7 Beau wrote the journal article.
8 The paper was rejected by the publisher because it was written in the wrong style.

8 Watch Part 3 of the talk. Answer the questions. ▶ 5.3

1 How did the research finally get published?
2 What was the reaction to the research?
3 What were two lessons that Amy learned?

9 Amy says that changing the way a person thinks about something can be easy or hard. Explain why you think it would be easy or hard to change the way people think about:

- what they eat.
- what they watch on TV.
- where they shop.

10 **MY PERSPECTIVE**

Did the TED Talk change your views about science and scientists at all? In what way?

11 **VOCABULARY IN CONTEXT**

a Watch the clips from the TED Talk. Choose the correct meanings of the words and phrases. ▶ 5.4

b Work in pairs. Talk about:

- a time you received a *reward* for doing something.
- a time you regret *not bothering* to do something.
- an interesting or possible *link* that scientists have discovered in recent times.
- a time you had to *adapt* to a new situation.
- people you think should be given more of *a voice*.

CHALLENGE

Beau and Amy do not explain much about how the experiment worked, apart from showing the one pattern of flowers. Work in groups. Discuss how you would:

- give rewards to bees for going to "good flowers."
- identify which bees are going to which flowers.
- train the bees to learn the pattern of one color surrounded by another.
- check that the bees aren't just "smelling" the good flowers.
- check that the bees aren't just choosing the good flowers by color.
- check that the bees aren't just choosing the flowers in the middle.

Read the paper about Blackawton Bees and see exactly how the children set up the experiment and what they discovered. It's available on the TED website.

5E Conducting Experiments

SPEAKING

Useful language

Staging

The first thing we'd need to do is...

We'd also need to make sure that we (didn't)...

I suppose then we should...

Preparing research questions

I wonder if / how / why...

It'd be good to know what / whether...

We'd need to try to figure out...

Hypothesizing

I'd expect the results to show...

I'd imagine that the data would probably reveal...

I would / wouldn't have thought it would be possible to prove that...

1 Work in pairs. Look at the questions. Discuss why it might be useful to know the answer to each of them. What do you think the answers are?

1 How much does homework improve exam results?
2 Do goldfish only have a ten-second memory?
3 How many words can you learn in an hour?
4 Does going out with wet hair cause colds or the flu?
5 Do boys get more attention in class? If so, why?
6 Are people who listen to pop music happier?
7 What is the quickest way to have people board a plane?

2 Work in groups. If you were going to design an experiment for a question like one of those in Activity 1, what steps would you need to complete?

3 Listen to a short lecture on how to design experiments. Note the six main steps. Then compare your answers with a partner. Use the light bulb experiment to explain each stage. 26

4 As a class, discuss why you think:

1 certain kinds of hypotheses are easier to prove than others.
2 proving a hypothesis wrong can be an important step towards learning.
3 it's important to record in detail how experiments are set up and conducted.
4 proving a hypothesis right in the way described could be seen as insufficiently scientific.

5 Work in pairs. Design an experiment to:

a find the answer to a question in Activity 1.
b see if one of the life hacks you learned about earlier actually works.
c test another life hack you have heard about.

Use some of the language in the Useful language box. Decide:

- how you would set the experiment up.
- what kind of data you would record.
- what points of comparison you would need.
- what you would expect the results to prove.

6 Work with another pair. Explain the design of your experiment. Can your partners see any way in which it could be improved?

How can you find out if goldfish really have a ten-second memory?

WRITING A scientific method

7 WRITING SKILL Describing a process

Work in pairs. How do you think writing about a process is different from telling a story? Is the guidance typical of stories or scientific reports?

1. You avoid using personal pronouns, such as *I*, *he*, or *she*.
2. You use a wide variety of words and descriptive language.
3. You use a lot of passive sentences.
4. You write steps in the order they happened.
5. You define words you think your reader may not know.
6. You use idioms and colloquial language.
7. You summarize what you are going to tell people at the beginning.
8. You explain the reason for doing something.
9. You may add a diagram of what you are describing.
10. You have a final sentence or comment that summarizes the point of the text.

8 **Read about the process that was completed in preparation for the Blackawton Bee experiment on page 151. Which of the features in Activity 7 can you identify?**

9 **Look at the Useful language box. Use the language and these verbs to retell the process in the diagram on this page. Then look at the process on page 151 and check how well you did.**

let into	paint	pick up	place	put into
release	remove	return	turn off	warm up

10 **Write a method like the one on page 151, describing:**

- one of the experiments you designed in Activity 5.
- an experiment you have conducted at school.
- a famous historical experiment that you are interested in.

Useful language

Introducing the process

The experiment aimed to show that…

The purpose of the experiment was to find out if…

The diagram illustrates the process used to…

Figure one shows how…

Linking steps

First of all,…

Before starting the experiment,…

The bees were then released…

Once the bees had been released…

After being released, the bees…

Finally,…

Explaining the steps

They were marked **to** *identify them.*

They were marked **in order to** *identify them.*

They were marked **so that** *they* **could** *be identified.*

In order to do this,…

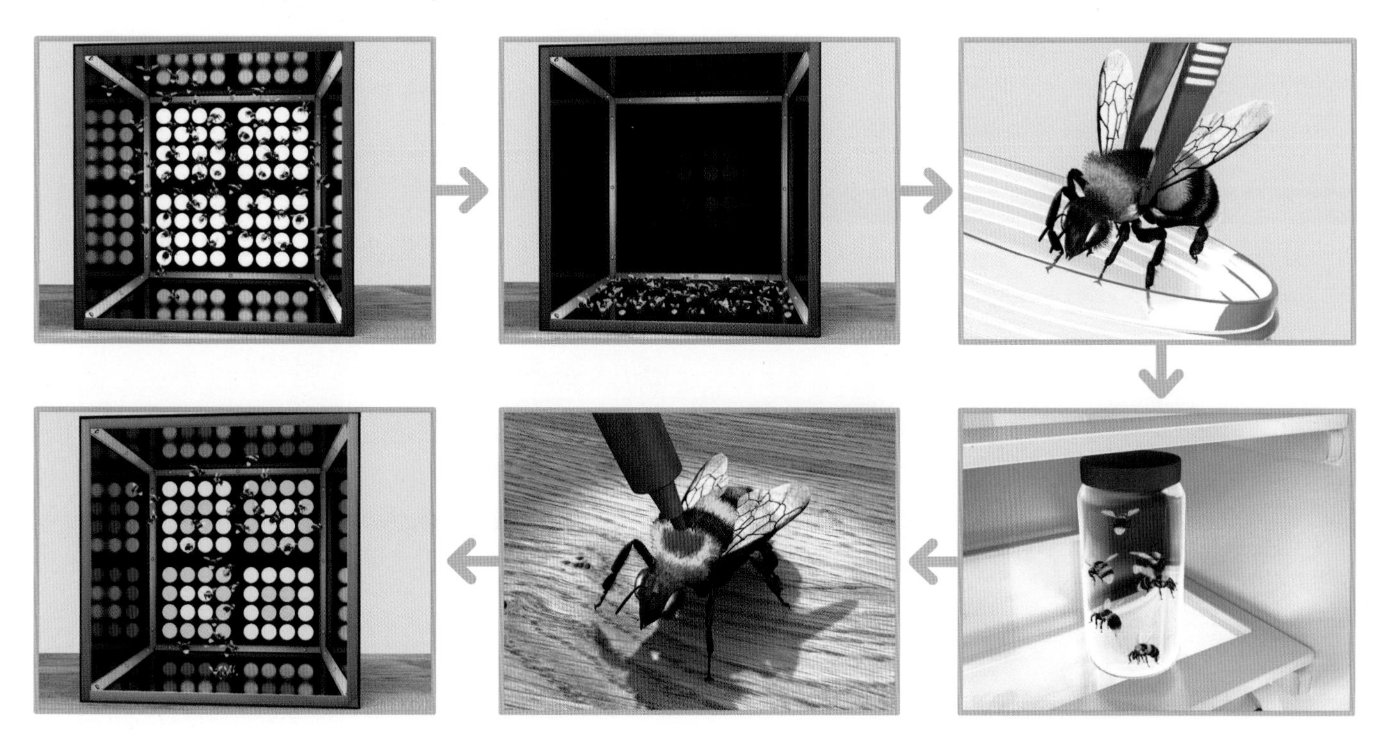

PRESENT AND PAST FORMS

Simple present

The simple present describes things that are generally true, habits, or permanent states.

*I **miss** my host family.*

The simple present also describes things scheduled to happen at a particular time in the future.

*We **arrive** at seven in the morning and then **leave** the following evening.*

Present continuous

The present continuous describes actions seen as temporary, in progress, or unfinished.

*We**'re talking** about study-abroad programs.*

The present continuous is also used to talk about things in the future that one has arranged to do with other people.

*I**'m meeting** some friends on Sunday.*

Simple past

The simple past is used to describe finished actions in the past, especially when there is one finished action after another.

*I **spent** six months in Berlin in 2015. Then I **came** home.*

Past continuous

The past continuous is used to emphasize an action in progress around a time in the past.

*I **was** actually **thinking** about canceling my trip before I left.*

Past perfect

The past perfect emphasizes that one thing happened before a particular point in the past.

*I**'d** never **left** Argentina.*

Past perfect continuous

The past perfect continuous (*had been* + *-ing*) is the preferred form for talking about something in progress over a period of time *up to* or *before* a particular point in the past. However, the past perfect can also be used in most of these cases.

*I**'d been wanting** to go there for ages.*

Remember that some "state" verbs that do not express action are not used in continuous forms.

USED TO AND *WOULD*

To talk about habits, regular actions, or events in the past, use *used to* and *would*. The simple past can also be used. Often, these habits or events no longer happen.

Would is more common than *used to*. *Used to* is often used to start a topic, and then *would* or the simple past is used to give extra details.

*I **used to do** it all the time when I was a student going home to visit friends… Often, when you **went** to some hitching spots, **you'd have to line up** behind several others already waiting for a ride… I often argued with my parents about the dangers of hitchhiking and **I would tell them** about all the amazing experiences I'd had.*

Used to or the simple past (not *would*) are used to describe past states existing over a period of time.

*Hitchhiking **used to be** / **was** / ~~**would be**~~ so common when I **was** / **used to be** / ~~**would be**~~ a student.*

Describe individual past events and situations with the simple past only. Do not use *used to* or *would*.

*I also **spent** / ~~**used to spend**~~ / ~~**would spend**~~ one summer hitching around South America.*

To form negatives, use *didn't* to show the past tense. Notice that *use to* is used in negatives.

*People **didn't use to worry** about sharing their space.*

It is common to form negatives using *never* instead of *didn't*. Notice that *used to* is used to indicate the past tense in this case.

*People **never used to worry** about sharing their space.*

When asking questions, use the auxiliary *did* to show the question is in the past tense. Notice that *use to* is used in questions.

***Did** you **use to go** there?*

There is no present form of *used to*. The adverb *usually* or the verb *tend to* is used.

*People **don't** ~~used to~~ **usually** hitchhike now.*

1 Choose the correct option.

I (1) *was going / went* on a student exchange to France recently. I (2) *was staying / stayed* with a French boy named Olivier and his family for three weeks over Easter. I (3) *had / was having* an amazing time there. They (4) *were taking / took* me skiing for ten days, which was incredible! I (5) *didn't go / hadn't been* before, but (6) *I'd been taking / I was taking* lessons to get myself ready, so I wasn't completely clueless when I got there. Over the next few weeks, both my skiing and my French (7) *had improved / improved*. The only bad thing about the trip was that while we (8) *had been staying / were staying* in the mountains, I got really sick. I don't know if it was food poisoning or what, but I (9) *felt / had felt* really bad. Olivier (10) *has been coming / is coming* here in July. I'm a little worried because I can't take him to do exciting things like skiing! Most of the time here, (11) *I just hang out / I'm just hanging out* with my friends. (12) *I still look / I'm still looking* forward to seeing him, though.

2 Complete the sentences. Use the past perfect continuous form of the verb if appropriate. If not, use the past perfect.

1 My sister ___________ (talk) about doing a student exchange for years, so it's great that she finally went.

2 We ___________ (know) each other for years before we decided to travel together.

3 I got really badly sunburned. I ___________ (lie) around on the beach all day and just forgot to put sunscreen on!

4 I ___________ (see) a lot of the country during my time there, but that was my first time in the capital.

5 This was my third time in the city. I ___________ (enjoy) it the other two times but didn't have much of a feel for it yet.

6 They were so nice. We ___________ (stay) in a B&B, but they said we could sleep at their place.

3 Complete the text about HitchBot with *would*, *used to*, or the simple past.

HitchBot was a special robot designed by scientists at two Canadian universities as an experiment to see how humans react to robots. They (1) ___________ send the robot on hitchhiking trips with instructions to try to visit certain places along the way. They (2) ___________ leave the robot at the side of the road, and when someone pulled up to see what it (3) ___________ (be), the robot (4) ___________ read a message explaining what it wanted to do. The driver then had to pick up the robot, put it in their car, and then leave it by the side of another road to be picked up by someone else. The vast majority of people (5) ___________ (treat) the robot well and it (6) ___________ (complete) four trips in Canada, Holland, Germany, and the United States.

4 Rewrite each sentence using *used to* or *would* and the word in bold.

1 My grandparents usually came on vacation with us when I was younger. **come**
My grandparents ___________ on vacation with us when I was younger

2 In the past, most workers only had one day a week off. **work**
In the past, most workers ___________ six days a week.

3 In the 19th century, women usually traveled with someone. **travel**
Women ___________ on their own in the 19th century.

4 My hair's a lot longer now. **have**
I ___________ shorter hair.

5 My dad gave up playing soccer professionally because he got injured. **to be**
My dad ___________ a professional soccer player until he got injured.

5 Complete each pair of sentences with the correct form of the verb in bold, and a pronoun. Use the adverb in parentheses, if given. Put one sentence in a past form and the other in a present form.

leave

1a When I went to Mexico in 2016, it was the first time ___________ my country. (ever)

1b ___________ ? You've hardly seen the city. (already)

get used to

2a I was in the UK for almost nine months, but I can't say I ___________ the food. (ever)

2b It's taken a while, but ___________ speaking in Spanish. Hopefully, I'll be fluent by the time we leave. (slowly)

stay

3a I was a little worried because ___________ with a host family before, but it was fine. (never)

3b Where ___________ on your study-abroad trip next year?

get

4a We took a wrong turn back there. ___________ way off the beaten path.

4b We went to seven cities in four days, so ___________ a feel for the places. (hardly)

PRESENT PERFECT FORMS AND SIMPLE PAST

Present perfect

The present perfect is used:

- to introduce or list experiences connected to a present situation / discussion.
- to refer to a completed event within a period of time including now.
- to talk about the duration of something that is still true now.

Most successful entrepreneurs ***have failed*** *at least once.*

Entrepreneurs ***have always needed*** *the confidence to recover from failure.*

The present perfect continuous is used:

- to talk about duration of activities that are still true now.
- to emphasize the process (not the completed action).

The number of entrepreneurs ***has been growing*** *over the last few years.*

Kickstarter ***has been running*** *for several years now.*

The continuous form is preferred when talking about duration, but the simple form can also be used with no difference in meaning.

The number of entrepreneurs ***has been growing*** *over the last few years.*

The number of entrepreneurs ***has grown*** *over the last few years.*

The simple form is usually used when talking about a completed action, while the continuous form is usually used to emphasize the process. This is why the simple form is preferred with specific amounts.

Since it started, Kickstarter ***has*** *~~been raising~~* ***raised*** *two billion dollars.*

*He'****s*** *~~been starting~~* ***started*** *ten different companies over the last fifteen years.*

Simple past

The simple past is used:

- to tell a story of completed events.
- with time phrases that show completed time.
- to talk about the duration of completed events.

D'Aloisio's first investor ***contacted*** *him via email from Hong Kong.*

She ***wrote*** *for ten years without success.*

VERB PATTERNS (*-ING* OR INFINITIVE WITH *TO*)

The *-ing* form is commonly used with the following verbs.

admit	avoid	can't stand	consider
delay	enjoy	finish	keep
mind	miss	practice	recommend

The infinitive with *to* is commonly used with the following verbs.

agree	arrange	decide	expect
fail	hope	intend	need
offer	plan	promise	refuse

Objects before *-ing* and *to*

Some verbs can have an object before an *-ing* form or an infinitive with *to*.

catch sb/sth *-ing*	discover sb/sth *-ing*	feel sb/sth *-ing*
find sb/sth *-ing*	got sb/sth *-ing*	hear sb/sth *-ing*
imagine sb/sth *-ing*	leave sb/sth *-ing*	mind sb/sth *-ing*
notice sb/sth *-ing*	remember sb/sth *-ing*	see sb/sth *-ing*

advise sb/sth *to*	allow sb/sth *to*	ask sb/sth *to*
beg sb/sth *to*	cause sb/sth *to*	challenge sb/sth *to*
convince sb/sth *to*	dare sb/sth *to*	expect sb/sth *to*
force sb/sth *to*	get sb/sth *to*	hire sb/sth *to*
invite sb/sth *to*	order sb/sth *to*	pay sb/sth *to*
permit sb/sth *to*	prepare sb/sth *to*	remind sb/sth *to*

Negatives can be made using *not*.

I hate ***not having*** *a cell phone with me.*

Verbs with two objects

These verbs are commonly followed by two objects.

ask	book	bring	build
buy	cook	find	get
give	lend	make	owe
pass	save	show	tell

With most verbs that can be followed by two objects, the order of the objects can be reversed if *for* or *to* is put in front of the person / group of people. The preposition used depends on the initial verb.

Can you ***email me the report*** *sometime today, please?*

Can you ***email the report to me*** *sometime today, please?*

1 **Do the time phrases show a completed time (a), a time period that includes now (b), or both (ab)?**

a The company's profits rose ____________.
b The company's profits have been rising ____________.

1 over the last five years
2 last year
3 in 2015
4 in the past few months
5 since they found a different distributor
6 when we did the marketing campaign
7 for a long time
8 over the last year

2 **Complete the summary with one word in each space.**

Madison Forbes has (1) ____________ loved drawing and design, and (2) ____________ 2010, she's been turning her designs into a successful business called Fishflops, which produces flip flops with Madison's cute sea characters on them. She came up with the name in 2006—(3) ____________ she was just eight years old—and, with the help of her father, (4) ____________ up the business, which now sells to clothing stores like Nordstrom as well as to the Association of Zoos and Aquariums (AZA). Over the (5) ____________ few years, they have also started producing shoes and T-shirts, and the company has (6) ____________ several million dollars in sales—not that Madison has been (7) ____________ a life of luxury with the profits; instead, she (8) ____________ saved most of the money to pay for college. The company also gives to several charities, and a portion of the AZA sales goes to protect endangered animals.

3 **Explain the use of these verb forms from Activity 2.**

1 Madison Forbes has always loved drawing...
2 She's been turning her designs into a successful business...
3 She came up with the name...
4 They have also started producing shoes...
5 The company has made several million dollars in sales...
6 Not that Madison has been living a life of luxury...

4 **Are the sentences correct (C) or incorrect (I)? Correct the incorrect sentences.**

1 I need to practice giving this presentation before class.
2 We've almost finished to raise the money we need.
3 Have you considered to pay someone who can do it?
4 I'm going to keep to write to them until I get an answer!
5 He admitted sending thousands of spam emails.
6 I'd recommend to report it. It doesn't look right.
7 I tried to get a better deal, but they basically just refused negotiating.
8 That report needs checking before you send it.

5 **Complete the sentences with the correct form of the verbs.**

1 I can't imagine him ____________ (post) something like that! It's so out of character.
2 I accidentally downloaded a virus and it caused the whole system ____________ (crash).
3 Our teacher always forces us ____________ (speak) in English in class.
4 I got some bad feedback on my project. It left me ____________ (feel) very upset.
5 We'd like to remind you ____________ (change) your password within the next two weeks.
6 Websites ____________ (play) music while they load is so annoying!
7 I can still remember begging my parents ____________ (buy) me my first Xbox!
8 They caught him ____________ (try) to access the school's online records.
9 If I could, I'd hire someone ____________ (take) my science exam so I didn't have to study for it.
10 I just can't see them ____________ (win). They have too many players injured.

6 **Look at each first sentence. Add three words to complete each second sentence so that it has a similar meaning to the first.**

1 My parents didn't let me use social media until I was 16.
My parents never allowed ____________ social media when I was younger.
2 That video really made me think. Online companies have so much power over us!
That video really got ____________ how much power online companies have!
3 I warned her about sending her details, but she didn't listen!
I begged ____________ send her personal details, but she didn't listen.
4 Every time you enter the site, they make you change your password.
Every time you enter the site, they ____________ change your password.
5 That video is amazing. How could anyone not like it?
I can't imagine ____________ that video! It's so amazing!
6 Don't let me forget how terrible that site is!
____________ to use that site again! It's awful!

DETERMINERS

Determiners are words used before nouns. They have two main functions:

- to show which noun is being referred to.
- to show how much / how many of something.

Articles

The indefinite article is used:

- before nouns when they are one of several, when it is not important which one is meant, or when something is mentioned for the first time.
- to say what people or things are / were.

The definite article is used:

- before nouns when it is thought to be clear which thing or things is / are meant.
- before superlative adjectives.
- as part of some fixed expressions.

No article is used:

- before uncountable nouns.
- with plural nouns to talk about things in general.
- after prepositions in many expressions with places.
- before the names of most cities, countries, continents, street names, airports, or stations.

Quantifiers

Quantifiers are determiners that show *how much* or *how many* of something. Some can only be used with uncountable nouns or plural countable nouns.

Both is used to talk about two people and / or things.

Either and *neither* are followed by singular countable nouns. They are used before a noun to talk about two choices or possibilities. *Neither* is a negative, so it is not used with *no* or *not*.

Every and *each* are used only with singular countable nouns. Sometimes it is not important which word is used, but generally:

- *each* is used to focus on individual things in a group, or to list two or more things.
- *every* is used to talk about a group or to list three or more things.
- *all* is used to talk about the whole of something. *All* is followed by uncountable or plural nouns.
- *any* is used in positive sentences when it is not important to specify the exact person or thing, because what is being said applies to everyone or everything.
- when quantifiers are used with pronouns, *of* is added after the quantifier.

COMPARATIVES AND SUPERLATIVES

Comparatives and superlatives can be made with adjectives, adverbs, or nouns.

To emphasize that something is "less than," the comparative form ...*not as X as*... is often used.

Their training was ***not as hard as*** *it is now.*

Size differences can be shown by modifying the comparative with a number or measurement, or a modifier.

On average, shot putters are now ***two and a half inches taller*** *and* ***130 pounds heavier*** *than they were in the past.*

Over a thousand more people *have run sub-four-minute miles since Bannister did it.*

Big difference	**much / a lot / a great deal / far**	better more efficient
Small difference	**a little / slightly**	

We can also add modifiers to "not as" comparatives.

not nearly as fast — *not nearly as many*
not quite as good — *not quite as much*

Remember, *many* and *few* go with countable nouns, and *much* and *little* go with uncountable nouns.

The pattern *the more... , the more...* can be used to show how two or more changes happen together or affect each other.

Comparative	Clause remainder	Comparative	Clause remainder
The longer and thinner	*your legs are,*	*the more energy-efficient*	*they are to swing.*

Look at the box to see how situations now are compared with the past.

Athletes are training harder and more intelligently than	*they used to do.* *before.* *in the past.* *they did before.*
Elite shot-putters now are two and a half inches taller than	*they were in the past.* *they used to be.* *40 years ago.*

1 Choose the correct option.

1. Mia Hamm started playing soccer when she was living in *the Italy / Italy*. Later, when she was in *the junior high school / junior high school*, she played on *the boys' team / boys' team*.
2. Hamm has done a lot to promote *a women's / the women's / women's* soccer.
3. To tell you *the truth / truth / a truth*, I'm not really interested in *motorcycles / the motorcycles*, but I admire Valentino Rossi. He has *charm / a charm / the charm* and *a lovely personality / lovely personality / the lovely personality*.
4. Jesse Owens was born in *the Alabama / Alabama* in 1913. He was *the youngest / youngest / a youngest* of ten children, and his father was *farmer / the farmer / a farmer*.
5. As *the teenager / teenager / a teenager*, Owens helped his family by delivering *the groceries / groceries* and working in *a shoe repair shop / shoe repair shop / the shoe repair shop*.
6. Susi Susanti now runs *company / the company / a company* selling *the badminton rackets / badminton rackets*. She imports *a material / the material* for *rackets / the rackets* from Japan, and they're then produced in China.

2 Choose the correct option. In some cases, both may be correct.

1. There's *not much / only a few* difference between the two teams.
2. I have *almost no / hardly* interest in sports, to be honest.
3. *Very few / Not many* talented young athletes actually become successful.
4. I've never really had *no / any* talent for sports.
5. I don't have *very much / very little* respect for most soccer players.
6. *A lot of / Most* medals we win at the Olympics are in long-distance running.
7. When the World Cup is on, I usually try to watch *all / every* game.
8. I couldn't see much because there were *a lot of / so many* people in front of me.

3 Complete the sentences with these determiners.

all	any	both	each
either	every	neither	no

1. I like the fact that you can play the game anywhere. ___________ special equipment is needed.
2. Mia Hamm was named FIFA's World Player of the Year in ___________ 2001 and 2002.
3. ___________ his school nor his family had the money to send Jesse Owens to the 1932 Olympics.
4. My brother can name ___________ player who's played for the team in the last ten years!
5. I admire ___________ athlete who works hard and has a good attitude.
6. It's a very close game. ___________ team could win, but I still think Brazil looks stronger.
7. ___________ my friends are really into boxing, but I can't stand it!
8. There's a website that shows you how much ___________ player earns.

4 Complete each second sentence so that it has a similar meaning to the first sentence, using the word in bold and two or three extra words.

1. This season they have scored 65 goals and we've only scored 30.
   This season they've scored ___________ we have. **far**
2. Usain Bolt actually ran only slightly faster than Jesse Owens.
   Jesse Owens ___________ as Usain Bolt. **fast**
3. I used to play basketball a lot, but I hardly ever play now.
   I don't play basketball ___________ I used to. **much**
4. No one has ever won as many gold medals in swimming for her country as she has.
   She is our ___________ ever. **successful**
5. If you continue to play, your injury will only get worse.
   The ___________ worse your injury will get. **longer**
6. The number of professional athletes has increased dramatically.
   There ___________ athletes in the past. **far**

5 Complete the comparatives using your own ideas.

1. I'm slightly ___________ than ___________.
2. I'm nowhere near ___________.
3. Young people these days are far more ___________.
4. There ___________ as ___________ as there ___________ in the past.
5. I ___________ than I used to.
6. ___________, the more successful you will be.

FUTURE FORMS 1

Be going to + verb is usually used to talk about what has already been planned. Unless an adverb like *probably* is used, it means it is a definite plan.

*They**'re going to** build a new museum in our town.*

***I'm going to** stay in tonight and study.*

The present continuous is also often used, particularly with plans and arrangements involving other people.

***I'm** meeting a friend of mine later.*

Sometimes *will* is used to talk about scheduled plans.

*The coach **will arrive** at nine and **will take** everyone to the museum, where the tour **will start** at ten.*

Will + infinitive is usually used at the moment of making a decision.

A: What's your flight number?

*B: I don't know. I**'ll check** later and I**'ll send** you a text with it.*

Will is usually used to make promises, threats, refusals, etc. (see Unit 6).

Will or *be going to* can be used to talk about predictions. Unless an adverb like *probably* or *possibly*, or an introductory verb such as *think* or *guess* is used, they both mean the speaker is certain about their prediction. *May* / *might* can also be used to show less certainty.

Certain	Less certain
*It**'s going to create** jobs.*	*It**'s possibly going to create** jobs.*
*It**'s going to be** a disaster.*	*It**'s probably going to be** a disaster.*
*They**'ll go** over budget.*	*They**'ll probably go** over budget. / I think they**'ll go** over budget.*
*They **won't get** many visitors.*	*They **might not get** many visitors.*

The future continuous is used to emphasize that an action is ongoing / unfinished in relation to a particular point in time or a second future action. The future continuous is *will be* + *-ing*. (*Be going to be* + *-ing* is also used.)

*It's going to create jobs and they**'ll be employing** local artists.*

When a future time clause is used, the verb is in the simple present or present perfect.

*But what about once it**'s been completed**?*

Be about to is sometimes used to talk about a plan, arrangement, or prediction concerning what is going to happen in the immediate future. *Just* is sometimes added to emphasize it is the next thing planned.

***We're about to** hold a community festival.*

***He's just about to** leave, but if you rush you might catch him before he does.*

FUTURE FORMS 2

The future in the past

When the future is talked about as seen from a time in the past, *was / were going to*, *would* as the past tense of *will*, and the past continuous can all be used.

*My son was struggling, and I was worried he **was going to** drop out of school and maybe end up hanging out with the wrong kids.*

*He went several steps further and promised those 11 students that he **would** turn the orchestra into a world leader!*

*Abreu had managed to get 50 music stands for the 100 children he **was expecting** to come and rehearse.*

Future perfect

The future perfect is formed using *will / won't* + *have* + past participle.

*Soon, over 10 million people **will have seen** it.*

The future perfect emphasizes actions completed by a certain time.

*I'll call you after six. I**'ll have finished** work by then. (= already finished before six)*

The future perfect continuous is formed using *will / won't* + *have been* + *-ing*.

*It**'ll** soon **have been running** for 70 years.*

The future perfect continuous emphasizes an ongoing action that is taking place in the present and will continue up until a point in the future.

*By the end of this course, I **will have been studying** English for ten whole years!*

The future perfect is usually accompanied by a time reference such as *before the weekend*, *by Thursday*, etc.

1 **Complete the sentences using the two future forms in bold and the verbs in parentheses. Decide which form is the best for each space.**

present continuous / *be going to*
The festival ___________ (be) great because some of my favorite bands ___________ (play).

The festival *is going to be* great because some of my favorite bands *are playing*.

1 simple present / *will*
What do you think you ___________ (do) after you ___________ (leave) school?

2 simple present / future continuous
Let's hope that when we ___________ (have) the concert outside, it ___________ (not / rain).

3 present perfect / *going to*
They ___________ (start) the project once they ___________ (raise) enough money.

4 present continuous / present perfect
We ___________ (go) on a school trip to Hong Kong after we ___________ (finish) all our exams.

5 *will* / future continuous
I ___________ (not do) much this weekend, so I ___________ (show) you around the city, if you want.

6 present perfect / *be about to* / *will*
I'm sorry, the movie ___________ (start). I ___________ (call) you when it ___________ (finish).

2 **Complete the second sentences using 3–5 words—including the words in bold—so that they have the same meaning as the first sentences.**

I'll come over to your house after I have finished my homework. **am**

I'll come over to your house, but *I am going to finish* my homework first.

1 The tickets are going to sell out immediately. **soon**
The tickets will sell out almost ___________ gone on sale.

2 First they're going to repair the houses and then they'll paint them. **before**
They're going to repair the houses ___________ them.

3 They need to raise a lot of money so they can complete the project. **to**
If ___________ the project, they have to raise a lot of money.

4 I don't think that the project will be a failure. **should**
The project ___________.

5 I could meet you when I go shopping in town on Saturday. **be**
I ___________ in town on Saturday, so I could meet you then.

3 **Complete the summary with these words.**

expected	going	than	wasn't	were	would

In many ways, Sheffield and Bilbao are similar. By the 1990s, both were post-industrial cities wondering how they were (1) ___________ to cope in the coming years. Like the Guggenheim, the National Centre for Popular Music was (2) ___________ to be a landmark building that (3) ___________ boost tourism in the city. Bosses at the Centre (4) ___________ hoping for 400,000 visitors a year, but numbers were far lower (5) ___________ expected, with only around 140,000 showing up in the first 12 months. People soon realized that the center on its own (6) ___________ going to be enough to transform the city, and it closed down before even reaching its second birthday.

4 **Complete the second sentences using the words in parentheses and 1–3 additional words.**

1 I had high hopes for it, but it was actually sort of a letdown.
It wasn't as good as ___________ (thought) be.

2 I had high expectations, but it totally exceeded them.
It was even better than ___________ (expecting) to be.

3 They ended up with three million visitors—far more than initially expected.
They ___________ (hoping) to get around a million visitors, but ended up with three times that!

4 I'd planned to go out and meet some friends, but in the end I was too tired.
I ___________ (going) to go out and meet some friends, but in the end I was too tired.

5 I hadn't planned to return yet, but I ran out of money.
I ___________ (stay) longer, but I ran out of money.

5 **Choose the correct option.**

1 Hurry up! The movie will *start* / *have started* by the time we get there, if we don't get moving!

2 *I'm going* / *I will have gone* to a concert tomorrow night, so can we meet on Friday instead?

3 *I'm helping* / *I'll have helped* a friend with something tomorrow, but *I'll have finished* / *I'm finishing* by five, so I'll call you then.

4 *I'll have been living* / *I'm going to live* here for the last five years in July.

5 I read somewhere that by the time you're 60, you will have *been sleeping* / *slept* for twenty years!

PASSIVES 1

The passive is used to focus on who or what an action affects. The passive is also used when it is unclear or unimportant who performs an action. The passive is formed using *be* + a past participle.

Simple present

The cup ***is*** *then* ***left*** *far away from your bed.*

The machines ***are exported*** *all over the world.*

Present continuous

If your phone ***is being*** *charged…*

The wrong questions ***are being*** *asked.*

Present perfect

I ***have*** *just* ***been sent*** *an email by Maxine.*

It ***has been designed*** *to track your sleep patterns.*

Simple past

I ***was*** *recently* ***given*** *this lovely new smartphone.*

We ***were*** *only* ***told*** *about it at the last minute.*

Past continuous

There was a power outage while the experiment ***was being carried out****.*

They ***weren't being produced*** *in Mexico, so I saw an opportunity.*

Past perfect

I wanted to produce them, but a patent ***had*** *already* ***been taken out****.*

After modals

*You****'ll be forced*** *to get up.*

It ***would be thrown*** *around all over the place.*

After prepositions

I'm scared of ***being asked*** *questions I can't answer.*

Some verbs have two objects: the <u>direct object</u> and an **indirect object**.

My parents gave ***me*** *<u>a great new smartphone</u>.*

Maxine sent ***me*** *<u>an email</u>.*

A passive sentence can be made in two ways when there are two objects.

I *was recently given <u>this great new smartphone</u>.*

<u>A new smartphone</u> was given ***to me****.*

I *have just been sent <u>an email</u> by Maxine.*

<u>An email</u> has just been sent ***to me*** *by Maxine.*

PASSIVES 2

Passive reporting verbs

A passive structure is often used to report general knowledge, beliefs, and assumptions. There are two common patterns after the passive.

The brain	is thought	to have over 12,000 miles of blood vessels.
	was believed	to be controlled by four different elements or "humors."
	is estimated	to weigh six and a half pounds.
	is known	to recover from serious damage.
It	is thought	(that) the brain works like a watch.
	is claimed	(that) the brain is like a computer.
	is assumed	(that) people know what they are doing.
	is well known	(that) smoking causes cancer.

In the second pattern, *it* is impersonal. It is there because in English sentences with a verb need a subject.

Causative *have* and *get*

Have / *get* + something + past participle is a passive construction, similar in meaning to the sentences in **b**. However, with this structure the person or thing that causes the action or is affected by the action can be brought in (*I* and *My brother* in the sentences in **c**). This structure is used to show that someone else does something for or to the subject.

a	*Someone stole my bag.*	*The hairstylist dyed my brother's hair.*
b	*My bag was stolen.*	*My brother's hair was dyed.*
c	*I* ***had*** *my bag stolen.*	*My brother* ***got*** *his hair dyed.*

Causative *get* is usually:

- less formal and uncommon in writing.
- used when the subject is the cause of the action. (My brother paid the hairdresser to dye his hair.)

1 Complete the sentences with the correct active or passive form of the verbs in parentheses.

1. Language (1) __________ obviously __________ (exist) for many thousands of years before writing (2) __________ (invent), but the existence of written records really (3) __________ (mark) the beginning of history as we know it. The earliest writing (4) __________ (find) in part of what (5) __________ now __________ (call) Iraq.
2. The printing press (1) __________ often __________ (call) one of the most important inventions of all time. Of course, books (2) __________ (produce) before Johannes Gutenberg (3) __________ (present) his first creation to the world, but always by hand! Before too long, thousands of books (4) __________ (print) and (5) __________ (distribute) all over Europe.
3. If you're worried about your phone (1) __________ (steal), here's a helpful hack. A special app can (2) __________ (install) so that you can (3) __________ (track) the phone if it's lost or stolen. You'll also be able to see if the phone (4) __________ (use). It can even (5) __________ (wipe) clean remotely, to stop criminals from (6) __________ (get) hold of your data.
4. The first self-driving car only (1) __________ (hit) the road very recently, but it's quite possible that cars as we know them will soon (2) __________ (replace) by this new model. Over recent years, much of the research into these cars (3) __________ (fund) by Elon Musk, a TED speaker who (4) __________ (start) lots of different companies. Thousands of self-driving cars (5) __________ already __________ (build)—and they (6) __________ (get) more sophisticated.

2 Complete each sentence by making these verbs with two objects into the passive.

---

award Ahmed Zewail the Nobel prize in Chemistry
give me it
give us some tricky questions
~~show the queen one of the first telephones~~
teach us how to do it

---

1. In January 1878, one of the first telephones *was shown to the queen* by its inventor, Alexander Graham Bell.
2. In 1999, the Nobel prize in Chemistry __________, who was the first Egyptian to receive the prize.
3. The science test was sort of a nightmare because we __________!
4. I can type very fast because we __________ in elementary school.
5. I had my watch stolen, and I was really upset because it __________ by my grandparents.

3 Complete each pair of sentences using the word in bold. One sentence should be in the active form and the other should be in the passive form.

1. **accept**
   - **a** It __________ now that increases in global temperatures are due to human activity.
   - **b** Most scientists __________ that we need to take action to reduce global warming.
2. **not know**
   - **a** We __________ exactly how many stars there are in the solar system.
   - **b** It __________ exactly how stars were first formed.
3. **think**
   - **a** Some researchers __________ that it could be possible to live on Mars.
   - **b** Mars __________ to have water under its surface.
4. **believe**
   - **a** In the past, many diseases __________ to be caused by having too much blood in the body.
   - **b** Doctors in the past __________ that they could cure diseases by removing blood from the body.

4 Complete the short report with one word in each space.

The government is (1) __________ air quality tested because high levels of pollution (2) __________ thought to (3) __________ increasing. The government is also having research (4) __________ in schools to try to find out whether air pollution is having any effect on students' performance. Air pollution is known (5) __________ affect health and is estimated to (6) __________ thousands of deaths each year. (7) __________ is also claimed (8) __________ it affects the development of the brain and young people's intelligence, but more research is needed to determine if there is a clear link.

IRREGULAR VERB LIST

INFINITIVE	SIMPLE PAST	PAST PARTICIPLE
arise	arose	arisen
beat	beat	beaten
become	became	become
bend	bent	bent
bet	bet	bet
bite	bit	bitten
blow	blew	blown
break	broke	broken
breed	bred	bred
bring	brought	brought
broadcast	broadcast	broadcast
build	built	built
burn	burned	burned
burst	burst	burst
cost	cost	cost
cut	cut	cut
deal	dealt	dealt
dig	dug	dug
dream	dreamed	dreamed
fall	fell	fallen
feed	fed	fed
fight	fought	fought
flee	fled	fled
forget	forgot	forgotten
forgive	forgave	forgiven
freeze	froze	frozen
grow	grew	grown
hang	hanged/hung	hanged/hung
hide	hid	hidden
hit	hit	hit
hold	held	held
hurt	hurt	hurt
keep	kept	kept
kneel	knelt	knelt
lay	laid	laid
lead	led	led
lend	lent	lent
let	let	let
lie	lay	lain
light	lit	lit
lose	lost	lost
mean	meant	meant

INFINITIVE	SIMPLE PAST	PAST PARTICIPLE
misunderstand	misunderstood	misunderstood
must	had to	had to
overcome	overcame	overcome
rethink	rethought	rethought
ring	rang	rung
rise	rose	risen
sell	sold	sold
set	set	set
shake	shook	shaken
shine	shone/shined	shone/shined
shoot	shot	shot
shrink	shrank	shrunk
shut	shut	shut
sink	sank	sunk
slide	slid	slid
smell	smelled	smelled
spell	spelled	spelled
spend	spent	spent
spill	spilled	spilled
split	split	split
spoil	spoiled	spoiled
spread	spread	spread
stand	stood	stood
steal	stole	stolen
stick	stuck	stuck
strike	struck	struck
swear	swore	sworn
tear	tore	torn
throw	threw	thrown
upset	upset	upset
wake	woke	woken
win	won	won

UNIT 1 A review

When writing reviews, it is common to use relative clauses beginning with *which* in order to express personal comments or beliefs.

1 Wu and Ting Ting were incredibly welcoming and did everything that they could to make me feel at home, although during the stay I was often left to my own devices because they were busy working. I had a lovely big room, my own TV, and a desk to study at. I was a little far from my school, though, which wasn't ideal.

2 I can't complain about the place as a whole. There were plenty of rides, which kept the kids satisfied, but given that the price for a family of four for the day was $195, it's just not worth it. Not when you realize that Fantasyland is cheaper. What's more, the lines are longer than at Fantasyland, as it is packed with locals. If it hadn't been as full, and we'd actually been able to go on more than three rides in seven hours—and it was less expensive—it might have been worth it. As it is, though, I'd skip it and go to Fantasyland instead.

3 After I'd checked in and been given my key, I found that my room wasn't much bigger than a shoebox! Feeling that this wouldn't work for a four-night stay, I went back down to the front desk and asked for a larger room. They then tried to charge me €40 per night to upgrade to a suitable room, which was ridiculous. We finally agreed on €9 per night for the upgrade. On top of that, parking was €15 a day! Terrible place with terrible service. They're trying to make as much extra money as they can. I'm scared to ask for another pillow, which is necessary since the bed only has one!

4 If you like to see and be seen, then grab yourself one of the outdoor seats here, order a coffee, sit back, and enjoy! Looking out over the main square, and close to the museum and the market, this is a great people-watching spot—and it does great breakfasts, lunches, and snacks as well, which is perfect if you're feeling hungry. I can't recommend it enough.

UNIT 2 A persuasive article

Grab the reader's attention by asking a *have you ever…* question to stimulate a shared experience.

Young Entrepreneur Trying to Turn a Nightmare into a Dream Business

Have you ever spent hours working on a project and saved it to your flash drive only to then lose your drive and all your work? You know you should have backed it up, but it's easy to forget, isn't it? And then you have to explain it to your teacher or boss. Awful! Well, all that might soon be a thing of the past thanks to the bright idea of a 16-year-old entrepreneur from Northern Ireland.

Persuade the reader to continue reading by saying that you will present a solution.

Mason Robinson has invented a piece of software that automatically backs up your work to the cloud when you save your work to a flash drive. As Mason says, "It has a unique aspect in saving people's work twice!"

Present factual information related to the solution.

He developed the *i-save USB* idea as part of a summer project at a local science park. Now he is trying to raise two thousand dollars through a Kickstarter campaign to improve the product and distribute it.

So why don't you support Mason to make his business dreams a reality and, at the same time, end the nightmare of lost homework and research?

Provide a reason why the reader should take action in the final paragraph.

UNIT 3 A survey

Start reporting findings by referring the reader to the source of results and explaining the aim of the investigation.

Explain the most important statistics related to your aim.

This bar chart shows the results of a survey carried out on 50 people aged between 13 and 55. The aim of the survey was to find out levels of participation in exercise in the four weeks before the interview.

During this time, 68 percent of those interviewed walked for health and recreation, about one in six biked, and over half did some kind of sport. As can be seen from the chart, the most popular sports during this month were swimming and diving, with almost 15 percent of those asked trying it at least once. This was followed closely by various health and fitness activities.

Obviously, these results were determined to at least some degree by the weather. If the survey were to be repeated in the summer rather than the winter, we might, for instance, expect the popularity of soccer and golf to increase.

Among the people who did not take part in any exercise during the month in question, the main reasons given for not participating were lack of time, cost, and general poor health.

Account for the results and explain how one might make the statistics more reliable.

You may choose to give a further description of interesting findings.

UNIT 4 A *for* and *against* essay

In the opening paragraph of a *for* and *against* essay, demonstrate why the subject is relevant now.

State the advantages of the topic first and follow this with the limitations.

Over recent years, tourism has become more important to the local economy. As the area attracts more tourists, it is only natural that local officials should be thinking about ways of promoting the region further. It has been claimed that the creation of a new museum would boost visitor numbers. However, I believe that such a plan would not have as positive an impact as other possible options.

One argument in favor of a big new museum is that it would put the region on the map and draw in visitors, who would then spend money on accommodation, transportation, and food. In addition to this, it would create jobs—initially in construction, and then within the building. Finally, museums are often seen as being good for the wider community as they help educate people.

However, a museum would be expensive. It might be better to spend that money on other areas of the local community. Local schools and hospitals could be improved greatly if a similar sum of money were made available, and this would benefit a wider range of people. In addition, it is worth asking how many local people would actually visit a new museum. There is already a small museum in town and it is almost always empty.

In conclusion, while a new museum might bring limited benefits and lead to the creation of some jobs, other choices are preferable. Investment in vital facilities may not bring more tourists, but would create a more skilled, healthier, and happier society.

Introduce your opposing argument or point of view by using the passive, and signal you disagree by using words or phrases like *however*. Then provide your own opinion.

Finally, take notice of both sides of the argument and state your position.

UNIT 5 A scientific method

When writing a scientific method, start by introducing the process.

Words linking the steps of the process are used.

Use phrases like *in order to* to explain why certain steps were taken in the process.

The Blackawton Bee Experiment

The experiment aimed to discover if bees could think in the same ways as humans. The experiment was carried out using a large transparent box called the Bee Arena. The arena contained colored circles representing flowers which had small holes in them that could be filled with sugar water to attract the bees. Before the experiment was started, the bees were marked individually to identify them. In order to do this, forager bees (bees that fly around looking for and collecting pollen) were let into the bee arena. Once all the bees were inside the arena, the lights were turned off in order to make them stop flying. The bees were then picked up using tweezers and put into a pot with a lid. The pot was then placed in a fridge so that the bees would fall asleep. Once they had fallen asleep, the bees were removed from the pot one at a time and painted with different colored dots. Finally, the bees were returned to the pot and warmed up before being released back into the bee arena.

UNIT 1

accessible (adj) /æk'sɛsəbəl/
anxiety (n) /æŋ'zaɪəti/
B&B (n) /'bi ən 'bi/
ban (v) /bæn/
basically (adv) /'beɪsɪkli/
be up for (phr v) /bi 'ʌp ˌfɔr/
break down (phr v) /'breɪk 'daʊn/
budget (n) /'bʌdʒɪt/
cause (v) /kɔz/
come across (phr v) /'kʌm ə'krɔs/
come down to (phr v) /ˌkʌm 'daʊn tu/
community (n) /kə'mjunɪti/
culture shock (n) /'kʌltʃər ˌʃɒk/
date back (phr v) /'deɪt 'bæk/
deal (n) /dil/
decline (n) /dɪ'klaɪn/
established (adj) /ɪ'stæblɪʃt/
evaluate (v) /ɪ'vælјuˌeɪt/
extensive (adj) /ɪk'stɛnsɪv/
fluent (adj) /'fluənt/
food poisoning (n) /'fud ˌpɔɪzənɪŋ/
genuinely (adv) /'dʒɛnjuɪnli/
get a real feel for (phr v) /ˌgɛt ə 'rɪəl 'fil fɔr/
get used to (the food) (phr v) /ˌgɛt 'juzd tu/
grand (adj) /grænd/
hang out (phr v) /'hæŋ 'aʊt/
hiking (n) /'haɪkɪŋ/
honesty (n) /'ɒnɪsti/
host family (n) /'hoʊst 'fæməli/
ideal (adj) /aɪ'dɪəl/
incredibly (adv) /ɪn'krɛdəbli/
independence (n) /ˌɪndɪ'pɛndəns/
individual (n) /ˌɪndɪ'vɪdʒuəl/
influence (v) /'ɪnfluəns/
investment (n) /ɪn'vɛstmənt/
keep in touch (idiom) /'kip ɪn 'tʌʧ/
left to (your) own devices (idiom) /'lɛft tu (yər) 'oʊn dɪ'vaɪsɪz/
legal (adj) /'ligəl/
lie around (phr v) /'laɪ ə'raʊnd/
look after (phr v) /'lʊk 'æftər/
look back (phr v) /'lʊk 'bæk/
major (adj) /'meɪdʒər/
media (n) /'midiə/
move on (phr v) /'muv 'ɒn/
necessarily (adv) /ˌnɛsə'sɛrəli/
negotiate (v) /nɪ'goʊʃiˌeɪt/
opt (v) /ɒpt/
overseas (adv) /'oʊvər'siz/
participant (n) /pɑr'tɪsəpənt/
perspective (n) /pər'spɛktɪv/
pick up (phr v) /'pɪk 'ʌp/
reinforce (v) /ˌriɪn'fɔrs/
reliability (n) /rɪˌlaɪə'bɪlɪti/
reputation (n) /ˌrɛpjə'teɪʃən/
resource (n) /'risɔrs/
restriction (n) /rɪ'strɪkʃən/
revolution (n) /ˌrɛvə'luʃən/
ridiculous (adj) /rɪ'dɪkjələs/
robbery (n) /'rɒbəri/
roots (n) /ruts/
rush (v) /rʌʃ/
servant (n) /'sɜrvənt/
sights (n) /saɪts/
simply (adv) /'sɪmpli/
spread (v) /sprɛd/
standard (n) /'stændərd/
stare (v) /stɛər/
step out (phr v) /'stɛp 'aʊt/
strongly (adv) /'strɔŋli/
trip up (phr v) /'trɪp 'ʌp/
turn out (phr v) /'tɜrn 'aʊt/
tutor (n) /'tutər/
upgrade (n) /'ʌpˌgreɪd/
upgrade (v) /ʌp'greɪd/
vice versa (adv) /'vaɪsə 'vɜrsə/
wealth (n) /wɛlθ/
welcoming (adj) /'wɛlkəmɪŋ/
worry (n) /'wɜri/

UNIT 2

(a) matter (of) (idiom) /(ə)'mætər (əv)/
adapt (v) /ə'dæpt/
aspect (n) /'æspɛkt/
assume (v) /ə'sum/
attach (v) /ə'tætʃ/
automatically (adv) /ˌɔtə'mætɪkli/
backup (n) /'bækˌʌp/
banking (n) /'bæŋkɪŋ/
bargain (n) /'bɑrgɪn/
barrier (n) /'bæriər/
be based (phr v) /bi 'beɪst/
beg (v) /bɛg/
businessperson (n) /'bɪznɪsˌpɜrsən/
campaign (n) /kæm'peɪn/
capable (adj) /'keɪpəbəl/
climate change (n) /'klaɪmɪt ˌʧeɪnʤ/
code (n) /koʊd/
confirm (v) /kən'fɜrm/
corporate (adj) /'kɔrpərɪt/
cut down (phr v) /'kʌt 'daʊn/
data (n) /'deɪtə/
demonstrate (v) /'dɛmənˌstreɪt/
detect (v) /dɪ'tɛkt/
discourage (v) /dɪs'kɜrɪdʒ/
distant (adj) /'dɪstənt/
distribute (v) /dɪ'strɪbjut/
distribution (n) /ˌdɪstrə'bjuʃən/
diverse (adj) /dɪ'vɜrs/
edit (v) /'ɛdɪt/
email (n) /'iˌmeɪl/
entrepreneur (n) /ˌɒntrəprə'nʊər/
executive (adj) /ɪg'zɛkjətɪv/
expand (v) /ɪk'spænd/
export (v) /'ɛkspɔrt/
failure (n) /'feɪljər/
filter (n) /'fɪltər/
fund (n) /fʌnd/
fund (v) /fʌnd/
gender (n) /'dʒɛndər/
go too far (idiom) /'goʊ ˌtu 'fɑr/
guarantee (n) /ˌgærən'ti/
handle (v) /'hændl/
harvest (v) /'hɑrvɪst/
illegal (adj) /ɪ'ligəl/
impressive (adj) /ɪm'prɛsɪv/
inbox (n) /'ɪnˌbɒks/
infect (v) /ɪn'fɛkt/
intrigue (v) /ɪn'trig/
invent (v) /ɪn'vɛnt/
investor (n) /ɪn'vɛstər/
knock on the head (idiom) /'nɒk ɒn ðə 'hɛd/
leadership (n) /'lidərˌʃɪp/
market (v) /'mɑrkɪt/
network (v) /'nɛtˌwɜrk/
origin (n) /'ɔrɪdʒɪn/
out of hand (idiom) /'aʊt əv 'hænd/
post (v) /poʊst/
potential (n) /pə'tɛnʃəl/
pressure (n) /'prɛʃər/
profile (n) /'proʊfaɪl/
profit (n) /'prɒfɪt/
publisher (n) /'pʌblɪʃər/
put together (phr v) /'pʊt tə'gɛðər/
raise money (phr v) /'reɪz 'mʌni/
reality (n) /ri'ælɪti/
recover (v) /rɪ'kʌvər/
risk (n) /rɪsk/
scam (n) /skæm/
social media (n) /'soʊʃəl 'midiə/
solar (adj) /'soʊlər/
source (n) /sɔrs/
spam (n) /spæm/
statement (n) /'steɪtmənt/
store (v) /stɔr/
strategy (n) /'strætɪdʒi/
summarize (v) /'sʌməˌraɪz/
supplier (n) /sə'plaɪər/
tribe (n) /traɪb/
turn up (phr v) /'tɜrn 'ʌp/
victim (n) /'vɪktɪm/
wealthy (adj) /'wɛlθi/

UNIT 3

accelerate (v) /æk'sɛləˌreɪt/
advance (n) /æd'væns/
agree with (phr v) /ə'gri ˌwɪð/
amount (n) /ə'maʊnt/

anticipate (v)	/æn'tɪsə,peɪt/
athletic (adj)	/æθ'lɛtɪk/
attitude (n)	/'ætɪ,tud/
awareness (n)	/ə'wɛərnɪs/
billion (n)	/'bɪljən/
brand (n)	/brænd/
bronze (adj)	/brɒnz/
captain (v)	/'kæptən/
championship (n)	/'tʃæmpiən,ʃɪp/
change the face of (idiom)	/'ʧeɪnʤ ðə 'feɪs əv/
closely (adv)	/'kloʊsli/
compete (v)	/kəm'pit/
conquer (v)	/'kɒŋkər/
debt (n)	/dɛt/
determine (v)	/dɪ'tɜrmɪn/
elite (adj)	/ɪ'lit/
energetic (adj)	/,ɛnər'dʒɛtɪk/
entire (adj)	/ɛn'taɪər/
essentially (adv)	/ɪ'sɛnʃəli/
establish (v)	/ɪ'stæblɪʃ/
evolution (n)	/,ɛvə'luʃən/
evolve (v)	/ɪ'vɒlv/
expense (n)	/ɪk'spɛns/
fade away (v)	/'feɪd ə'weɪ/
fame (n)	/feɪm/
formal (adj)	/'fɔrməl/
forward (n)	/'fɔrwərd/
funding (n)	/'fʌndɪŋ/
gardening (adj)	/'gɑrdnɪŋ/
glory (n)	/'glɔri/
goal (n)	/goʊl/
greatly (adv)	/'greɪtli/
hold (a record) (v)	/hoʊld/
host (v)	/hoʊst/
injury (n)	/'ɪndʒəri/
instantly (adv)	/'ɪnstəntli/
intensively (adv)	/ɪn'tɛnsɪvli/
junk food (n)	/'dʒʌŋk ,fud/
largely (adv)	/'lɑrdʒli/
long-term (adj)	/'lɔŋ,tɜrm/
marathon (n)	/'mærə,θɒn/
medal (n)	/'mɛdl/
muscle (n)	/'mʌsəl/
nation (n)	/'neɪʃən/
participate (v)	/pɑr'tɪsə,peɪt/
pay off (phr v)	/'peɪ 'ɔf/
percentage (n)	/pər'sɛntɪdʒ/
personality (n)	/,pɜrsə'nælɪti/
popularity (n)	/,pɒpjə'lærɪti/
positive role model (phrase)	/'pɒzɪtɪv 'roʊl ,mɒdl/
preferably (adv)	/'prɛfərəbli/
principle (n)	/'prɪnsəpəl/
psychological (adj)	/,saɪkə'lɒdʒɪkəl/
quote (n)	/kwoʊt/
ranking (n)	/'ræŋkɪŋ/
real passion (phrase)	/'rɪəl 'pæʃən/
recreation (n)	/,rɛkri'eɪʃən/
represent (v)	/,rɛprɪ'zɛnt/
role model (n)	/'roʊl ,mɒdl/
roughly (adv)	/'rʌfli/
schedule (n)	/'skɛdjul/
season (n)	/'sizən/
select (v)	/sɪ'lɛkt/
set (a new record) (v)	/sɛt/
set up (v)	/'sɛt 'ʌp/
shrink (v)	/ʃrɪŋk/
slightly (adv)	/'slaɪtli/
slow down (phr v)	/'sloʊ 'daʊn/
smash (v)	/smæʃ/
specialize (v)	/'spɛʃə,laɪz/
specific (adj)	/spə'sɪfɪk/
spirit (n)	/'spɪrɪt/
stamina (n)	/'stæmɪnə/
status (n)	/'steɪtəs/
subsequently (adv)	/'sʌbsɪkwəntli/
subway (n)	/'sʌb,weɪ/
suit (v)	/sut/
sum (n)	/sʌm/
surface (n)	/'sɜrfɪs/
tackle (v)	/'tækəl/
target (n)	/'tɑrgɪt/
technique (n)	/tɛk'nik/
technological (adj)	/,tɛknə'lɒdʒɪkəl/
tend to (phr v)	/'tɛnd tu/
terminal (n)	/'tɜrmɪnl/
throughout (prep)	/θru'aʊt/
top (adj)	/tɒp/
vast (adj)	/væst/

UNIT 4

actual (adj)	/'æktʃuəl/
authority (n)	/ ə'θɔrɪti/
behind (prep)	/bɪ'haɪnd/
boost (v)	/bust/
carnival (n)	/'kɑrnɪvəl/
choir (n)	/kwaɪər/
claim (v)	/kleɪm/
comedy club (n)	/'kɒmɪdi ,klʌb/
commitment (n)	/kə'mɪtmənt/
confidence (n)	/'kɒnfɪdəns
construction (n)	/kən'strʌkʃən/
costume (n)	/'kɒstum/
creation (n)	/kri'eɪʃən/
creativity (n)	/,krieɪ'tɪvɪti/
demolish (v)	/dɪ'mɒlɪʃ/
desperate (adj)	/'dɛspərɪt/
discipline (n)	/'dɪsəplɪn/
diverse social background (col)	/dɪ'vɜrs 'soʊʃəl 'bæk,graʊnd/
dramatic (adj)	/drə'mætɪk/
duration (n)	/dʊ'reɪʃən/
economist (n)	/ɪ'kɒnəmɪst/
economy (n)	/ɪ'kɒnəmi/
emphasize (v)	/'ɛmfə,saɪz/
engagement (n)	/ɛn'geɪdʒmənt/
expression (n)	/ɪk'sprɛʃən/
factor (n)	/'fæktər/
fatal (adj)	/'feɪtəl/
festival (n)	/'fɛstɪvəl/
figure out (phr v)	/'fɪgjər 'aʊt/
found (v)	/faʊnd/
foundation (n)	/faʊn'deɪʃən/
fulfill (v)	/fʊl'fɪl/
gallery (n)	/'gæləri/
gang (n)	/gæŋ/
generate (v)	/'dʒɛnə,reɪt/
hard work (col)	/'hɑrd 'wɜrk/
impact (n)	/'ɪmpækt/
income (n)	/'ɪnkʌm/
industrial (adj)	/ɪn'dʌstriəl/
initially (adv)	/ɪ'nɪʃəli/
innovative (adj)	/ɪnə,veɪtɪv/
inspiration (n)	/,ɪnspə'reɪʃən/
lead to (phr v)	/'lid tu/
leading orchestra (col)	/'lidɪŋ 'ɔrkɪstrə/
literally (adv)	/'lɪtərəli/
low income (adj)	/'loʊ 'ɪnkʌm/
mayor (n)	/meɪər/
minister (n)	/'mɪnɪstər/
minority (n)	/mɪ'nɔrɪti/
mixed results (phrase)	/'mɪkst rɪ'zʌlts/
museum (n)	/mju'ziəm/
official (adj)	/ə'fɪʃəl/
organizer (n)	/'ɔrgə,naɪzər/
parade (n)	/pə'reɪd/
physical (adj)	/'fɪzɪkəl/
poverty (n)	/'pɒvərti/
pride (n)	/praɪd/
private company (col)	/'praɪvɪt 'kʌmpəni/
process (n)	/'prɒsɛs/
professional (n)	/prə'fɛʃənl/
public art (col)	/'pʌblɪk 'ɑrt/
redevelopment (n)	/,ridɪ'vɛləpmənt/
rehearse (v)	/rɪ'hɜrs/
reject (v)	/rɪ'dʒɛkt/
relic (n)	/'rɛlɪk/
remarkable (adj)	/rɪ'mɑrkəbəl/
rhythm (n)	/'rɪðəm/
run over (phr v)	/'rʌn 'oʊvər/
sell out (phr v)	/'sɛl 'aʊt/
signal (v)	/'sɪgnl/
skilled (adj)	/skɪld/
stand for (phr v)	/'stænd fɔr/
straightforward process (col)	/,streɪt'fɔrwərd 'prɒsɛs/
strict set (col)	/'strɪkt 'sɛt/
struggling (adj)	/'strʌgəlɪŋ/
supposedly (adv)	/sə'poʊzɪdli/
take charge (phr v)	/'teɪk 'ʧɑrʤ/
theater (n)	/'θiətər/
venue (n)	/'vɛnju/
violence (n)	/'vaɪələns/
vital (adj)	/'vaɪtl/
volunteer (n)	/,vɒlən'tɪər/
widely (adv)	/'waɪdli/

UNIT 5

alter (v)	/ˈɔltər/
arm (v)	/ɑrm/
assignment (n)	/əˈsaɪnmənt/
beautiful (adj)	/ˈbjutəfəl/
belief (n)	/bɪˈlif/
bother (v)	/ˈbɒðər/
browser (n) /	/ˈbraʊzər/
bubble (n)	/ˈbʌbəl/
bulb (n)	/bʌlb/
capacity (n)	/kəˈpæsɪti/
chemical (n)	/ˈkɛmɪkəl/
circumstance (n)	/ˈsɜrkəmˌstæns/
conduct (v)	/kənˈdʌkt/
consume (v)	/kənˈsum/
cooperation (n)	/koʊˌɒpəˈreɪʃən/
cooperative (adj)	/koʊˈɒpərətɪv/
curiosity (n)	/ˌkjʊəriˈɒsɪti/
deadline (n)	/ˈdɛdˌlaɪn/
determining (adv)	/dɪˈtɜrmɪnɪŋ/
discovery (n)	/dɪˈskʌvəri/
dissolve (v)	/dɪˈzɒlv/
dominant (adj)	/ˈdɒmɪnənt/
downwards (adv)	/ˈdaʊnwərdz/
effective (adj)	/ɪˈfɛktɪv/
electrical (adj)	/iˈlɛktrɪkəl/
embrace (v)	/ɛmˈbreɪs/
engage (v)	/ɛnˈgeɪdʒ/
evidence (n)	/ˈɛvɪdəns/
function (n)	/ˈfʌŋkʃən/
genius (n)	/ˈdʒiniəs/
grasp (n)	/græsp/
helpful (adj)	/ˈhɛlpfəl/
hopeful (adj)	/ˈhoʊpfəl/
identify (v)	/aɪˈdɛntəˌfaɪ/
imaginative (adj)	/ɪˈmædʒənətɪv/
increasingly (adv)	/ɪnˈkrisɪŋli/
innovation (n)	/ˌɪnəˈveɪʃən/
innovative (adj)	/ˈɪnəˌveɪtɪv/
intelligence (n)	/ɪnˈtɛlɪdʒəns/
journal (n)	/ˈdʒɜrnl/
labor (n)	/ˈleɪbər/
lid (n)	/lɪd/
link (n)	/lɪŋk/
listener (n)	/ˈlɪsənər/
make matters worse (phrase)	/ˈmeɪk ˈmætərz ˈwɜrs/
mark (v)	/mɑrk/
mature (v)	/məˈtʃʊər/
mechanical (adj)	/mɪˈkænɪkəl/
medical (adj)	/ˈmɛdɪkəl/
mode (n)	/moʊd/
movement (n)	/ˈmuvmənt/
myth (n)	/mɪθ/
network (n)	/ˈnɛtˌwɜrk/
place (v)	/pleɪs/
pleasurable (adj)	/ˈplɛʒərəbəl/
pleasure (n)	/ˈplɛʒər/
practical (adj)	/ˈpræktɪkəl/
previously (adv)	/ˈpriviəsli/
ray (n)	/reɪ/
reaction (n)	/riˈækʃən/
reference (n)	/ˈrɛfərəns/
release (v)	/rɪˈlis/
researcher (n)	/rɪˈsɜrtʃər/
return (v)	/rɪˈtɜrn/
reward (n)	/rɪˈwɔrd/
sample (n)	/ˈsæmpəl/
scan (n)	/skæn/
social (adj)	/ˈsoʊʃəl/
society (n)	/səˈsaɪəti/
sophisticated (adj)	/səˈfɪstɪˌkeɪtɪd/
submit (v)	/səbˈmɪt/
substance (n)	/ˈsʌbstəns/
surgeon (n)	/ˈsɜrdʒən/
surgery (n)	/ˈsɜrdʒəri/
surround (v)	/səˈraʊnd/
survey (n)	/ˈsɜrveɪ/
theory (n)	/ˈθɪəri/
threat (n)	/θrɛt/
transform (v)	/trænsˈfɔrm/
transparent (adj)	/trænsˈpærənt/
tremendous (adj)	/trəˈmɛndəs/
ultimate (adj)	/ˈʌltəmɪt/
uncertainty (n)	/ʌnˈsɜrtənti/
use (n)	/jus/
useful (adj)	/ˈjusfəl/
voice (n)	/vɔɪs/

PERSPECTIVES 3

Workbook

Australia • Brazil • Mexico • Singapore • United Kingdom • United States

Perspectives 3

Publisher: Sherrise Roehr

Executive Editor: Sarah Kenney

Project Manager: Katherine Carroll

Senior Technology Product Manager: Lauren Krolick

Director of Global Marketing: Ian Martin

Senior Product Marketing Manager: Caitlin Thomas

Sr. Director, ELT & World Languages: Michael Burggren

Production Manager: Daisy Sosa

Senior Print Buyer: Mary Beth Hennebury

Composition: Lumina Datamatics, Inc.

Cover/Text Design: Brenda Carmichael

Art Director: Brenda Carmichael

Cover Image: The Hive at Kew Gardens, London. ©Mark Hadden

Perspectives 3 Workbook

ISBN: 978-1-337-29730-1

National Geographic Learning
20 Channel Center Street
Boston, MA 02210
USA

National Geographic Learning, a Cengage Learning Company, has a mission to bring the world to the classroom and the classroom to life. With our English language programs, students learn about their world by experiencing it. Through our partnerships with National Geographic and TED Talks, they develop the language and skills they need to be successful global citizens and leaders.

Locate your local office at **international.cengage.com/region**

Visit National Geographic Learning online at **NGL.Cengage.com/ELT**
Visit our corporate website at **www.cengage.com**

Photo Credits:
2 Lutz Jaekel/laif/Redux, **4** emei/Shutterstock.com, **7** Ersler Dmitry/Shutterstock.com, **8** GoodMood Photo/Shutterstock.com, **14** Rawpixel.com/Shutterstock.com, **16** Fred Turck/Shutterstock.com, **19** chombosan/Shutterstock.com, **20** Juergen Faelchle/Shutterstock.com, **26** Stefan Schurr/Shutterstock.com, **28** (tl) Petr Toman/Shutterstock.com, (bl) grmarc/Shutterstock.com, **31** Leonard Zhukovsky/Shutterstock.com, **38** Kjeld Friis/Shutterstock.com, **40** Anton_Ivanov/Shutterstock.com, **43** Skreidzeleu/Shutterstock.com, **45** Oscity/Shutterstock.com,**52** WilcoUK/Shutterstock.com, **55** Monkey Business Images/Shutterstock.com, **63** Manu M Nair/Shutterstock.com, **64** Photobac/Shutterstock.com, **67** Juan Aunion/Shutterstock.com, **68** Andrew Sutton/Shutterstock.com, **71** (tl1) TPm13thx/Shutterstock.com, (tl2) Nick Fox/Shutterstock.com, (tl3) Kit Korzun/Shutterstock.com, (tl4) Rich Carey/Shutterstock.com, **76** Tupungato/Shutterstock.com, **79** Svitlana-ua/Shutterstock.com, **81** Golubovy/Shutterstock.com, **87** Kzenon/Shutterstock.com, **88** Thoai/Shutterstock.com, **91** bokehart/Shutterstock.com, **100** (cl) VCG/Visual China Group/Getty Images, (cr) Justin Hobson/Shutterstock.com, **103** Oliver Foerstner/Shutterstock.com, **112** Kleber Cordeiro/Shutterstock.com, **115** wawritto/Shutterstock.com, **117** hxdbzxy/Shutterstock.com, **119** (cr) Tomsickova Tatyana/Shutterstock.com, (br) Antonio Guillem/Shutterstock.com.

Text Credits:
4 "Rescuing an Icon", by A.R. William, National Geographic Magazine, August 2015, p.14., **16** "Big Ideas, Little Packages", by Margaret G. Zackowitz, National Geographic Magazine, November 2010, p.24., **16** "Power to the People", by Chris Costas, National Geographic Traveler, August-September 2015, p.18., **28** "To Greeks We Owe Our Love of Athletics", March 1944, p.315., **40** "Street Dreams: Edinburgh Scotland", by Alexander McCall Smith, National Geographic Traveler, February-March 2015, p.11., **52** "Accents and Perception", by Luna Shyr, National Geographic Magazine, June 2011, p.42., 52 "Curiosity and a Cat", by Steve Boyes, National Geographic Magazine, March 2014, p.42., **64** "Baboon Troop Adapts to Survive in Desert", National Geographic Magazine, February 1992, p4., **67** "Shadow Cats", National Geographic Magazine, February 2017, p.104., **76** "Cities are the Key", by Keith Bellows, National Geographic Traveler, May-June 2011, p.26., **79** "A Thing or Two About Twins", by Peter Miller, National Geographic Magazine, January 2012, p.46., **88** "A World Together", National Geographic Magazine, by Erla Zwingle, August 1999, p.12., **88** "Cultures", text from a National Geographic map, 2014. **100** "Tracking a Tornado's Damage from Every Angle", by Daniel Stone, National Geographic Magazine, October 2016, p.22., **103** "Reader Fixes an African Bridge", National Geographic Magazine, October 2002, p32., **112** "The Art of Recovery", by Susan Goldberg, National Geographic Magazine, February 2015., **115** "A Cure in Sight", by David Dobbs, National Geographic Magazine, September 2016, p.30.

Printed in the United States of America
Print Number: 02   Print Year: 2021

CONTENTS

1 Travel, Trust, and Tourism

1A Cultural Exchange

VOCABULARY Experiences abroad

1 Review Complete the chart with these words.

a bike ride	a taxi	a trip	college
my bus	my train	two hours	work

get to	go for

take	catch

2 Review Complete the sentences with these words.

backpacking	commute	cruise	destination
flight	ride	route	voyage

1 Tim Peake went on a long ________________ into space.
2 We need to take a different ________________ because there's been an accident.
3 Most people ________________ to work by car.
4 You have reached your ________________.
5 Could you give me a ________________ to work, please?
6 They're traveling on a ________________ ship.
7 It was cheap to go ________________ around Australia.
8 The earlier ________________ gets to the airport at 7:00pm.

3 Read the sentences. Are they logical (L) or illogical (I)?

1 Let's go to all the major sites tomorrow—I want to get off the beaten path! ____
2 I love having a host family stay with me. ____
3 She won't try street food because she's afraid she'll get food poisoning. ____
4 Yumi lost weight in Russia because it took a while to get used to the food. ____
5 Travelers who are outgoing often hang out with the local people. ____
6 Don't wear any expensive jewelry because you might get robbed. ____
7 Ignacio likes to travel so he can lie around the house all day. ____
8 Liu didn't find the people very welcoming and made lots of new friends. ____

4 Choose the correct option (a–d) to complete each sentence.

1 I got huge culture ____ the first time I visited Asia.
a scare **b** shock **c** fear **d** clash

2 There wasn't enough time to get a real ____ for the place.
a look **b** sight **c** feel **d** emotion

3 She always tries to get off the beaten ____ to escape the tourists.
a path **b** road **c** street **d** walk

4 We got ____ outside the hotel.
a theft **b** robbed **c** taken **d** stolen

5 Did you hang _____ with any local people?
a out
b up
c in
d by

6 I'd prefer to be _____ to my own devices on vacation and not have a guide.
a used
b found
c taken
d left

5 **Match the two parts of the sentences.**

1 I don't find the locals
2 I've never had food
3 It's relaxing to lie
4 The children quickly got used
5 We're staying in
6 I want to see

a poisoning.
b around the house all day.
c all the sights tomorrow.
d the same B&B.
e very welcoming.
f to the different food.

6 **Complete the sentences with the correct forms of these verbs.**

be	find	get	go	lie	stay

1 I don't want to ________________ food poisoning.
2 We're going to ________________ with a host family.
3 Let's ________________ hiking in the mountains.
4 We'll probably ________________ around on the beach most of the week.
5 Did you ________________ the locals welcoming?
6 Do you want to ________________ left to your own devices?

7 **Find the mistake in each sentence and write the correct word.**

1 We stayed with a B&B. ________________
2 It took a while to get using to the food. ________________
3 I found the people really welcome. ________________
4 She got food poisoned. ________________
5 We were left to his own devices. ________________
6 They saw all the sight. ________________
7 Have you ever got culture shocking? ________________
8 They were robbery the first night. ________________

8 **Extension** Complete the sentences with these words.

amenities	availability	down time	excursion
overbooked	secluded	tourist traps	wander

1 After visiting Cuzco, we went on an amazing ________________ to Machu Picchu.
2 The resort was in a very ________________ part of the island. It had its own beach!
3 When we got to the hostel, they didn't have any ________________. All the beds were taken.
4 What do you like to do when you have ________________?
5 He's happiest when he's left to his own devices to ________________ around the city.
6 The flight was ________________ but no one wanted to give up their seat.
7 The new hotel has all the ________________ you want—wifi, large flat-screen television, an excellent restaurant.
8 The guide advised us that the shops on the waterfront are ________________.

PRONUNCIATION

9 Listen to the sentences. Does the *'d* contraction you hear represent *would* or *had*? 2

1 **a** would **b** had
2 **a** would **b** had
3 **a** would **b** had
4 **a** would **b** had
5 **a** would **b** had
6 **a** would **b** had
7 **a** would **b** had
8 **a** would **b** had

LISTENING

10 Listen to a short environmental report about the Taj Mahal in India. Match the two parts of the phrasal verbs that you hear. Then practice saying the verbs. 3

1 pass	**a** out
2 given	**b** after
3 took	**c** up
4 carried	**d** with
5 stirred	**e** away
6 came	**f** on
7 deal	**g** up
8 looking	**h** out

11 Listen to the report again. Are the statements true (T) or false (F)? Practice saying the true statements. 3

1 The Taj Mahal is a tomb for Princess Mumtaz Mahal. ____
2 The princess died having her fourth child. ____
3 The Taj Mahal is made of white ivory. ____
4 The appearance of the building has changed over time. ____
5 Scientists were able to work out the likely cause of the discoloration. ____
6 Human activity has created problems for the building. ____
7 Mike Bergin is a well-known architect. ____
8 The government in Agra acted to help reduce air pollution. ____

12 Choose the correct options. Listen again if necessary. 3

1 Why was the Taj Mahal built?
a as a resting place for a princess
b to attract foreign visitors and boost the economy
c to hold many of India's finest art masterpieces

2 What city is the closest to the Taj Mahal?
a Delhi
b Agra
c Mumbai

3 What was the original color of the building?
a brown
b yellow
c white

4 How many countries participated in the research?
a 1
b 2
c 3

5 What is an example of a fossil fuel?
a oil
b animal waste
c wood

6 What is Mike Bergen's job title?
a architectural engineer
b environmental engineer
c air quality engineer

7 What kind of fuel did Agra switch many trucks to?
a propane
b diesel
c natural gas

13 Complete the sentences with a word or short phrase. Listen again if necessary. 3

1 The Taj Mahal is the ____________________ of Princess Mumtaz Mahal.
2 The building was constructed with ____________________ marble.
3 The ____________________ of Agra has been growing rapidly.
4 The Taj Mahal's marble began to ____________________.
5 Research found two likely causes of the discoloration: ____________________.
6 The research findings were discussed in the Indian ____________________.
7 People in Agra have started using ____________________ to cook with.

GRAMMAR Present and past forms

14 Find and correct the mistakes in the sentences. Some sentences have more than one possible correct answer. There are two sentences that are correct.

1 While we were waiting for the bus, I was seeing a poster for tours at the art museum.

____

2 Melissa wanted to explore the city center while it didn't rain.

____

3 Enzo shared his photos from Singapore; he was hoping to make his friends jealous.

____

4 Luis and I were stared at the painting for ten minutes, but we never figured out what it was.

____

5 Ana was suffering from culture shock because she was being away from home for the first time.

____

6 The manager offered me a discount when I called to purchase my ticket.

____

7 While Eva and Eduardo were hanging out at the cafe, Lucas and Rafael were checked the train timetable.

____

8 We listen to the tour guide's explanation, but my parents were buying postcards.

____

15 Complete the sentences with the correct forms of the verbs in parentheses.

1 Giovanni ______________ (study) English for many years before he ______________ (move) to Canada last month.

2 Before we ______________ (realize) it, Salma ______________ (rush) to the front of the line and bought our tickets.

3 Ali ______________ (read) yet another guidebook about New Zealand because she really ______________ (want) to visit Auckland next year.

4 Because Amelia ______________ (take) a photography course, she ______________ (know) exactly which camera to take on her last trip.

5 Before he ______________ (visit) the castle, Paul ______________ (already, read) several books about its history.

6 Before Jakob ______________ (tour) the museum, he ______________ (get) a real feel for Athens from walking around its markets.

7 Julia ______________ (examine) the painting with great interest because she ______________ (study) art history in college many years before.

8 Chen ______________ (hike) for eight hours before he ______________ (find) a good place to set up his tent.

9 Emma ______________ (buy) some more souvenirs while her boyfriend ______________ (wait) for his cell phone to charge.

16 Put the words in the correct order to make sentences and questions.

1 ever / Jasmin / abroad / has / traveled

______________________________?

2 to spend / in / semester / was / Ravi / this / Bologna / planning

______________________________?

3 is / has / he / Nico / never / scared of / been / because / surfing / the ocean

______________________________.

4 very / with / has / food / Kari / poisoning / been / sick

______________________________.

5 for / Valparaiso / a / you / get / feel / real / did

______________________________?

6 happy / devices / to / to / own / her / left / Akita / wasn't / been / have

______________________________.

7 wanting / Minjoo / Sydney / years / to / for / visit / been / had

______________________________.

17 Write a sentence about something you are doing, were doing, or had done at the following times.

1 January 1st ______________________________

2 last weekend ______________________________

3 last summer ______________________________

4 10:30 this morning ______________________________

5 9:00 last night ______________________________

6 right now ______________________________

1B A Place to Stay

VOCABULARY BUILDING Phrasal verbs

1 Put the words in the correct order to make sentences and questions.

1 you / make sure / look / your / sister / after / the / at / pool

____.

2 line / where / we / up / to / get / do / tickets / train

____?

3 close / to / were / when / down / broke / Las Vegas / we / car / the

____.

4 hanging / park / at / the / out / amusement / is / fun / lots of

____.

5 over / where / drivers / pull / on / road / this / can

____?

6 for / enough / whether / it / to / down / trip / comes / have / I / money / the

____.

7 airport / the / who / going / is / to / up / him / pick / from

____?

READING

2 Read the article. Sentences a–g provided here have been removed from the article. Decide which sentence belongs in each place (1–6). One sentence is extra.

1 ____
2 ____
3 ____
4 ____
5 ____
6 ____

a Along these lines, you need to decide what type of lodging you are going to offer.
b Make sure you plan your business with your customer in mind.
c An empty hotel will not stay in business for long.
d Why do people visit this community, and how can your hotel become a part of it?
e How can your hotel make more money than you spend?
f Have you dreamed of opening a hotel of your own somewhere beautiful?
g Next, you need to decide what services your hotel will offer.

3 Do the statements match the information in the article? Is the information true (T), false (F), or not given (NG)?

1 A hotel owner should charge enough for rooms to cover the costs of running the hotel. ____
2 Customers who pay more for rooms will be less concerned about service. ____
3 Offering the right special services to customers can bring more business to a hotel. ____
4 The Philippines offers the best diving in Asia. ____
5 Opening a new hotel can help people living in the local community. ____

4 Find a word from the article that matches each definition.

1 something that doesn't succeed ____________
2 to charge less than something is worth ____________
3 an amount of money that is charged ____________
4 a short pleasure trip ____________
5 the feeling of a place ____________

Living the Dream 4

1 Have you ever visited a hotel or B&B so peaceful that you thought about never leaving? (1) You are not alone. Most people have a fantasy of escaping their daily life for a new and exciting adventure, but a few people actually do it. So what does it take to start a small hotel or a B&B? What separates success stories from failures?

2 First, you have to choose a location that will attract plenty of guests. (2) Additionally, those guests need to be willing to pay enough money for their rooms to cover the hotel's costs. Some new hotel owners underprice their rooms, or they open their hotel in a place so far off the beaten path that tourists won't spend enough on lodging to keep the hotel open. Often a hotel's success comes down to being in the right location.

3 (3) Will you have a luxury resort charging high prices or a relaxing hostel where travelers can meet and make friends? (4) For example, travelers paying expensive room rates will expect the highest quality service, while those looking for an informal experience will be more satisfied by a friendly atmosphere than by expensive sheets. Give your customers what they want, and they will come back again and again.

4 (5) Will you have a restaurant? Will you offer excursions like snorkeling trips or guided tours? If so, these services will cost money, and you need to make sure you charge enough to cover the expense. On the other hand, special services can be a major attraction for tourists. When Gabrielle and Matthew Holder left the UK for the Philippines to open their own resort, they chose a site where the diving is fantastic. Tourists travel from around the world to dive in this part of the Philippines, and they are attracted to a resort that offers organized diving tours.

5 Finally, consider the community you are opening your hotel in. (6) Jonathan Baldrey spent three years renovating his hotel in Santo Domingo in the Dominican Republic to reflect the neighborhood's fascinating history. Now it appeals to travelers who want to get a sense of the Dominican Republic's culture when they visit.

6 Whether your dream is to own a luxury hotel or to open a peaceful B&B where you can meet and entertain guests from all over the world, the recipe for success is the same. Do your research, pick the perfect location, work out pricing and costs, and offer the right services and atmosphere for your customers. Do these things, and you too could be living your dream!

1C On the Road

GRAMMAR *Used to* and *would*

1 A word is missing in each sentence. Read the four answer choices and choose the correct option to complete each sentence.

1 I _____ to go to Namibia to visit my family every December.
a would **c** use
b used **d** has

2 When _____ get ready to leave for Namibia, my family would remind me to prepare for the heat—temperatures in northern Namibia can reach 122 degrees Fahrenheit!
a I'd **c** I use
b I used **d** I had

3 When we finally got to Namibia, sometimes _____ go climbing on the Brandberg Mountain.
a we had **c** we used
b we use **d** we'd

4 _____ admire Brandberg's ancient rock paintings.
a We had **c** We used
b We use **d** We'd

5 I _____ to stand for hours and study the ancient artwork.
a would **c** use
b used **d** has

6 Bushman/San hunter gatherers, people who _____ to live in the area more than 2,000 years ago, made this incredible art.
a would **c** use
b used **d** has

7 They _____ make images of things from their everyday life, for example, the jewelry they wore and the animals they must have seen such as giraffes, elephants, and snakes.
a would **c** use
b used **d** has

8 I _____ to imagine a hunter hiding out in the very caves I was visiting, painting the scenes I was seeing so many years later.
a would **c** use
b used **d** has

2 Complete the sentences with these phrases. Use correct capitalization as necessary.

but she used to speak Malayalam
my mother used to live on Kakkathuruthu
she used to paint pictures
used to love eating curries made with coconut and cinnamon
would light lamps and fish in the lagoons
would wear beautiful saris

1 When she was a girl, ______________________, a tiny island in Kerala (a state in southern India).
2 My mother speaks mostly English now, ______________________ with her family and friends.
3 ______________________ of the many beautiful flowers around her home, such as purple water hyacinths drifting on the lakes.
4 My mother ______________________, served on banana leaves.
5 On Kakkathuruthu, my grandmother and her friends ______________________ when they went to the market.
6 At night, fishermen ______________________.

3 Listen and choose the correct full form for the contracted *'d* form you hear. 5

1 **a** They would **b** They had
2 **a** She would **b** She had
3 **a** I would **b** I had
4 **a** we would **b** we had
5 **a** he would **b** he had
6 **a** I would **b** I had

Metal pails collect sap on a maple tree.

4 **Choose the correct option to complete the text.**

I live in Vermont, in the United States, and, when I was younger, I (1) *used to help / used to helping* my parents make maple syrup every spring. We (2) *used to love / would love to* pouring the sweet, sticky syrup on everything from pancakes and waffles to ice cream! But making the syrup (3) *would took / took* a lot of work. The cold nights and warm days of spring got the maple trees ready to provide the sap (a thin, sugary liquid stored inside the trees) that we (4) *collected / use to collect* to make our syrup.

To start, we (5) *would pull on / used pull on* our snow boots and warm jackets. Then we (6) *would go / used to* outside and make holes in the trees about an inch deep. Next, (7) *we had hang / we'd hang* buckets on the trees to collect the sap that would drip out of the holes. My grandparents used to have horses to pull the wagon holding the buckets from tree to tree, but we used a tractor. Once we had all the sap gathered, we (8) *would boil / would boiled* it for hours and hours in a special building called a sugarhouse until it (9) *was / used to* sweet, sticky, and golden—it took about 35 gallons of sap to make one gallon of syrup! I (10) *never use to think / used to think* the sugarhouse was like a sauna, with all the heat and steam. Every year, when the syrup (11) *use to be / was* ready, we used to have a big party for all our friends to share the first batch.

5 **Put the words in the correct order to make sentences and questions. Use the correct verb form.**

1 use / called / be / Constantinople / Istanbul / to
Istanbul used to be called Constantinople.

2 on / you / post / a / social media / lot / of / to / use / do / photos
______________________________?

3 do not / cream / we / to / ice / after / school / use / get
______________________________.

4 the / I / TV / would / all / time / watch
______________________________.

5 space / use / think / couldn't / people / to / everybody / go / into
______________________________.

6 I / to / lot / read / a / of / novels / mystery / use
______________________________.

7 use / we / vacations / skiing / never / to / go / on
______________________________.

8 hair / your / be / use / did / to / blond
______________________________?

6 **Read the letter Petra wrote to her grandfather when she studied in Croatia a few years ago. Then write about Petra using *would* and *used to.***

March 19, 2015

Dear Grandpa,

I love being an exchange student in Croatia! There's so much going on. Every day before class, I meet my friend Lorena for coffee. Then I ride my bike to school, while Lorena goes to her job at the hospital. On Mondays, Wednesdays, and Fridays, I study English and chemistry. On Tuesdays and Thursdays, it's math and history. I study every night at the library, but I never study on weekends.

On weekends, I like to hang out with my friends—sometimes we go snorkelling or hiking. Last weekend, we went to see the ancient city walls in Dubrovnik. And next weekend, I think we're going to Lokrum, a beautiful island with amazing forests.

In your last letter, you asked if I'd been going out to listen to music. Well, my friends and I don't go to concerts because they're too expensive. We usually just enjoy streaming music at home.

Love,

Petra

While studying in Croatia in 2015…

1 ______________________________
every day before class.

2 ______________________________
bike to school.

3 On Mondays, Wednesdays, and Fridays,
______________________________.

4 ______________________________
on Tuesdays and Thursdays.

5 ______________________________
at the library.

6 ______________________________
on weekends.

7 ______________________________
hang out with her friends on weekends.

8 ______________________________
because they were too expensive.

1D How Airbnb Designs for Trust

TEDTALKS

AUTHENTIC LISTENING SKILLS

1 **Listen and complete the extract with the words you hear.** 6

(1) ________________ the day after graduating from design school and (2) ________________ having a yard sale. And this guy (3) ________________ up in this red Mazda and he (4) ________________ looking through my stuff. And he (5) ________________ a piece of art that I made. And it turns out (6) ________________ alone in town for the night, driving cross-country on a road trip before he goes into the Peace Corps.

WATCH

2 **Number the statements about Joe's life in order.**

____ **a** Joe and Brian build a website and launch their business, Airbed and Breakfast.

____ **b** Now, 785,000 people in 191 countries use Airbnb each day.

____ **c** Joe moves to San Francisco and, after two years, is unemployed.

____ **d** Joe learns that online reviews help to build trust and reduce social bias.

____ **e** Joe suggests to his roommate, Brian, that they host people in their home during a major design conference.

____ **f** Joe hosts his first house guest shortly after finishing design school.

3 **Choose the correct option to complete the sentences.**

1 Joe *had / used to have* a yard sale when he finished design school.

2 The "Peace Corps guy" *would buy / bought* a piece of art from Joe.

3 Joe and Brian *used to be / would be* roommates in San Francisco.

4 On the old website, people *didn't use to write / would write* negative reviews.

5 In the early days, Joe *would take / had taken* the customer service calls himself.

6 One time, some hosts *used to take / took* their guest to the hospital when he had a heart attack.

7 According to Joe, good design *has helped / used to help* people to overcome their biases.

4 **Read the sentence and paragraph provided here. In which place (a–d) could the sentence be added to the paragraph?**

This information comes in two forms: information the host shares about themselves and customer reviews.

Joe Gebbia argues that design is able to change the way people relate to one another. (a) By creating hidden guidelines for users, such as the size of a response box, the website encourages people to share just enough information about themselves to create trust, but not so much that people become frightened. (b) Gebbia recognizes that people don't naturally trust strangers and need to learn more about them before opening their homes. (c) Gebbia had to experiment with the review process before arriving at the current format, but he learned that the best approach was to wait until both host and guest had written their reviews before the reviews are revealed. (d) This way, reviewers are not biased by what the other person has written and give more honest feedback.

VOCABULARY IN CONTEXT

5 **Match the words and phrases (1–6) with the sentences that illustrate them (a–f).**

1 keep in touch ____
2 broke ____
3 rush ____
4 anxiety ____
5 up for it ____
6 trip up ____

a Mark gets so **nervous** when he travels that he has difficulty sleeping.

b Leticia didn't notice how much money she had been spending until she saw **a zero balance** in her bank account.

c When So-Jin first started studying English, the different accents she heard really **confused** her.

d My uncle didn't wake up when his alarm rang, and he had to **hurry** to get to his appointment on time.

e My cousins and I don't live in the same city, but we make sure to **call each other every week** to see how things are going.

f I wanted to see the new movie last night, so I called my friends to see if they were **interested in joining me.**

1E Trip Advice

SPEAKING

Useful language

Making suggestions

If sightseeing is their thing, then the best place to go is…

If they want to experience a genuine local night out, I'd suggest trying…

If they're only staying here for a little while, they should probably…

If you ask me, the one place they really have to go to is…

Reacting to suggestions

If they'd rather try something different,… might be worth a shot.

I wouldn't bother going to…, personally.

They'd be better (off) going to…

1 Complete the sentences with these phrases. Then listen to check your answers. 7

a little while	be better (off)
'd suggest trying	experience a genuine
rather try something	's their thing
the best places	the one place
they should probably	worth a shot
wouldn't bother going	you ask me

If sightseeing (1) ______________________, then (2) ______________________ to go are Lombard Street and the Golden Gate Bridge. If they want to (3) ______________________ local night out, I (4) ______________________ Union Square. If they're only staying here for (5) ______________________, (6) ______________________ see Alcatraz Island. If (7) ______________________, (8) ______________________ they really have to go to is the beach. If they'd (9) ______________________ different, Chinatown might be (10) ______________________. I (11) ______________________ to the wax museum personally. They'd (12) ______________________ going to the aquarium or zoo.

2 Match the beginnings (1–8) with the endings (a–h) to make recommendations from a TV travel show about Barcelona. Then listen and check your answers. 8

Barcelona truly is one of the world's best-loved destinations.

1 If you're only staying here for a little while, ____
2 And if you ask me, ____ The nature-inspired cathedral designed by Antoni Gaudi is still being built more than 135 years later.
3 If you'd rather try something outside, ____
4 If sports are your thing, then ____
5 Barcelona is famous for its cuisine, but if you want to buy some fresh food, ____
6 You'd be best off going to La Boqueria, ____
7 If you want to experience a genuine local night out, ____
8 Then, head down La Rambla to the Plaça Reial to enjoy some more amazing tapas in one of the many small and friendly cafes, ____

a before finding a club to dance the night away.
b I wouldn't bother going to the supermarkets, personally.
c I'd suggest starting with some traditional tapas in a restaurant in the Raval district.
d one of the last covered markets in Europe, and sampling the wonderful range of food and drink on offer.
e Park Guell will definitely be worth a visit. This sculpted garden is a favorite with locals and tourists alike.
f the best place to go is the Olympic stadium. Home to the 1992 Games, this beautiful stadium also has great views over the city.
g the one place you really have to go to is the Sagrada Familia.
h you should probably hop on the *Bus Turistic* and see all the most famous attractions from an open-top double-decker bus.

3 Some friends from another country are coming to visit your city. Make notes on the best advice and recommendations you can give them for what to do in the area. Use the useful language.

4 Listen to a conversation between a student and a school counselor, and then answer the question. 9

Question: Make notes on how you would briefly summarize the issue the two speakers are discussing. Then add notes about which solution you recommend and give reasons to explain why. Speak for one minute and record yourself.

Then listen to the sample answer. 10

WRITING A review

5 **Read the extracts from all four reviews. Then give each one a different star-rating, from one (★☆☆☆) to four (★★★★) stars.**

1 The outdoor market was one of the highlights of the trip. We enjoyed browsing the stalls and looking at all the local goods and crafts. Unfortunately, they charge higher prices to tourists, but I imagine that happens everywhere. It's still a good place to buy souvenirs, and well worth a visit. ☆☆☆☆

2 The dining area was too dark, and the service was terrible. Our food took a long time to arrive, and when it did, the wrong dish was served to my sister. Also, everything was cold and poorly presented. What's more, it was expensive! I'd skip this restaurant if I were you. ☆☆☆☆

3 The walking tour of the city was a bit disappointing. It was advertised as a one-hour event but it finished after 45 minutes, which was surprising. Some of the sights were cool, but the tour guide didn't really give us much information about them. For $10, it's just not worth it. ☆☆☆☆

4 The three-day art course was the best thing I did all summer! The teacher was excellent and encouraged us all to try new art styles and techniques. I can't believe how much I learned in just a few days. Doing this course gave me so much confidence. I can't recommend it enough. ☆☆☆☆

6 **Complete the review with these words and phrases.**

arranged	enjoyed
fun	love
On top of that	One other thing was the fact that
recommend	special
what's more	which

Adventure-Break is an organized vacation in Scotland that offers a range of adventure sports and other activities. Two of my friends and I booked an *Adventure-Break* last month. In the beautiful and wild Scottish countryside, we (1) ______________ a variety of outdoor activities, including canoeing, mountain biking, hiking, and even kayaking. It was a memorable experience for all the best reasons! What I particularly like is that everything is (2) ______________ for you, (3) ______________ is very convenient. You choose your accommodation in advance—camping or staying in a chalet—and the adventure starts as soon as you arrive. (4) ______________, they have their own chefs who cook the most delicious meals for everyone. The guides do everything they can to make sure you enjoy your vacation and, (5) ______________, they're great (6) ______________. You can do as many activities as you want every day. (7) ______________ we met lots of people from different countries. We became really good friends with some of them, which was (8) ______________. If you like doing outdoor activities and meeting new people, you'll (9) ______________ *Adventure-Break*. I can't (10) ______________ it enough!

—Javier Sanchez, Spain

7 **Read Javier's review again. Are these statements true (T) or false (F)?**

1 *Adventure-Break* is good for people who enjoy doing sports. ____
2 Javier and his friends went on an *Adventure-Break* last year. ____
3 Most of the activities are done outside. ____
4 Javier tells us that the *Adventure-Break* was unforgettable. ____
5 People going on *Adventure-Breaks* have to find and arrange their own accommodation. ____
6 *Adventure-Break* participants take turns cooking for each other. ____
7 Javier was impressed with the guides. ____
8 There is no daily limit to the number of activities participants can sign up for. ____
9 *Adventure-Break* is only available to people from Spain. ____
10 Overall, Javier gives the experience a very positive review. ____

8 **You see this announcement on a travel website.**

Travel reviews wanted

Have you taken a vacation to a place you found particularly impressive or disappointing? Write us a review saying where you went and explain why. Tell us whether or not you would recommend this place to others. The best reviews will be published on our website.

Write your review.

Review

1 Choose the correct options to complete the email.

Hi Yumi,

We've just got back! At first, we stayed in a (1) ___. It was in the mountains, and the view (2) ___ my mind. However, I got food (3) ___ in the first week, so we looked for somewhere else to (4) ___ with Airbnb. Next year, I'm (5) ___ camping—then I'll be able to get off the (6) ___ path more and get a better feel for the place.

–Tania

1	**a** B&A	**b** B&B	**c** A&B	**d** B&C
2	**a** blew	**b** rushed	**c** shocked	**d** left
3	**a** poison	**b** poisoner	**c** poisoned	**d** poisoning
4	**a** lie around	**b** stay	**c** live	**d** hang out
5	**a** being	**b** doing	**c** going	**d** getting
6	**a** beat	**b** beating	**c** beats	**d** beaten

2 Complete the words in the sentences. Some of the letters are given for you.

1 It was a real c_____ t_______ shock at first.
2 The locals were so friendly and w_____ c___________.
3 They saw most of the s___________ in the first few days.
4 Sitting by the plane window reduces my a___________.
5 It's too bad that we didn't keep in t_________ after the vacation.

3 Put the words in the correct order to make questions.

1 your / package / Jamaica / tour / meals / did / in / include
_______________________________________?
2 about / long / how / at the end of the road / they / known / the private beach / have
_______________________________________?
3 rented / who / to / beach / house / their / you
_______________________________________?
4 lunch / where / guide / us / the / after / meet / telling / is / to
_______________________________________?
5 taken / climb / souvenirs / have / what / as / their / of / trekkers
_______________________________________?

4 Match the two parts of the sentences.

1 Every day—well, most days!—___
2 Because I have a meeting tomorrow, ___
3 Yesterday ___
4 My leg hurt while ___
5 By the time my older brother got home, ___
6 When my friend started coming with me to work out, ___
7 When I had classes in the afternoon, ___

a I'd come back from the gym.
b I would go to the gym in the morning.
c I'd already been going to the gym for a while.
d I go to the gym.
e I was running at the gym.
f I'm going to the gym today.
g I went to the gym.

5 Decide if the words in bold are correct or incorrect. Write the correct word(s).

1 When I lived in Costa Rica, I **would go jogging** every morning before breakfast. ___________
2 **Did you used** to eat beans for breakfast? ___________
3 I **would to want** to study abroad. ___________
4 She didn't **would to have** short hair. ___________
5 My grandmother **used tell** me stories about when she was growing up in Shanghai. ___________
6 Did you **use to ride** your bike to school? ___________
7 I **never use to eat** a lot of sugary snacks. ___________
8 He didn't **used to study** at the library. ___________

2 The Business of Technology

2A Young Business

VOCABULARY Setting up a new business

1 Review Cross out the mistake in each sentence and write the correct word.

1 She is in charge for the marketing team.
______
2 I work on the construction industry.
______
3 The job market is very competition.
______
4 I'm looking for a fully-time job.
______
5 Cleaning is not a very well-pay job.
______
6 He's responsible at sales.
______
7 Farming is a physically demanded job.
______
8 Doctors have to work extremely long hour.
______

2 Review Complete the sentences with these words.

charge flexible industry part-time prospects responsible stressful

1 Are you ______ for the advertising?
2 The job is so ______ I'm not sleeping very well.
3 Our new engineers have excellent career ______.
4 Our manager is in ______ of over 100 people.
5 They want ______ people who don't mind change.
6 It's a ______ job, from 9 to 2.
7 Do you work in the sports ______?

3 Match the words to make phrases connected to business.

1 handle
2 deal with a
3 raise
4 put together
5 negotiate
6 invent

a a good deal
b money
c stress and pressure
d a team of people
e something new
f range of people

4 Do you connect these activities more with people or with products? Complete the table.

distribute invent market meet negotiate network

People	Products

5 Choose the correct option (a–d) to complete each sentence.

1 The company needs to ______ another million dollars from the investors.
a raise
b deal
c lend
d figure

2 Don't forget to hand out your business card when ________________.
  a inventing
  b networking
  c getting on
  d putting together

3 We ________________ a good price with the supplier.
  a managed
  b got on
  c negotiated
  d handled

4 The company was able to ________________ from a bad year of sales.
  a redesign
  b accept
  c repair
  d recover

5 I'm responsible for ________________ the marketing department.
  a dealing with
  b distributing
  c getting on
  d negotiating

6 The manager ________________ together a team of engineers for the project.
  a hold
  b put
  c send
  d manage

6 Complete the sentences with the correct word. The first letter is given for you.

1 Positive comments on social media can r________________ a new company's profile significantly.
2 Remember, you can n________________ anything.
3 The director puts a lot of p________________ on the managers.
4 We're planning to d________________ our products in Europe.
5 How do you plan to m________________ your new product?
6 The t________________ they put together includes sales people in Europe and Asia.
7 The company is based in an o________________ in the city center.
8 It's important to n________________ with people from other companies when you go to a conference.

7 Extension Are the statements true (T) or false (F)?

1 The **founder** of a company has established it. ____
2 If you describe yourself as **proactive**, you enjoy working outdoors. ____
3 To **outsource** means to use suppliers outside your company for goods and services. ____
4 If negotiations are **delicate**, it means they are difficult. ____
5 A **self-starter** is someone who starts new companies. ____
6 A **team player** gets on well with other people at work. ____
7 The **chair** of a meeting is an important piece of furniture. ____
8 A **systematic** employee is good at planning. ____

8 Extension Complete the sentences with these words.

chair	delicate	founder	outsourced
proactive	self-starter	systematic	team player

1 She isn't a ________________ and is difficult to work with.
2 The ________________ is going to introduce the speakers.
3 We're having ________________ talks with our partners at the moment, so it's a bit risky.
4 I'm not very ________________ so the project looks a bit disorganized.
5 The company is looking for a ________________ for this role.
6 She is the ________________ of the business, which has been going since 2005.
7 The hotel ________________ the cleaning to a local company.
8 I'm very ________________ and good at making things happen.

PRONUNCIATION

9 **Listen to the questions. Does the intonation rise or fall at the end of the question? Practice saying the questions.** 11

1 Isn't there a more secure way to shop online?

____

2 You fell for an online scam? ______________

3 Do you think it's a good idea to post that?

____

4 Wouldn't it be great to start your own company?

____

5 What do you want to do with that?

____

6 Wouldn't it be better to help people in need?

____

7 Haven't you ever had that problem?

____

8 Why aren't they marketing the product yet?

____

LISTENING

10 **Listen to the speaker. Complete the sentences about the short lecture.** 12

1 Good ______________ might save the world one new idea at a time.

2 Designers have always dreamed up ______________ goods.

3 New products include ______________ roof tiles, electric motorcycles, and more.

4 The ______________ Design for Extreme Affordability course is at Stanford University.

5 Some entrepreneurs are taking a look at the concerns of people in ______________.

6 Designers are creating products to meet communities' most ______________.

7 Problems from health care to ______________ water can have affordable, beautifully designed solutions.

orange breasted sunbird

11 **Now listen to the description of four innovative products. Match the description with the product.** 13

1 gives hours of safe heat	a Q Drum
2 costs around a dollar	b The Embrace
3 holds almost 13 gallons of water	c Respira
4 stops harmful bacteria and viruses	d LifeStraw

12 **Listen to the speaker. What is the main idea of her talk?** 14

a the positives and negatives of sustainable eco-tourism
b the benefits brought by conservation entrepreneurs
c the need for entrepreneurs to protect the natural world
d the entrepreneurial spirit of young African people

13 **Listen again and choose the correct options.** 14

1 What example does the speaker give of *sustainable eco-tourism*?
a national parks
b plant and animal habitats
c private nature reserves

2 What species does she describe as rare?
a coral lagoons
b the Fynbos plant
c orange-breasted sunbirds

3 Who refers to the area the speaker describes as the "Cape Floral Kingdom"?
a botanists
b Lutzeyer
c natives

4 How did the Lutzeyers raise money for the reserve?
a they raised the money themselves
b they used banks in nearby Cape Town
c they sold the abandoned farms and lands

5 How would you describe the attitude of the local people living near the reserve?
a unconvinced
b suspicious
c supportive

6 What does the speaker describe Grootbos as being part of?
a a conservation effort
b a worldwide trend
c our natural world

GRAMMAR Present perfect forms and the simple past

14 Choose the correct options to complete the conversation.

A: What (1) *are you learning / did you learn / have you learned* since starting your own company?

B: The most important thing I (2) *have learned / have been learning / learned* is that you have to be able to deal with failure in this business. But you can learn from failure.

A: When (3) *did you start / have you started / have you been starting* your company?

B: In 2012, my friends and I (4) *have started / started / have been starting* creating what eventually became our app. We had been working on it for two years before we (5) *have decided / have been deciding / decided* to get serious and quit our jobs to work on the app full-time.

A: And how do you define your current success?

B: For me, it (6) *wasn't / hasn't been being / hasn't been* about earning tons of money or having power or influence. I'm successful because I like what I do, and I have fun doing it. When it stops being fun, that's when I'll consider doing something different.

15 Complete the sentences with these words and phrases.

claimed	dreamed
has invented	have been attracting
have failed	have run
have risen	haven't been advertising
made	

1 Companies like ours ________________ in print magazines or newspapers.
2 The company's founder ________________ that he slept only three hours a night.
3 Many businesses ________________ because they ________________ out of money.
4 Technology companies ________________ the attention of investors for years.
5 The competition ________________ an app that works faster than ours.
6 In the late 1990s many people ________________ of becoming tech millionaires.
7 Our profits ________________ 5% in the last year thanks to automation.
8 We ________________ a profit for the first time after three years in business.

16 Complete the article with the correct forms of the verbs in parentheses.

Young Entrepreneurs in India

In recent years, kids in India (1) ________________ (make) a difference in important ways. A number of high school students (2) ________________ (become) entrepreneurs. Young entrepreneurs, sometimes called "schoolpreneurs," (3) ________________ (realize) that starting businesses is important for India's economic development.

Possibly the most famous young technology entrepreneurs in India are Shravan and Sanjay Kumaran, brothers and high school students from Chennai. They (4) ________________ (create) GoDimensions in 2011—when they were just 12 and 10 years old. In total, they (5) ________________ (develop) seven apps that are available in the Apple App Store and three Android apps for the Google Play Store. People (6) ________________ (download) the apps more than 70,000 times! Shravan and Sanjay claim to be the youngest cell phone app developers in India at 16 and 14 years of age. They (7) ________________ (give) presentations at a TedX Youth conference in 2015, and plan to donate 15% of their profits to charity.

Fortunately, investors (8) ________________ (be) willing to take a risk with young entrepreneurs—they are more interested in good business ideas than in the age of the entrepreneur!

17 Complete the sentences using the correct forms of the verbs in parentheses.

1 For as long as she can remember, people ________________ (ask) Leanna Archer what makes her hair look so beautiful.
2 Leanna ________________ (decide) to try to sell her all-natural hair product to people she ________________ (know).
3 She ________________ (put) the special hair product in small containers and ________________ (give) samples to her friends and their parents.
4 They ________________ (like) it so much, they were willing to pay for it!
5 So Leanna ________________ (start) her own hair-care company, Leanna's Essentials, when she ________________ (be) just thirteen.
6 Since then, thousands of people ________________ (be able) to enjoy Leanna's products.

2B Spreading Fast

VOCABULARY BUILDING Adjective and noun collocations

1 Complete the sentences with these adjectives.

distant	luxury	normal	official
personal	second-hand	well-paid	

1 Be careful with your ________ details so criminals cannot steal your identity.
2 I like to stay at ________ hotels when I travel; they're expensive, but it's worth it.
3 These shoes were only half the ________ price, so I bought them right away.
4 I've been researching online to try to find some of my ________ relatives and get in touch.
5 Has the university sent you your ________ letter of acceptance yet?
6 Jana has got an interesting and ________ job for the summer.
7 I'd like to buy a good ________ car when I graduate.

READING

2 Read the information. Match the information (a–f) with the paragraphs (1–5). Paragraph numbers may be used more than once.

a an example of a successful emotional advertisement ____
b details of advertising fifty years ago ____
c examples of advertisements that used the same marketing strategy ____
d context for how companies can succeed in advertising today ____
e restates information given in other sections ____
f discusses how games and advertising are related ____

3 Complete each sentence with the correct ending based on information from the text.

1 Viral marketing campaigns usually ____
2 Playworld was able to ____
3 Lay's contest to create a new chip flavor ____
4 Chipotle's Scarecrow game ____
5 Emotional responses to advertising content ____
6 A successful advertising campaign ____

a take advantage of the reasons that people share information on social media.
b is appealing to a wide range of people.
c received millions of entries.
d get free advertising by getting communities involved.
e was downloaded thousands of times.
f cause people to share the content with others.

4 Do the statements match the information in the article? Write true (T), false (F), or not given (NG).

1 Companies can make more money through advertising now than they could fifty years ago. ____
2 A company has to understand why people share on social media in order to make a successful advertisement. ____
3 An advertisement that gets an emotional reaction from consumers is less likely to be a success. ____
4 The Dove advertisement was successful because women felt emotionally connected to its message. ____
5 Prizes are more effective than games at getting consumers to share an advertisement. ____

Going Viral 15

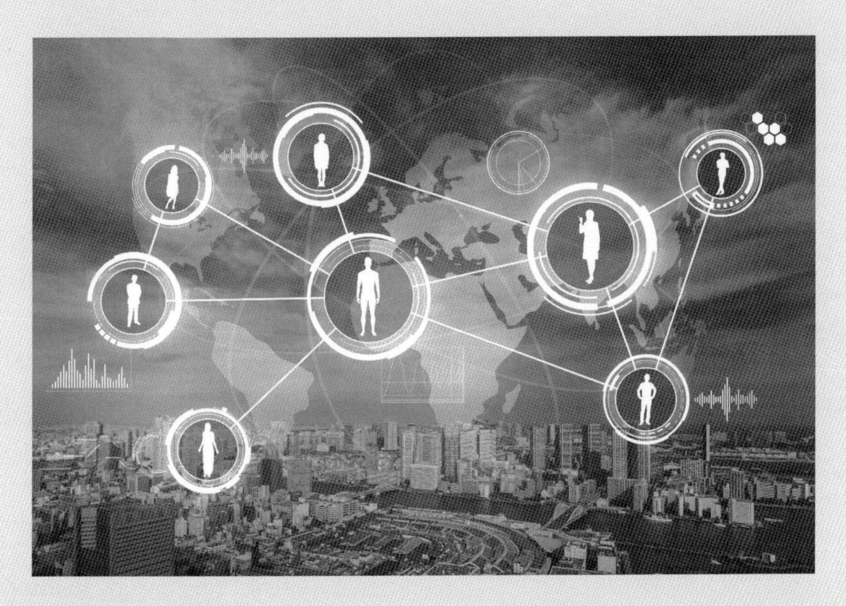

1 Fifty years ago, companies trying to increase awareness of their products knew exactly how to reach consumers. They focused their advertising efforts on television, newspapers, and magazines, and spent time developing creative advertisements that they knew millions of people would see. But today's consumers are flooded with information on a daily basis. In the age of social media, over 4.75 billion pieces of content are added to social media sites every 24 hours. How do companies and their products get noticed? Getting social media users to share content is important to success. Going viral, or having content shared quickly with many users, can make millions of dollars for a company. But how can a company create a viral marketing campaign? It has to understand why people share information and then use that in its advertising.

2 Emotion is a powerful reason that social media users share content. When a user feels a strong connection to an advertisement, whether that emotion is joy, sadness, or even anger, they are much more likely to share that advertisement with others. Take, for example, the advertising campaign about "real women" by the beauty brand Dove. In this advertisement, an artist draws two pictures of a woman without seeing her. One picture is based on that woman's description of herself, and the other is based on a description from someone who knows the woman. The pictures clearly show how the woman is critical of herself while others see her in a much more positive light. This advertisement appealed to the emotions of a diverse range of women, who could relate to its message. It was shared nearly 3.8 million times in a month.

3 But an advertisement doesn't have to be serious to get attention and shares. Some companies have had great success by offering games or prizes to social media users. The fast-food chain Chipotle Mexican Foods released an advertisement called "The Scarecrow" that had both a short film and a free game that users could download. The game had more than 250,000 downloads within four days of its release. This type of advertising is even more effective because a user is reminded of the company every time they open the app to play the game.

4 Social media users also love prizes. The snack food company Lay's increased its sales in the United States by 12% with a viral campaign asking users to create a new flavor of potato chips. The winning flavor, cheesy garlic bread, was selected from almost four million ideas. The playground manufacturer Playworld offered two free playgrounds to users who liked the company's social media page and wrote an essay about why they wanted to bring a playground to their community. Not only did visits to the company's social media page increase significantly, many communities worked together to try to win the playground, and local newspapers and TV news shows covered the contest at no cost to Playworld.

5 For an advertising campaign to succeed today, it has to appeal to people of many ages in many places. The companies producing the most successful advertisements are those that understand the reasons why people share and make their advertisements with those reasons in mind. Advertising is certainly different to what it was fifty years ago, but the profits from a great campaign can still be huge.

2C Tech My Advice

GRAMMAR Verb patterns (*-ing* or infinitive with *to*)

1 Choose the correct option to complete the sentences.

1. Nacho won't admit *using / to use* social media.
2. She decided *closing / to close* her social media account.
3. He hopes *receiving / to receive* a letter from the university soon.
4. Esteban needs *planning / to plan* carefully for the future.
5. When a website says it uses cookies, do you agree *continuing / to continue* using it?
6. Her parents want her to delay *using / to use* social media for as long as possible.
7. I didn't intend *offending / to offend* anyone with the post I wrote.
8. Eva refused *accept / to accept* Ivan's friend request on social media.

2 Choose the correct option to complete the sentences.

1. 3-D printing is something experts expect ________ a big role in the future.
   a play
   b to play
   c playing
2. Some people hear about amazing objects made by 3-D printers and start ________ they can make the same things themselves.
   a believing
   b believe
   c to believe
3. 3-D printers allow designers ________ new concepts.
   a to test
   b testing
   c test
4. Experts think ________ human tissue with 3-D printers is a distant possibility.
   a to produce
   b produce
   c producing
5. With 3-D printers, researchers can avoid ________ costly mistakes.
   a make
   b to make
   c making
6. If a student needs ________ a model for a science project, a 3-D printer can be useful.
   a to make
   b making
   c make

3 Are the words in bold correct or incorrect? Correct those that are incorrect.

1. For several decades, robotics companies in Japan have been working toward their ambitious goal—they intend **creating** a perfect humanoid robot. ________
2. They hope, one day, **being** able to make androids look exactly like humans. ________
3. Some scientists are also trying **to give** their androids a personality. ________
4. However, there are people who simply refuse **accepting** a future where robots and humans live and work side by side. ________
5. Other people don't mind **to think** about a future where robots play an important role. ________
6. Personally, I think I would enjoy **to interact** with a robot that can think, act, and relate to humans. ________
7. If asked, I'd certainly agree **to have** an android do chores around my house. ________
8. The question is, will we ever regret **to make** robots so much like humans? ________

4 Complete the conversation using the correct form of the verbs in parentheses. Use verb + *-ing* or infinitive with *to*.

A: Have you heard of the Hubble Space Telescope?
B: Yes, I have! It's used (1) ________ (study) our solar system.
A: Do you know how big the telescope is?
B: I know that the Hubble designers dreamed of making a bigger telescope, but they had to compromise. In the end, they managed (2) ________ (design) a smaller telescope that orbits 350 miles above Earth.

A: Did they do a lot of tests before sending it up in space?

B: They did. In fact, one astronaut wanted (3) ________________ (guarantee) the telescope could be fixed in space, so he went to the Smithsonian's National Air and Space Museum and practiced (4) ________________ (fix) its Hubble replica.

A: What does the Hubble do?

B: Well, one thing is that it allows us (5) ________________ (see) stars that are billions of light years from Earth. Hubble researchers are determined (6) ________________ (keep) exploring our solar system.

5 **Write sentences that are true for you. Use these prompts and verbs with *-ing* or infinitive with *to*.**

1 I always try ________________

____

2 I avoid ________________

____

3 Sometimes I miss ________________

____

4 When I finish ________________

____

5 I am considering ________________

____

6 As soon as I can, I hope ________________

____

6 **Complete the sentences with the objects and the correct forms of the verbs in parentheses.**

1 The teacher asked ________________ (me, arrange) a meeting with my parents.
2 Our teacher expects ________________ (us, text) each other in English for more practice.
3 My father can't stand ________________ (me, check) my phone constantly.
4 Karl watched ________________ (her, carry) four heavy bags and didn't offer to help.
5 The neighbors invited ________________ (us, swim) in their pool.
6 The airline strike has delayed ________________ (me, travel) to Santiago.
7 You can't expect ________________ (him, be) happy with the decision.
8 The coach chose ________________ (her, play) in the game.

7 **Read the sentences. Circle the direct object and underline the indirect object.**

1 Can you email me the directions when you can?
2 His aunt gave him money for his class trip.
3 The teacher read the children a story.
4 Can you pass me a pen to write the list?
5 Here, I'll lend you my phone to call him.
6 Veronica bought her parents tickets for the opera.

8 **Complete the sentences with direct and indirect objects and/or verbs with *-ing* or infinitive with *to*.**

1 They promised ________________

____

2 I don't expect ________________

____

3 It bothers me when people ask me ________________

____

4 I'm going to lend ________________

____

2D This is What Happens When You Reply to Spam Email

TEDTALKS

AUTHENTIC LISTENING SKILLS

1 **Read statements from James Veitch's TED Talk. Practice reading the responses aloud using intonation and pitch to show surprise. Record and then listen to yourself.** 16

1. We shall be shipping gold to you.
   Response: Shipping gold to me?
2. There's no point doing this at all unless you're shipping at least a metric ton.
   Response: A metric ton?
3. I'm a hedge fund executive bank manager.
   Response: A hedge fund executive bank manager?
4. We're ready for shipping as much gold as possible.
   Response: As much gold as possible?
5. I was in Sainsbury's the other day and there were, like, 30 different varieties.
   Response: 30 different varieties?
6. When we email each other, we need to use a code.
   Response: A code?
7. Send £1,500 via a Giant Gummy Lizard.
   Response: A Giant Gummy Lizard?
8. I am Winnie Mandela, the second wife of Nelson Mandela, the former South African president.
   Response: Winne Mandela?

WATCH

2 **Choose the correct option to complete the sentences.**

1. James refused *accepting / to accept* only 25 kilograms of gold from Solomon.
2. Instead, he offered *to receive / receiving* a metric ton of gold.
3. James enjoyed *corresponding / to correspond* with Solomon so much that he canceled plans with friends.
4. Apparently, Solomon planned *spending / to spend* his earnings on buying property.
5. James doesn't mind to *waste / wasting* spammers' time.
6. In corresponding with spammers, James recommends *creating / to create* a separate email account.
7. James never agreed *to send / sending* money to the person who claimed to be Winnie Mandela.

3 **Choose the correct options.**

1. What is the main topic of the talk?
   - **a** Gold is a solid investment.
   - **b** Answering spam emails can sometimes be fun.
   - **c** More people should try hummus.
   - **d** Nelson Mandela was an important South African leader.
2. According to James Veitch, what do spammers often do to encourage people to participate in their schemes?
   - **a** They tell you they know where you live.
   - **b** They ask for personal information about you.
   - **c** They share their hopes to make you feel empathy.
   - **d** They offer more money in each email.
3. What does Veitch imply when he says "Don't use your own email address because that's exactly what I was doing at the start and it was a nightmare."?
   - **a** That a spammer will sell your email address to other spammers.
   - **b** That people send a lot of emails at night.
   - **c** That it's dangerous to reveal your real identity.
   - **d** That most people use only one email address.
4. What can be inferred about James Veitch?
   - **a** He thinks spammers don't cause any harm.
   - **b** He wishes he were a bank manager.
   - **c** He enjoys pointing out the absurdity in people's words and actions.
   - **d** He doesn't care about other people.

VOCABULARY IN CONTEXT

4 **Match the words and phrases (1–6) with the sentences that show their meaning (a–f).**

1 intrigues _____	**4** out of hand _____
2 turned up _____	**5** knock it on the head _____
3 matter _____	**6** gone too far _____

- **a** I will call my brother tonight. We have an important **issue** to discuss.
- **b** Kenneth keeps turning his homework in late, so Sheila told him he needs to **stop that behavior** and start taking his studies seriously.
- **c** Raquel was surprised when her sister **appeared** at her shop one afternoon.
- **d** Jaime was trying to tell jokes, but when nobody laughed, he realized that he had **said something wrong**.
- **e** Jasmine has always enjoyed studying science; biology particularly **interests** her.
- **f** When Gene saw the mess that the children had made, he was upset that the situation had got **out of control**.

2E Investment Opportunity

SPEAKING

Speaking strategy

Persuading

When we are persuading people, we sometimes turn our own experiences and opinions into a negative question to challenge the other person's ideas.

I think it will lose money.

Don't you think it'll lose money?

I'd find it really useful.

Wouldn't you find it really useful?

I have sometimes had that problem.

Haven't you ever had that problem?

1 **Listen and complete the useful language with the correct auxiliary verb, then write the original idea.** 17

1 ___*Do*___n't you think it'll be a mistake?
I think it'll be a mistake.

2 ________n't you find it really annoying?
____

3 ________n't you ever seen that happen?
____

4 ________n't it look weird if you do that?
____

5 ________n't that a bad idea?
____

6 ________n't we wait five more minutes, please?
____

7 ________n't you see her yesterday?
____

8 ________n't you finish your homework first?
____

2 **Write a negative question to challenge each of these opinions or ideas using the words in parentheses.**

1 I'm going to have another piece of cake.
(had enough already)
____

2 Climate change isn't my problem.
(all responsible / environment)
____

3 I'm going to buy the latest laptop.
(wait / a sale)
____

4 I want to be a famous actor.
(need / plan B)
____

5 I'm going to watch movies all day.
(play / basketball)
____

3 **Look at these situations and decide what your opinions are. Then use negative questions to express your comments on the situations.**

1 Your English teacher gives you four pieces of homework in one day.
____

2 The government is cutting funding to youth projects.
____

3 Scientists have found a way to change babies' eye color.
____

4 A friend of yours has found a bag containing $1,000 in the street.
____

5 A company is considering building a big hotel on a nature reserve.
____

6 A friend is too lazy to study for their exams.
____

4 **Your school wants to protect itself from cybercrime. Below are some ideas that they are considering and a question for you to discuss. Make notes and then talk about the benefits and drawbacks of these ideas. Record yourself. Remember to use the speaking strategy. Then listen to a sample discussion of the topic.** 18

What are the benefits and drawbacks of these IT security ideas?

- backing up computers every hour
- permanently recording all activity of every user
- only allowing students to use their own devices

WRITING A persuasive article

5 **Match the steps for writing a persuasive text (1–4) with the examples (a–d).**

1 Grab the reader's attention and stimulate a shared experience. ___
2 Persuade the reader to continue reading by saying that a solution will be provided. ___
3 Present factual information related to the solution. ___
4 In the final paragraph, provide a reason why the reader should take action. ___

a What we can offer you is a happy balance between relaxing under a palm tree and participating in some very worthwhile environmental projects.
b Well, luckily, our team has found a fantastic way to help you live the dream!
c So, why not click here and join one of our *HOLunteering* trips today? You'll be glad you did!
d Have you ever dreamed of going on vacation somewhere exotic… but can't afford it? Trust me, we all have!

6 **Read the persuasive text. Then put the information provided here in the correct order.**

University students aiming to bring you the ideal sauce

Do you love ketchup but find it a little too sweet? Do you enjoy hot sauce but find it a little too… hot? Most of us do! We've all been served a dish that would be perfect, except that it's missing *something*. Well, problem solved! That something special has finally been developed, you'll be pleased to know, and it has a tantalizing Korean twist.

Theo, Mike, Erica, Ryan and Alex—five classmates at the University of California, Los Angeles (UCLA)—have created K POP, the most exciting and delicious sauce you'll ever taste. K POP Sauce with its winning combination of flavors, including Korean chilli paste and Theo's grandmother's secret ingredient, is simply a condiment like no other.

But the K POP team needs your help. Their Kickstarter goal is to raise enough money to produce K POP Sauce in large quantities, and ship it worldwide.

So, why not support the guys and make a pledge to their Kickstarter campaign? You'll be helping an excellent business get off the ground and giving yourself and the world the delight that is K POP Sauce!

a Says who is involved in developing the product ____
b Points out what the reader's support will accomplish ____
c Establishes the topic with a descriptive title ____
d Explains what the makers of the product need ____
e Lets the reader know a solution has been found ____
f Describes the product ____
g Creates initial interest by describing a shared experience ____
h Invites the reader to get involved ____

7 **Read the article. Then listen to the lecture. Write an essay summarizing the points made in the lecture you just heard, explaining how they cast doubt on points made in the reading.** 19

Set up in 2009, the Kickstarter corporation may not be as popular as it once seemed.

People with creative ideas in one of 13 categories, including art, music, and technology, can use Kickstarter to describe their project and appeal for financial support. They set a target amount of money needed and a date by which it must be raised. Any member of the public can access the Kickstarter platform and offer to support an idea. Those who do so are called "backers." If backers pledge enough, that is, promise to donate enough cash to meet the required target within the deadline, then the project is funded. So far so good… or is it? The system certainly has flaws.

Firstly, major celebrities have started using Kickstarter to fund new film ventures or to record new albums. These have been heavily criticized by many who resent already wealthy people potentially taking away opportunities from smaller, unknown artists whose need for Kickstarter is arguably greater.

Secondly, can we really trust Kickstarter projects? Even when projects reach their financial goal, who can guarantee the money won't be used for other purposes? Indeed, it is not unusual for funded projects to soon fail due to poor planning or underestimated needs. This seems like a reckless waste of other people's money.

Lastly, many feel that backers are exploited by the Kickstarter system. No matter how much of their own money they pledge, they receive very little in return. This hardly seems fair, especially as thousands of Kickstarter projects have enjoyed enormous financial success.

Kickstarter may be a good service in some circumstances, but it is far from perfect.

Review

1 **Rewrite the sentences. Complete the sentences using the correct form of the word in capital letters. Use two or three words.**

1. He works in the Madrid office. BASE
   He ______________________ the Madrid office.
2. She's working alongside the partners in Asia. DEAL
   She's ______________________ the partners in Asia.
3. I have to find a good team for the presentation. PUT
   I have to ______________________ a good team for the presentation.
4. Entrepreneurs can accept failure and quickly move on. RECOVER
   Entrepreneurs can ______________________ failure quickly.
5. Meditation is useful for dealing with pressure. HANDLE
   Meditation is a good ______________________ pressure.

2 **Complete the sentences with the correct word. The first letter is given for you.**

1. The business uses a s __ __ __ __ __ __ __ in China to provide materials.
2. She managed to n __ __ __ __ __ __ __ __ __ a good pay raise with her manager.
3. They're using online advertising to m __ __ __ __ __ __ the language school.
4. N __ __ __ __ __ __ __ __ __ __ is an important part of building professional relationships.
5. Partners help to d __ __ __ __ __ __ __ __ __ __ __ your products in other regions.
6. I'm a social e __ __ __ __ __ __ __ __ __ __ __ __ __ __ working in the field of education.
7. Where is your company b __ __ __ __ __ ?
8. Successful companies i __ __ __ __ __ __ new things in response to customers' needs.

3 **Find and correct the mistakes in these sentences. Two sentences are correct.**

1. Organizations that has been using start-up companies to find solutions to social, cultural, or environmental problems are called "social entrepreneurs."
   ____
2. Traditionally, start-up companies have been measured their success by looking at profits or sales.
   ____
3. In contrast, social entrepreneurs have worked to end poverty, increase health care, and improve the quality of life. ______________________
4. Social entrepreneurs have using social networking to reach more people, spread information about their activities, and raise money. ______________________
5. Kiva.org been lending money to low-income entrepreneurs in 80 countries ($25 at a time) since 2005.
   ____
6. In 2009, Matt Damon has cofounded Water.org, which works to increase access to safe water and sanitation for people in developing countries. ______________________
7. For over 12 years, Khan Academy has made education available to people all over the world—for free!
   ____
8. Since 2000, the Bill & Melinda Gates Foundation is working to increase access to health care and reduce extreme poverty. ______________________

4 **Complete the sentences with the correct form of these verbs. There may be more than one correct answer.**

give	link	pick up	see	study

1. Students who like ______________________ science might be interested in bionics, which is the study of mechanical systems that function like living organisms or parts of living organisms.
2. Scientists have learned it's possible ______________________ machine and mind.
3. A tiny camera that communicates with her brain allows a blind woman ______________________ the shapes of trees.
4. A bionic arm can let a person move that arm ______________________ a fork.
5. Bionics represents a big leap forward. It enables researchers ______________________ people back a lot of what they've lost.

5 **Choose the correct options to complete the sentences. Both forms may be correct.**

1. I love *watching / to watch* old movies.
2. She advised me *going / to go* home because I wasn't feeling well.
3. I fail *seeing / to see* how I can help you.
4. I never allow anyone *looking / to look* at my homework.
5. Do you avoid *calling / to call* your father at work?
6. Did she ask you *going / to go* to her house?
7. Tang refuses *using / to use* social media.
8. Have you finished *studying / to study* for the test?

3 Faster, Higher, Stronger

3A Incredible Achievements

VOCABULARY Describing athletes

1 Review Read the email. Choose the correct options to complete the email.

Hi Juanita,

I just wanted to thank you for (1) _____ me to exercise more. I've been (2) _____ cycling every weekend and I also (3) _____ yoga every morning now. I'm feeling so much better. Are you still (4) _____ hard for the marathon next month? I heard that you (5) _____ your personal best last year and (6) _____ the silver medal. Good for you!

I also wanted to say that it's great that you're going to (7) _____ our charity in the race. All of the runners are (8) _____ an important role in helping us to raise money.

Thank you!

Regards,

Lara

1 **a** representing **b** achieving **c** encouraging **d** making
2 **a** doing **b** going **c** playing **d** training
3 **a** do **b** go **c** play **d** train
4 **a** going **b** encouraging **c** doing **d** training
5 **a** achieved **b** won **c** had **d** made
6 **a** beat **b** achieved **c** won **d** scored
7 **a** show **b** present **c** do **d** represent
8 **a** playing **b** making **c** doing **d** being

2 Review Circle the odd one out.

1	referee	court	spectator	coach
2	diving	sailing	kick	karate
3	pass	track	rink	court
4	throw	swing	bounce	kick
5	net	diving	court	tennis

3 Choose the correct option to complete the sentences.

1 My brother has a real _____ for cycling.
a attitude **b** passion **c** role **d** race

2 Serena Williams is one of the most _____ female tennis players of all time.
a skilful **b** technique **c** star **d** great

3 How many goals has Benzema scored in his _____?
a average **b** game **c** record **d** career

4 Usain Bolt currently _____ the world record for the 100 metres.
a wins **b** sets **c** holds **d** smashes

5 Who _____ the team in Brazil?
a was captained **b** did captain **c** captained **d** captain

4 Complete the sentences with these verbs.

captained	competed	had
played	scored	smashed
was	won	

1 As a player, he ________________ skillful technique.
2 I ________________ in a national athletics competition last year.
3 Jenny ________________ the star of the team.
4 She ________________ a bronze medal in the 100 meter swimming competition.
5 She ________________ the existing world record.
6 He ________________ the team during the European Championship.
7 He only ________________ one goal last season.
8 The whole team ________________ a role in winning.

5 Complete the sentences with these words and phrases.

competed in and won	energetic	played a key role
real passion	really great	scored a goal
set	attitude	won

1 Shauna's teammates chose her to be the captain because she has a ________________.
2 Tomas is not the greatest player on the team, but he has a ________________ for the game.
3 The swimmer ________________ a new Olympic record.
4 The defenders ________________ in the team's victory over Real Madrid.
5 Ronaldo has ________________ in each of his last 12 games.
6 The Australian sailing team ________________ a silver medal in the Olympics.
7 She is one of the most ________________ coaches in women's basketball today.
8 He ________________ the Tour de France last year.

6 Cross out the mistake in each sentence and write the correct word.

1 Young people need a positively role model.
____
2 The team won a golden medal.
____
3 He was a star of the championship.
____
4 He's holding the world record for long jump.
____
5 You need to improve your technical.
____

7 **Extension** Complete the table.

Noun	Adjective
	energetic
passion	
	skillful
awareness	
	positive
competition	

8 **Extension** Write answers that are true for you.

1 What is something you are passionate about?
____
____
2 Who is the most competitive person you know?
____
____
3 What are your most important skills?
____
____

PRONUNCIATION

9 **Listen to the sentences. Underline the words that you hear linked together. Then practice saying the sentences.** 20

1 We had the best time at the Olympics!
2 It's far easier than you think it is.
3 She had the fastest time in the race.
4 Soccer isn't as popular in the United States.
5 He's a lot better at it than I am.
6 They're the first team to win two years in a row.
7 We don't play as often as we used to.
8 It's more difficult for me than it was years ago.

A competitor in the show jumping event of the modern pentathlon

LISTENING

10 **Listen and choose the correct options.** 21

1 What Greek word means "competition"?
 a athlon
 b penta
 c deca
2 How many events are in the decathlon?
 a 5
 b 10
 c 15
3 What sporting event do the ancient and modern pentathlon have in common?
 a swimming
 b running
 c riding
4 What event is NOT part of our modern pentathlon?
 a shooting
 b fencing
 c wrestling
5 What are athletes awarded for each event in the pentathlon?
 a points
 b medals
 c money
6 Who receives the silver medal?
 a the athlete with the third highest score
 b the athlete with the highest score
 c the athlete with the second highest score

11 **Listen to a lecture. Indicate the sports that you hear mentioned.** 22

1 wrestling ____
2 running ____
3 swimming ____
4 javelin throwing ____
5 climbing ____
6 jumping ____
7 horseback riding ____
8 gymnastics ____
9 discus throwing ____
10 boxing ____

12 **Listen again. What is the main point that the speaker is trying to make?** 22

a the similarities of the ancient and modern world
b the brutality of human beings not changing over time
c the basic desire of all humans to compete and win
d the enduring influence of Greek culture on athletics

13 **Match the words with their definitions. Listen again if necessary.** 22

1 discus ____
2 halteres ____
3 stadion ____
4 sprint ____
5 javelin ____
6 pentathlon ____
7 decathlon ____

a an ancient measure of distance in racing
b a spear-shaped object thrown by an athlete
c an Olympic event with ten events
d a disc-shaped object thrown by an athlete
e an ancient weight made of stone or bronze
f an Olympic event with five events
g a short run at full speed

GRAMMAR Determiners

14 Write *a* or *an* in front of the noun phrase.

1 ________ huge crowd of people
2 ________ positive role model
3 ________ average of 15 points
4 ________ world record
5 ________ athlete from Peru
6 ________ decent game
7 ________ absolutely amazing win
8 ________ great attitude
9 ________ injury to her ankle
10 ________ pulled muscle
11 ________ unknown participant
12 ________ winning strategy

15 Circle the correct words to complete the text. Circle *x* if no word is necessary.

Young Olympic Athletes from Rio 2016

Every four years, athletes compete for their countries in the Summer Olympic Games, and young athletes show the world what they can do.

- 18-year-old Yusra Mardini competed for (1) *a / the / x* Refugee Team at (2) *x / every / the* 2016 Rio Olympics. She is a swimmer. She and her family escaped (3) *some / a few / the* war in Syria.
- At the same time, (4) *x / a / a few* sisters Leila, Liina, and Lily Luik are believed to be (5) *those / the / x* first triplets to compete in (6) *an / her / each* Olympics. They called themselves "(7) *his / these / the* Trio to Rio" and competed in (8) *the / those / my* women's marathon—against (9) *all / a / both* team of (10) *x / the / each* German twins! Even though the triplets didn't win (11) *all / any / this* medals, no one will ever forget them.
- 16-year-old Kanak Jha was (12) *that / his / the* youngest Olympian on (13) *some / every / the* entire US team in Rio. (14) *Your / His / These* sport is table tennis. When he was 14, he won (15) *this / neither / the* table tennis World Cup.

16 Complete the sentences with *a, an, the,* or *x* (if no article is needed).

Marjorie Gestring: Young Olympic Gold Medalist

(1) ______ springboard diver from the United States, Marjorie Gestring, was once (2) ______ youngest Olympic gold medalist. At the age of almost (3) ______ 14, she won (4) ______ gold medal for three-meter springboard diving at (5) ______ 1936 Summer Olympics in Germany. (Her exact age was 13 years, 268 days.) She was the youngest person ever to win (6) ______ gold medal (at that time). Today, she's still (7) ______ second youngest gold medalist ever.

Marjorie won (8) ______ major diving competition in 1936 and joined (9) ______ US Olympic diving team. At the 1936 Olympics, (10) ______ Americans won (11) ______ gold, silver, and bronze medals for springboard diving. After (12) ______ Olympics, Marjorie continued to compete. She became (13) ______ member of (14) ______ International Swimming Hall of Fame.

Today, the youngest gold medal winner is speed skater Kim Yun-mi from South Korea who won (15) ______ gold medal at the 1994 Winter Olympics. She was just 13 years old.

17 Complete the sentences with these words.

a few	a lot	any	both
each	how many	much	some

1 I didn't know ______________ about cricket until my friends decided to teach me the rules.
2 At our soccer games, the spectators always scream really loudly for ______________ and every goal.
3 ______________ points did the winning team get in the first half?
4 We saw ______________ people leave the stadium before the end of the game.
5 My friends and I support ______________ Real Madrid and Manchester United.
6 It's hard to believe, but ______________ of people enjoy watching bowling on TV.
7 Have your friends been to ______________ games so far this year?
8 ______________ people find it hard to believe that dressage ("horse dancing") is an Olympic sport.

18 Cross out the mistake in each sentence and write the correct word.

1 I really want to learn more about these sport I read about online. ______________
2 My younger brother wants to be a athlete when he grows up. ______________
3 Do you have some idea how hard it is to run a marathon? ______________
4 We don't have a real goal, so just kick the ball between that flags. ______________
5 Much of the fans were unhappy when they read that their favorite player had moved to another team. ______________
6 Only that most talented athletes can compete at the Olympics. ______________
7 We watched the basketball game with both our cousins. ______________

3B Think Like an Athlete

VOCABULARY BUILDING Synonyms in texts

1 **Complete the sentences using these synonyms for the words in bold.**

amounts	elite	establish
money	selected	talents

1 You should make the most of your **abilities** and try to become a professional athlete.
You should make use of your ________________ and try to become a professional athlete.
2 Only **the top** athletes can afford to live in great luxury.
Only ________________ athletes can afford to live in great luxury.
3 The school wants to **set up** a new after-school tennis club.
The school wants to ________________ a new after-school tennis club.
4 No young athlete can rise to the top without the **funding** to train.
________________ for training is important for young athletes who want to succeed.
5 The **sums** of money made by professional athletes are absolutely amazing.
Professional athletes make incredible ________________ of money.
6 If you want to be **chosen** for the team, you have to practice every day.
Only those who practice daily will be ________________ for the team.

READING

2 **Read the article on the opposite page. Then read the introductory sentence for a summary of the article. Choose three of the sentences below to complete the summary.**

Today's top athletes focus on mental as well as physical fitness.

1 Plato believed that mental fitness was more important for success than physical fitness.
2 Although some athletes initially resisted sports psychology, it is now more popular than ever.
3 Athletes in sports that require great focus have had tremendous success with sports psychology.
4 Laurie Hernandez won two medals in the Rio de Janeiro Olympics.
5 Goal setting is important for athletes in some sports and is an effective part of sports psychology.
6 Sports psychology uses breathing, visualization, and the setting of achievable goals to help athletes succeed.

3 **Choose the correct option according to the information in the article.**

1 According to paragraph 2, which of the following is true of elite athletes?
 a They have been resistant in the past to the idea of using sports psychology.
 b After 1920, they immediately began using sports psychology to train.
 c Their coaches were more open to the idea of using sports psychology than they were.
 d They used sports psychology more in the mid-1900s than they do today.
2 According to paragraph 3, it is NOT true that Simone Biles
 a used sports psychology to help overcome her lack of confidence.
 b used sports psychology to become one of the top athletes in the world.
 c has refused to speak publicly about using sports psychology in her training.
 d inspired her teammate to begin using sports psychology.
3 Which of the following can be inferred about Laurie Hernandez from paragraph 3?
 a She is a better gymnast than Simone Biles.
 b She would never have used sports psychology if not for Simone Biles.
 c Sports psychology helped her to win two Olympic medals.
 d Like Simone Biles, she suffered from a lack of confidence.

4 **Write the word from the text that matches each definition.**

1 to do better in an activity than others ________________
2 to slowly disappear or lose importance ________________
3 an activity performed regularly, sometimes as part of a ceremony ________________
4 to succeed in reaching a goal ________________
5 easy to see or understand ________________

Mental Gymnastics 23

Simone Biles

1 More than 2,000 years ago, the Greek philosopher Plato wrote that "Physical fitness is as important as intellectual fitness." Plato recognized the connection between the body and mind and believed that people should focus on being physically fit as well as being mentally fit. Today's athletes are more physically fit than ever. Everything from an athlete's diet to their training routine to how much they sleep at night is completely planned and controlled. But in the high-pressure world of professional sports, the best athletes often listen to Plato's advice and focus on taking care of their mind as well as their body.

2 The first sports psychology laboratory was founded in Berlin in the early 1920s, and since then, the study and practice of sports psychology has continued to increase. Although most elite athletes are looking for any way to outperform the competition, some were resistant to the idea of seeing a sports psychologist. Athletes have said they didn't want to discuss their fears and they worried about being asked to change their training routines. More importantly, they didn't want to seem "weak" to their competitors. Also, coaches were sometimes concerned about letting someone else control their athlete. But as more and more top athletes have spoken openly about the positive impact of sports psychology, this resistance has begun to fade. For example, after winning a championship in 2010, basketball great Ron Artest appeared on TV to thank his sports psychologist.

3 Almost every sport has athletes that use sports psychology, but athletes in sports that require tremendous focus, like golf, tennis, and gymnastics, use sports psychologists the most. American gymnast Simone Biles is sometimes described as the greatest athlete in the world today. She won five medals at the Olympic games in Rio de Janeiro, and four of them were gold. Biles has been open about how sports psychology has contributed to her success. In 2013, she was struggling with nerves and a lack of confidence. Her father called a sports psychologist, and three years later, Biles was a star of the Olympics. After seeing Biles's dramatic improvement, her teammate Laurie Hernandez started seeing the same sports psychologist. Hernandez won a gold and a silver medal in Rio.

4 So how does sports psychology actually work? Typically, an athlete meets regularly with a sports psychologist who gets to know them and understand their goals. Then the psychologist creates a specific plan for that athlete. This usually includes breathing exercises, visualization exercises—using your imagination to see yourself do something, and goal setting. Before she competes, Laurie Hernandez places one hand on her stomach and breathes deeply. This ritual calms her before she begins. Goal setting usually focuses on specific performance goals, like swimming half a second faster, instead of competitive goals, like winning a medal. By focusing on a specific goal, pressure decreases and the goal seems more achievable.

5 Today's top athletes know what Plato wrote about all those years ago. The body and mind must work together to achieve greatness. The majority of Olympic athletes now use mental training as a major part of their training routine, and the benefits of sports psychology are clear. To compete at the highest level today, your mental game must be as strong as your physical game.

3C Getting Better All the Time

GRAMMAR Comparatives and superlatives

1 Choose the correct option to complete the sentence.

1 There are ____ more baseball players at our school than there are football players.
a few **b** little **c** many **d** much

2 She spends ____ less time studying than she does practicing soccer.
a few **b** little **c** many **d** much

3 Busy students have ____ time to participate in sports.
a few **b** little **c** many **d** much

4 ____ tickets were sold for tonight's game—only 100.
a Few **b** Little **c** Many **d** Much

5 I keep asking him to join, but he's shown very ____ interest in becoming part of the basketball team.
a few **b** little **c** many **d** much

6 Very ____ fans were in the stands for this week's game because it was raining and cold.
a few **b** little **c** many **d** much

7 I couldn't believe I had to pay so ____ money for my tickets to the diving championships. They were expensive!
a few **b** little **c** many **d** much

2 Complete the sentences using comparatives and the cues in parentheses. There is more than one correct answer for each sentence.

1 The freezer is ____________ than the fridge. (cold, big difference)

2 It's ____________ today than it was yesterday. (hot, small difference)

3 I have ____________ pages to read for my history class than I do for math. (more, big difference)

4 A Lamborghini is ____________ than any car I'll ever buy. (expensive, big difference)

5 Joshi gets ____________ grades than I do. (good, big difference)

6 It takes ____________ to travel to Dubai than it does to get to Sharjah. (long, small difference)

7 I spend a ____________ time riding my bike than I do jogging. (more, big difference)

3 Use the information in the two sentences to complete the comparative sentence.

Example: Viktor can lift 285 pounds. Karim can lift 375 pounds. (90 pounds)
Karim can lift *90 more pounds than Viktor can.*

1 The first modern Olympics were held in 1896. The first World Cup football game was held in 1930. (34 years)
The first modern Olympics ____________
____________.

2 The world record in the women's long jump is about 24.5 feet (7.5 meters). The world record in the men's long jump is about 29.5 feet. (9 meters)
The men's long jump world record is about ____________
____________.

3 Approximately 111.3 million people watched the 2017 Super Bowl on TV. There were approximately 70,800 people at the stadium watching the game in person. (more than 111.22 million)
In 2017, approximately 70,800 went to the Super Bowl game, but ____________
____________.

4 Kai can swim for 60 minutes. Ruby can swim for 45 minutes. (15 minutes)
Kai can swim ____________
____________.

5 Our team scored nine points. The other team scored four points. (five points)
The other team scored ____________
____________.

4 Which option is closer in meaning to the original sentence?

1 The more I focus on eating healthily, the more my swimming endurance improves.
a My swimming endurance improves when I spend more time focusing on eating well.
b Because my swimming endurance improves, I spend more time focusing on eating well.

2 The more time I practice, the more compliments I get.
a When I get compliments, I want to spend more time practicing.
b When I spend more time practicing, I get more compliments.

3 The higher the mountain, the more time it takes to climb.
a Climbing higher mountains takes slightly less time than climbing lower mountains.
b It takes more time to climb a higher mountain than a lower mountain.

4 The noisier the concert, the less Gayle wants to go.
  a Gayle prefers going to noisy concerts.
  b If concerts are quite loud, Gayle is less likely to want to go to them.

5 The more challenging the class, the longer I have to study.
  a My classes are challenging before I study.
  b I have to study more for classes that are challenging than for those that are easy.

6 The more beautiful the painting, the more expensive it is.
  a You have to pay more for more beautiful paintings.
  b More expensive paintings aren't more beautiful.

7 The closer we get to Nagasaki, the more excited I am.
  a I'm getting more excited as we get closer to Nagasaki.
  b Because I am more excited, Nagasaki is closer.

8 The more points you score, the more rewards you get.
  a You score more points after you get more rewards.
  b You get more rewards when you score more points.

5 Choose the correct option to complete the sentences.

1 Elite marathon runners are faster these days; in the past, marathon runners were *not as fast / as fast*.

2 More people stream sports on their tablets than five years ago. Five years ago, *not as many / more* people streamed sports on their tablets.

3 Athletes are required to use safer equipment, though in the past, athletes' equipment was *not as safe / as safe* as today.

4 The team's uniforms are a lot more colorful this season, and I think these *not as colorful / more colorful* uniforms look great.

5 A great deal more women play soccer these days. Today there are *as many / more* women playing soccer.

6 Now that I've started practicing with the team, I'm a much better skier. Last year I *wasn't as good / was better* at skiing.

7 A lot fewer people are going to watch the team play. Today there are *not as many / more* people at the games.

6 Are the words in bold correct or incorrect? Correct those that are incorrect.

1 My friend Sahil is **a bit talented than** many Olympic athletes. ________________

2 Mount Sanquing in China **is as beautiful** any place on Earth. ________________

3 Getting enough sleep **as important as** eating well and exercising. ________________

4 This sushi **is slightly better then** the sushi we had last week at the new restaurant near our office.
____

5 Your joke **isn't as funny as** the one Yuri told in class yesterday. ________________

6 Oslo, Norway, **is not nearly hot** as Colombo, Sri Lanka.
____

7 Electric cars are **far more efficiency than** cars that use only gasoline. ________________

8 Many of the other artists of his time **weren't as innovative as** Picasso.
____

9 The Nile is **the most long** river in Africa.
____

7 Read the information about the 2016 Olympic athletes. Are the statements below true (T) or false (F)?

2016 Summer Olympics Results (partial)

Rank	Name	Country	Time
50km walk (men)			
1	Matej Toth	Slovakia	3:40:58
5	Wei Yu	China	3:43:00
7	Havard Haukenes	Norway	3:46:43
20km race walk (women)			
4	Antonella Palmisano	Italy	1:29:03
5	Shijie Qieyang	China	1:29:04
6	Ana Cabecinha	Portugal	1:29:23
Long jump (women)			
3	Ivana Spanovic	Serbia	7.08 m
5	Ese Brume	Nigeria	6.81 m
6	Ksenija Balta	Estonia	6.79 m
Hammer throw (men)			
5	Marcel Lomnicky	Slovakia	75.97 m
6	Ashraf Amgad Elseify	Qatar	75.46 m
7	Krisztian Pars	Hungary	75.28 m

1 In the 50km walk, Haukenes was a great deal faster than Toth. ____

2 Haukenes was not nearly as fast as Yu in the 50km walk. ____

3 In the 20km race walk, Palmisano was much faster than Qieyang. ____

4 Cabecinha was over a minute slower than Palmisano in the 20km race walk. ____

5 In the long jump, Brume didn't jump nearly as far as Spanovic. ____

6 Balta jumped nearly as far as Brume in the long jump. ____

7 In the hammer throw, Pars was not quite as good as Lomnicky. ____

8 Pars threw the hammer a bit further than Elseify. ____

3D Are athletes really getting faster, better, and stronger?

TEDTALKS

AUTHENTIC LISTENING SKILLS

1 **Listen to the excerpts from David Epstein's TED Talk, and circle the words he uses to mark contrast.** 24

1 Rather than the same size as the average elite high jumper, the average elite shot-putter is two and a half inches taller and 130 pounds heavier.
2 So, in sports where large size is prized, the large athletes have gotten larger. Conversely, in sports where diminutive stature is an advantage, the small athletes got smaller.
3 These men are seven inches different in height, but because of the body types advantaged in their sports, they wear the same length pants.
4 The Kalenjin make up just twelve percent of the Kenyan population but the vast majority of elite runners.
5 That's the power that's contained in the human body. But normally we can't access nearly all of it.
6 Ultra-endurance was once thought to be harmful to human health, but now we realize that we have all these traits that are perfect for ultra-endurance.

WATCH

2 **Complete the sentences with a word or short phrase.**

1 The winner of the 2012 ________________ ran two hours and eight minutes.
2 I want you to pretend that Jesse Owens is in ________________.
3 That's the difference that track ________________ has made.
4 Eddy Merckx set the ________________ for the longest distance cycled in one hour at 30 miles, 3,774 feet.
5 While we haven't evolved into a new species in a century, the ________________ within competitive sports certainly has changed.
6 The financial incentives and fame and glory afforded ________________ skyrocketed and it tipped toward the tiny upper echelon of performance.
7 In some cases, the search for bodies that could push athletic performance forward ended up introducing into the ________________ populations of people that weren't previously competing at all.
8 This is a vertical ________________ of more than 8,000 feet, and Kílian went up and down in under three hours.

3 **Match these sports with the statements. Two sports are used more than once.**

cycling	marathon	sprinting	swimming

1 The 2012 Olympic winner finished in two hours and eight minutes. ________________
2 This sport favors a body type similar to a canoe. ________________
3 The Kalenjin tribe have been particularly successful in this event. ________________
4 In this sport, the governing body decreed that competitors had to use the same technology as in 1972. ________________
5 Starting blocks were an important innovation in this sport. ________________
6 Scientists estimate that Jesse Owens would have finished less than one stride behind Usain Bolt in this sport, if he'd been using the same technology. ________________

4 **Choose the correct option to complete the sentences.**

1 Every year, runners seem to get *faster / fastest*.
2 More sophisticated training methods mean that today's athletes are often *stronger / strongest* than the winners from one hundred years ago.
3 In cycling, the *longer / longest* distance traveled in one hour is only about 800 feet further than the record set by Eddy Merckx in 1972.
4 Michael Phelps is seven inches *taller / tallest* than Hicham El Guerrouj, even though their legs are the same length.
5 Today's gymnasts are significantly *shorter / shortest* than competitive gymnasts from several decades ago.
6 The *better / best* athletes in the world have more specialized body types today than they used to.
7 Humans are better suited to ultra-endurance sports than *more / most* primates.

VOCABULARY IN CONTEXT

5 **Match the words and phrases (1–6) with the sentences where a synonym is used (a–f).**

1 shrunk ____
2 fade away ____
3 the entire ____
4 essentially ____
5 change the face of ____
6 throughout ____

a Widespread use of specialized swimsuits has completely **changed the nature of** competitive swimming.
b Athletes at university are **basically** training at a professional level.
c The distance between certain records **has got smaller** over the years.
d **In all parts of** the world, technology gives people the opportunity to watch huge sporting events.
e Some people worry that certain sports will **disappear** from public notice if they are not included in the Olympics.
f I wonder whether **the whole** difference between Jesse Owens' and Usain Bolts' records can be explained by technology?

3E Surveys

SPEAKING

Useful language

Introducing main findings

The most surprising / interesting thing we found was that…

You won't be surprised to hear that… but one thing that was interesting was…

The main thing we discovered was…

(By far) the most popular… was…

Introducing other points

Another thing that was interesting was…

Apart from that, we found that…

Some other things worth mentioning are…

1 **Put the words in parentheses in the correct order to complete the presentation. Then listen to check your answers.** 25

Hello. We're here to present the findings of the class sports survey we conducted.
(1) (discovered / thing / was / the / we / main) ________

____

people do at least three hours of individual exercise a week.
(2) (most / the / thing / was / we / surprising / that / found) ________

____

everyone does at least two sports regularly. By far the most popular individual sport was swimming.
(3) (we / that, / that / found / from / apart) ________

____

one-third of the class go to the gym at least once a week.
(4) (was / another / was / that / interesting / thing) ________

____

the number of people who like mountain biking. A third of the class go mountain biking regularly, and over three-quarters do it from time to time.
Focusing on team sports, (5) (to / you / be / that / surprised / won't / hear) ________

____

most of the males play football, (6) (was / one / thing / was / but / that / interesting)

____

____

that over half of the females we surveyed play soccer regularly.

(7) (things / are / worth / some / mentioning / other) ________

____

that spinning classes were more popular with females than males, and that ten percent of the class play more than three team sports, including basketball.

2 **Look at the data about Cybercrime. Prepare some notes for a presentation on this information. Remember to include the useful language. Then listen to the sample answer and compare your ideas.** 26

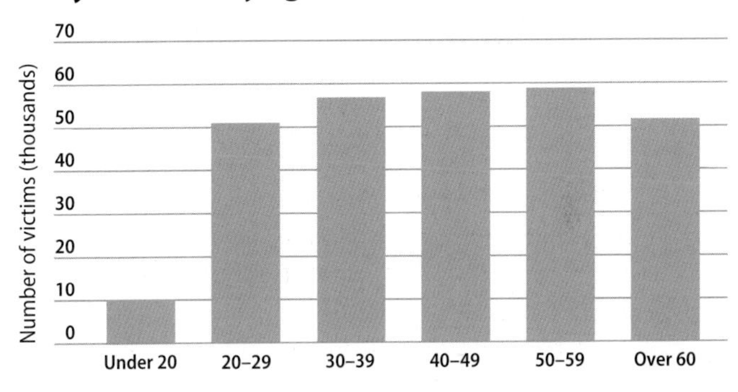

Source: U.S. Department of Justice / Federal Bureau of Investigation Statistics shown are for 2015.

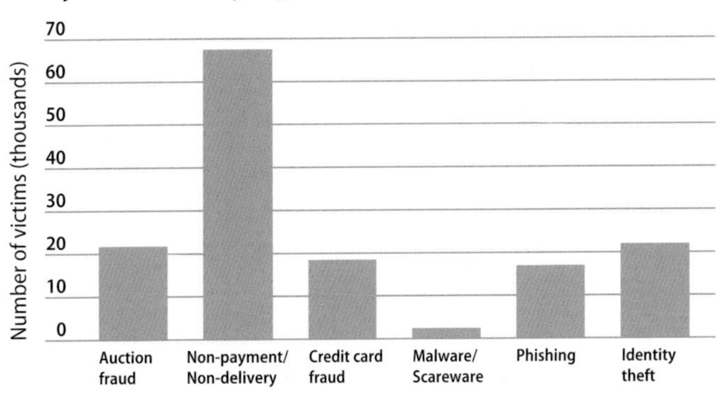

3 **You have been asked to talk about a sport that is typical in your country. Make notes about this topic. Use the useful language. Then listen to the sample answer.** 27

Your comments should include:

- what the sport is
- how you play or do it
- when and how often people do it
- why you consider it a typical sport for your country

WRITING A survey

4 **Choose the correct option to complete the sentences.**

1 *More then half / More than half* of the participants were under 16.
2 *Under just two-thirds / Just under two-thirds* of the sports are free.
3 *Roughly a quarter / Roughly the quarter* of all scheduled events were canceled.
4 We can see that membership *double / doubled* in May.
5 *One on four / One in four* runners dropped out of the marathon.
6 The *vast majority of / vast majority in* students prefer doing team sports.
7 *Almost 40 percent of / 40 percent of almost* those surveyed live in cities.
8 Funding for sports *increased by / increased in* 15 percent over the period.

5 **Look at the bar chart. Then complete the text with the missing phrases a–h.**

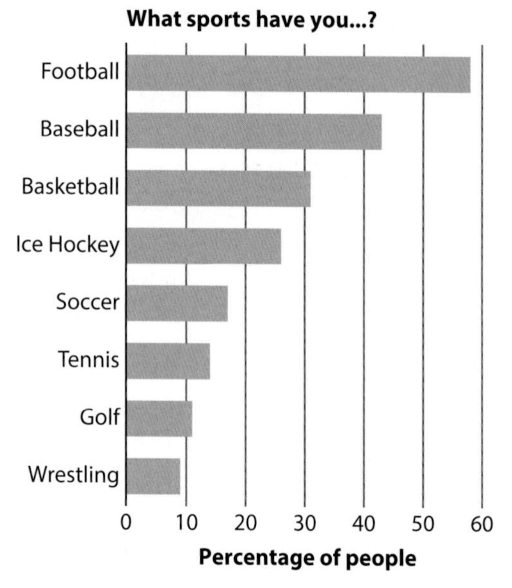

This bar chart shows the results of a survey carried out in a local city last year. A hundred adults participated in the survey, (1) _____.

All participants in the survey attended at least some spectator sports during the year. As can be seen from the chart, (2) _____. The lowest attendance was at wrestling, (3) _____. More than a quarter went to watch ice hockey, with almost one in three going to watch basketball games. The football statistics are not entirely surprising, given that the popularity of football is well documented. (4) _____ second most popular spectator sport in the survey.

(5) _____, as a highly successful baseball team is based in the region in which the surveyed city is located.

(6) _____, the numbers attending ice hockey were unexpected. The reason given by those interviewed was support for their children or other family members (7) _____. A lack of developed facilities in the local area has been suggested as the reason for the lower numbers (8) _____.

a Being higher than the national average
b with fewer than one in ten participants attending wrestling matches
c attending wrestling events
d which aimed to discover levels of annual attendance at sporting events
e Baseball was the
f well over half of those interviewed attended football matches
g participating in ice hockey
h This may be explained by geography

6 **Read the text again. Then answer the questions.**

1 What was the purpose of the survey?
  a to find out how many people are playing sports
  b to find out how many people are watching sports
2 How many people interviewed did not attend any sporting events?
  a none of them   **b** at least one
3 Which statistics are first mentioned in the text?
  a the national average for attendance at these sports
  b the sports with the best and worst attendance
4 Which sport did roughly one-third of all participants attend?
  a basketball   **b** golf
5 What reason is suggested for the high numbers attending football matches?
  a that the local team in this city is very successful
  b that football is known to have high levels of support
6 According to the text, why did so many people go to watch ice hockey?
  a because their relatives play ice hockey
  b because their city has extremely well-developed facilities for ice hockey

7 **The chart below gives information about a group of people who were surveyed about their attitudes to gym class. Summarize the information by selecting and reporting the main features, and make comparisons where relevant.**

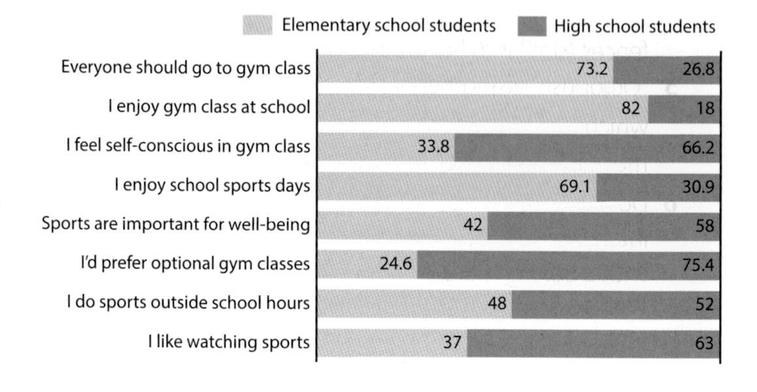

Review

1 Match the two parts of the sentences.

1 You scored a
2 He hasn't got a real
3 We competed
4 He's a skillful
5 She's a positive
6 I won
7 I want to set
8 You played a

a player.
b key role in the team.
c a new world record.
d passion for golf.
e in the championship.
f great goal.
g the race.
h role model.

2 Complete the sentences with the missing word.

1 I won a silver ______________ at my school sports day.
2 He has a real ______________ for gymnastics.
3 She smashed the world ______________ by three minutes.
4 He didn't ______________ any goals on Saturday.
5 Messi was the youngest player to ______________ Argentina.
6 He played a key ______________ in the team from the start.
7 They have a really great ______________ towards their opponents.
8 Who ______________ the championship?

3 Complete the sentences with these words. Write *x* if no word is necessary. Some words can be used more than once.

a	a few	a lot of
many	the	x

1 In the sport of extreme ironing, which started in England, people travel to ______________ remote places to iron their clothes there.
2 At the Cooper's Hill Cheese-Rolling and Wake, "athletes" chase a wheel of cheese down a hill; the winner gets to keep ______________ cheese.
3 Snow polo, ______________ Swiss sport in which players play polo on a snowy field, is now played in other parts of the world.
4 Sweden gave us *kaninhop* (Bunny Jumping) in which ______________ trained rabbits jump over small fences (similar to horses in show jumping).
5 "Octopush" is another name for underwater hockey in which ______________ swimmers use a "pusher" to move a hockey puck into the goal.
6 Do you know ______________ people who are interested in chessboxing? It combines a game of chess with a boxing match.

4 Choose the correct option to complete the sentences.

1 _____ of my friends are interested in trying out for the basketball team.
a Far few
b Hardly any
c Every

2 The Shanghai Tower isn't the world's _____ building any more.
a as tall as
b quite a bit tallest
c tallest

3 I couldn't go to the match because I had _____ homework.
a many
b a lot of
c too

4 Star soccer player Cristiano Ronaldo was born in _____.
a a Madeira, Portugal
b the Madeira, Portugal
c Madeira, Portugal

5 I didn't see _____ my friends at the match.
a any of
b any
c every of

6 Our team lost the match because we didn't score _____ the other team did.
a as much points as
b as many points as
c slightly fewer points as

7 I am two years _____ my sister.
a as older then
b older than
c the oldest

5 Complete the comparative sentences with the information given.

1 Lima's population: almost ten million; Bogota's population: around nine million (slightly / big)
Lima is ______________ Bogota.
2 the red shirt: $9.99; the blue shirt: $11.50 (not / quite / cheap)
The blue shirt ______________ as the red shirt.
3 Always Dreaming time: 2:03.59; Smarty Jones time: 2:04.06 (fast)
The 2004 Kentucky Derby winner, a horse named Smarty Jones, ______________ the 2017 winner Always Dreaming.
4 Brad: 5 feet 9 inches; Jackie: 4 feet 9 inches (quite / tall)
Brad is ______________ than Jackie.
5 money China spent on Beijing Olympics: $40 billion; money Russia spent on Sochi Olympics: $50 billion (not / quite / expensive)
The Beijing Olympics ______________ the Sochi Olympics.
6 River Volga length: 2,265 miles; River Congo-Chambeshi length: 2,920 miles (long)
The River Volga ______________ as the River Congo.

4 Cultural Transformation

4A Putting the Town on the Map

VOCABULARY Cultural events

1 Review Choose the correct option to complete the sentences.

1 We saw a fantastic *broadcast / production* of *Hamlet* at the theater yesterday.
2 The photographs are on display in the *art gallery / concert hall*.
3 They are rehearsing in their new music *cultural center / studio*.
4 Can you write down the *sculpture / lyrics* of that song, please?
5 He painted a *mural / portrait* of the queen.
6 How many *listeners / viewers* watched the documentary on TV?

2 Review Are these words connected with art or music? Complete the table.

concert hall, lyrics, mural, painting, portrait, verse

Art	Music

Roskilde Festival Denmark

3 Complete the sentences with these verbs.

attend, attracts, boost, brings, generates, holds

1 Roskilde Festival is a music festival in Denmark that ________ music lovers from around the world every year.
2 Organizers expect thousands of people to ________ the week-long event next summer.
3 The arrival of tourists going to the festival will ________ the country's broader economy.
4 It's also a humanitarian event that ________ people together.
5 The festival ________ events that include a vote for which charities should receive support from the festival.
6 Attendees visit local restaurants and attractions during their stay, which ________ income for the local economy.

4 Choose the correct option to complete the sentences.

1 The event organizers are putting *on / in / by* a parade.
2 The large number of visitors has a big impact *to / at / on* the city.
3 There is wide support *with / for / to* public art.
4 Thousands of people take part *on / by / in* carnivals around the country.
5 Street artist Banksy helped to put his home town, Bristol, *on / at / in* the map.
6 The exhibit creates a sense of pride *to / for / in* their history.

5 Choose the correct option (a–d) to complete the sentences.

1 The new music venue has had a negative ____ on transportation.
   a support **b** opportunity **c** impact **d** sense
2 Cultural events are great for ____ people together.
   a putting **b** bringing **c** offering **d** attracting
3 Having public art creates a ____ of pride in the local area.
   a sense **b** parade **c** festival **d** venue
4 Local people had the opportunity to take ____ in the organization.
   a place **b** together **c** role **d** part
5 The film festival has put Cannes on the ____.
   a map **b** party **c** road **d** menu

6 The art gallery generates over one million _____ in income.
a tourists
b events
c opportunities
d dollars

7 The many cultural events _____ tourists from all over the world.
a put on
b boost
c generate
d attract

8 Many people _____ several events every day.
a support
b attend
c generate
d attract

6 **Match the events or activities (1–8) with the benefits each one accomplishes (a–f). You can use the letters more than once.**

1 Have a party for the planners of a music festival. _____
2 Advertise the different groups that will perform. _____
3 Sell tickets for the event. _____
4 Hire teens and young people to work at the festival. _____
5 Organize volunteers for the festival. _____
6 Sell merchandise at the festival. _____
7 Hold a party after the festival for everyone who worked and performed. _____
8 Film a documentary about the music festival. _____

a attracts tourists
b creates sense of pride
c brings people together
d boosts the economy
e generates income
f offers young people opportunities

7 **Extension** **Read the clues and complete the crossword puzzle with these words.**

Across
2 a performance of music
5 a person who directs the performance of an orchestra
6 a school where musicians are trained
8 a movie with singing and dancing in the story

Down
1 a style of popular music, originally from the United States
3 a person who writes music
4 a piece of music played in a particular way
7 a live performance by a musician or comedian

arrangement	composer	conductor	conservatory
gig	jazz	musical	recital

8 **Extension** **Choose the correct options to complete the text.**

Every May, we organize a "fringe festival" that runs alongside the main festival in Brighton. There are hundreds of different events that are held over the five-day period. There is stand- (1) _____ comedy at the Bizarre Comedy Club, where there is also an (2) _____mic for people who want to try stand-up comedy. There will be showing of the best of (3) _____ cinema, and poetry (4) _____ from new writers. There are also free events including dozens of outdoor (5) _____ performances and a (6) _____ launch on Saturday, where you can meet local authors and get signed copies of their books. Finally, come along to the City (7) _____ Hall to see a display of local children's artwork.

1 a off
b in
c up
d down

2 a public
b closed
c private
d open

3 a independent
b main
c fringe
d public

4 a writings
b readings
c launches
d exhibits

5 a hall
b movie
c park
d street

6 a comedy
b art
c book
d photography

7 a Exhibit
b Exhibition
c Exhibiting
d Exhibited

PRONUNCIATION

9 **Listen to the sentences. Underline the word that you hear using contrastive stress. Then practice saying the sentences.** 28

1 We were going to take the subway to the festival, but it was mobbed.
2 The forecast said it was going to be a chilly evening, but it was freezing.
3 I thought there would be about twenty guests, but loads of people showed up.
4 They thought the tickets would cost ten dollars, but they were way more expensive.
5 She was going to meet me there, but she never showed up.
6 He said he would sing a song for us, but he's got a terrible voice.
7 The parade was going to start at 9, but we waited for hours.
8 My friend promised the show would be great, but it was awful.

LISTENING

10 **Listen to some people describing eight different cultural events. Choose the best answer.** 29

1 Where is the man talking about going?
  a a music festival
  b a museum
  c a magic show
2 Where does the woman want to take her friend?
  a a comedy club
  b a night club
  c a music club
3 What is the man describing?
  a a music festival
  b a symphony orchestra
  c a parade
4 Where did the woman go?
  a an art gallery
  b an art museum
  c an art festival
5 Where was the woman going to meet the man?
  a the comedy club
  b the art gallery
  c the theater
6 What is the woman describing?
  a a night club
  b a food festival
  c a parade
7 What did the man go to see?
  a a movie
  b a play in a theater
  c a symphony orchestra

Georgian architecture in Edinburgh, Scotland

11 **Listen to a talk about Edinburgh, Scotland. Match the adjectives with nouns to form the collocations that you hear.** 30

1 rolling	**a** streets
2 artistic	**b** museum
3 narrow	**c** appeal
4 elegant	**d** center
5 architectural	**e** proportions
6 residential	**f** design
7 aesthetic	**g** hills
8 pleasing	**h** area
9 cultural	**i** transformation

12 **Listen again and answer the questions.** 30

1 How many artistically interesting cities does the speaker mention?
  a one
  b two
  c three
2 What does the speaker say Edinburgh is known for?
  a its rolling hills
  b its cultural festivals
  c its romantic landscape
3 What was the motivation to construct New Town?
  a its foundation in the 12th century
  b an architectural competition
  c the unhealthy conditions in Old Town
4 What style of architecture is New Town?
  a Georgian
  b Scottish
  c British
5 What residential area does the speaker mention?
  a Dundas Street
  b Scotland Street
  c Cumberland Street

GRAMMAR Future forms 1

13 **Correct the errors in the sentences. There is one error in each sentence.**

In the future…

1 people will to read more digital books than print books.
2 we going to rely on our smartphones more than we expected.
3 people will subscribing to music streaming services rather than downloading songs.
4 people are going watch TV on the internet, not with cable.
5 you use your 3D printer to print things at home rather than buying them at a store.
6 electric cars is going to be "normal" cars.
7 drones are going deliver many of the products—and food!—that we order online.
8 self-driving cars will to take everyone to work.
9 we won't not use paper money anymore.

14 **Choose the correct options to complete the sentences.**

1 On Tuesday, my class *is attending* / *attends* a classical concert so we can learn more about the music.
2 Like most people, I *'ll be pretending* / *'m pretending* to understand the modern art when we go to the gallery.
3 The school choir *performs* / *is performing* several songs at the assembly today.
4 She *is about to wear* / *will be wearing* her costume when she walks home from school.
5 On Sunday, *I'm going to meet* / *'m about to meet* my friends at the food festival in the park.
6 I'll be really happy once we *will finish* / *finish* our exams.
7 My parents *are going to order* / *will order* a print of my favorite painting for my room.
8 Let's go! The teachers *are about to put* / *will put* the sculpture in the school lobby.

15 **Put the words in the correct order to make sentences and questions.**

1 on / evening / the lectures / Friday / start / .

____

2 be / the singer / the reporters / will / after / interviewing / the concert / ?

____

3 are / watch / we / about / the music video / on his laptop / to / .

____

4 when / on the art world / an impression / that young artist / make / starts / her show / will certainly / .

____

5 be / on / the musicians / working / tomorrow / will / their / song / new / ?

____

6 their drawings / going / the art class / to display / is / next week / in the hallway / .

____

7 think / he / be / time / don't / will / on / I / ready / .

____

8 my first book / have / ready / I / publish / enough / will / short stories / I / once / .

____

16 **Complete the questions about the future with the correct form of the verbs in parentheses. Sometimes there is more than one correct answer.**

1 ________ you ________ (know) when the documentary film about Salvador Dali will be shown?
2 When ________ the class ________ (film) the performance of the school musical?
3 ________ the band leader ________ (give) us a new song to learn for next week?
4 What time ________ your flight ________ (leave) on Saturday?
5 What ________ we ________ (do) this time next week?
6 ________ your friend ________ (dance) with the professional ballet dancers at the theater tonight?
7 It's late! ________ the show about ________ (finish)?

4B Painting the Town

VOCABULARY BUILDING Adjective and noun collocations 2

1 Choose the correct option to complete the sentences.

1 The students in my class are from *diverse* / *low* / *leading* backgrounds—everyone has a different perspective to share.
2 In this school we follow a *hard* / *strict* / *mixed* set of rules, and there are consequences if you break them.
3 With a lot of *driving* / *innovative* / *hard* work and effort, you can achieve all your goals.
4 My school is starting an *innovative* / *individual* / *mixed* program where students can volunteer to tutor other students who need extra help.
5 He won a scholarship that helps *mixed-* / *diverse-* / *low-*income students afford the fees at the private school.
6 She is a member of the *leading* / *straightforward* / *private* orchestra in the city, in which she plays the violin.
7 He never stops studying because of his *hard* / *leading* / *driving* ambition to get into the best college in the country.
8 Although the teacher worked hard to prepare the students, they received *straightforward* / *hard* / *mixed* results on the exam.

READING

2 Read the article. Sentences a–g below have been removed from the article. Decide which sentence belongs in each gap (1–6). There is one extra sentence that you do not need to use.

1 ____
2 ____
3 ____
4 ____
5 ____
6 ____

a They moved to the neighborhood, hired about twelve local residents and trained them to paint.
b They were built without any of the planning that makes cities functional and attractive.
c The Vila Cruzeiro project attracted attention from other cities trying to improve their struggling neighborhoods.
d Koolhaas and Urhahn hope to work in many more cities, all over the world.
e Koolhaas and Urhahn agree.
f However, they believe that bringing colorful art into disadvantaged neighborhoods does something else.
g While visiting these favelas, famous for their crime and drug problems, the artists saw something different—potential.

3 Choose the correct options according to the information in the article.

1 Why did Koolhaas and Urhahn want to paint the favelas?
a They wanted to make them inspiring places to live.
b They wanted to provide jobs for local workers.
c They were making a documentary about local artists.
d They enjoy street painting.

2 Who built most of the favelas in Brazil?
a skilled carpenters
b city planners
c the people who live there
d architects

3 Which of the following could replace the underlined word "accomplishment" in paragraph 4?
a buildings
b successful project
c employment
d stripes

4 Why do some people criticize Koolhaas and Urhahn's art projects?
a They think the artists take advantage of local workers.
b They do not believe that art can help local communities.
c They believe the art does not help with the biggest problems in the communities.
d They do not think that artists from another country can understand local communities.

5 What may be the best title for the article?
a Art in the Favelas
b Painting Buildings
c How do you paint neighborhoods?
d Can art save a neighborhood?

4 Do the statements match the information in the article? Write true (T), false (F), or information not given (NG).

1 Koolhaas and Urhahn grew up in neighborhoods like the ones they paint. ____
2 Koolhaas and Urhahn believe that painting can be done without much planning. ____
3 The majority of residents in Vila Cruzeiro were glad that the artists were painting their favela. ____
4 The project in Philadelphia took longer than the project in Vila Cruzeiro. ____
5 Urhahn believes that a painting project can help a neighborhood economically. ____

Painting the Town 31

A favela neighborhood in Rio de Janiero

1 Jeroen Koolhaas and Dre Urhahn, the pair of artists known as Haas and Hahn, grew up in Holland, far from the tough neighborhoods of Rio de Janeiro, Brazil, where they completed some of their most innovative street paintings. Koolhaas and Urhahn met as university students and began working together professionally when Koolhaas was making a documentary film about hip hop in Brazil's favelas—the informal, urban neighborhoods in which many of Brazil's very low-income families live. (1) What if they could paint the crumbling houses and dirty buildings and turn them into art? Could they help make these dangerous neighborhoods beautiful, inspiring places to live?

2 Most favelas in Brazil were built by the people who live in them as they moved to the cities in search of work. (2) Koolhaas and Urhahn wanted to do their paintings in the same way the favelas were built, using local people to paint and letting the paintings be created without too much planning.

3 First, they started spending a lot of time in Vila Cruzeiro, a favela neighborhood that they believed could become their first large painting project. The artists spent time in the neighborhood and got to know the people there. As local residents became excited about the project, Koolhaas and Urhahn began hiring local workers to plaster and paint the houses they selected. They worked together with the local artists for 18 months, and the result was colorful neighborhood paintings that cover dozens of buildings and bring art into one of Rio's poorest communities.

4 (3) After Vila Cruzeiro, Koolhaas and Urhahn were contacted by officials from North Philadelphia, one of the poorest neighborhoods in the United States. (4) The project took roughly two years to complete, but the new painters, along with Koolhaas and Urhahn, painted over 50 buildings to create a huge urban painting of colorful stripes. The City of Philadelphia recognized the efforts of the local painters by giving them an award for their accomplishment.

5 Critics of Koolhaas and Urhahn's art projects say that painting such troubled neighborhoods does not address the real problems they face, like poverty, unemployment, drugs, and crime. (5) They don't expect a painting to solve complex social and economic issues. (6) It inspires the local residents and gives them pride in their community. It changes attitudes.

6 So Koolhaas and Urhahn will continue to bring art to troubled communities. They have worked in Haiti and Curacao and receive emails from interested cities every week. They hope their work will encourage kids to pursue creative careers.

4C Things We Will Have Done and Learned

GRAMMAR Future forms 2

1 Match the two parts of the sentences.

1 She was going to play baseball,
2 It was starting to rain,
3 She promised
4 Yesterday my sister said
5 They were still playing baseball when it got dark,
6 She decided to go to the baseball game

a she was going to play baseball with her friends.
b because she hoped she would see her favorite player.
c but it started raining.
d so she knew she'd have to go inside soon.
e we would play baseball if it isn't too hot this afternoon.
f so we had to tell them to come inside.

2 Complete the sentences with these phrases.

I'll have cooked	I will have listened
she'll have visited	we'll have been swimming
will have been practicing	will have been studying

1 Once she gets to Greece next month, ________ nine different countries.
2 They ________ the songs for six weeks by the time they have their concert next month.
3 I ________ English for three years by the time I graduate.
4 After the birthday dinner I'm making for my mom next week, ________ all the recipes in Madhur Jaffrey's *Vegetarian India*.
5 ________ for an hour by the time you join us.
6 ________ to all of the band's music by the time I go to the concert next month.

3 Put the verbs in parentheses in the correct form of the future perfect simple or future perfect continuous.

1 By the time we go to the music festival in March, our band ________ (learn) several new songs.
2 I ________ (not have) time to finish all my homework by tomorrow.
3 Before the weekend, I ________ (pack) for the trip.
4 By the time our sister is able to meet us, we ________ (look around) the museum for about an hour.
5 They ________ (watch) the first movie in the series again before the second one comes out in June.
6 In ten minutes' time, we ________ (wait) for the train for two hours.
7 He ________ (take) acting lessons for six years by the time he graduates from high school.
8 I ________ (try out) for the school jazz band by the end of the month.

4 Put the words in the correct order to make sentences talking about the future in the past.

1 read / my / book / sister / to / but / couldn't / going / find / her / was
____
2 my / I / if / he / wondered / to / come / party / would
____
3 fell / I / to / going / call / was / you, / but / I / asleep
____
4 the / by the time / started / the / we / will / get / to / have / theater, / movie
____
5 have / sailing / two / by the time / arrive, / we'll / been / we / for / hours
____
6 saved / he'll / by the time / of / money / have / he / retires, / a lot
____

5 Which sentence, a or b, is closer in meaning to the original sentence?

1 They'll have set out all the food and put on some fun music by the time their friends arrive for the party.
   a When their friends arrive, there will be food out and music playing.
   b They'll turn on music and put out food after their friends arrive.
2 Niko told me he was going to camp in Yosemite National Park for a week with his family.
   a Niko told me he and his family camped for a week at Yosemite National Park.
   b When I talked to Niko, he hadn't gone camping with his family yet, but they were planning to go.
3 Once he goes to Yosemite, he'll have visited seven national parks.
   a He hasn't been to Yosemite yet, but he's planning to go. It will be the seventh national park he's visited.
   b He went to Yosemite once, and it was the seventh national park he'd visited.

4 By the time I put the bread in the oven, the beans will have been cooking for an hour.
   a Once I put the bread in the oven, the beans will cook for an hour.
   b The beans will cook for an hour. Then I'll put the bread in the oven.

5 He'll have been watching TV for 45 minutes by the time he has to go to bed.
   a He'll need to go to bed 45 minutes after he starts watching TV.
   b After 45 minutes of watching TV, he'll need to continue watching in bed.

6 Yen asked our teacher if we would visit the Louvre on our trip to Paris.
   a The trip to Paris occurred after Yen asked the question.
   b Yen asked the question while her teacher went to the Louvre.

7 By the time I go to my violin lesson on Tuesday, I'll have learned the song my instructor taught me last week.
   a I learned a new song from my instructor last week. I've been practicing it since then. I will know it well when I go to my lesson on Tuesday.
   b I will be practicing the song my instructor taught me last week when I go to my violin lesson on Tuesday.

6 **Complete the sentences about the future in the past with the correct form of the verb in parentheses.**

1. By the end of this week, I ________________ (finish) writing my paper on architecture in medieval Europe.
2. I knew you ________________ (plan to stay) in Hong Kong for a week, but I didn't know you were going to fly to Bangkok afterwards.
3. By the time we get to the south rim of the Grand Canyon, we ________________ (hike) for three days.
4. I ________________ (not read) JK Rowling's new book by the time I meet her at the book signing.
5. My pottery project ________________ (finish drying) by the time I get to class on Thursday, so I can start painting it then.
6. He said he ________________ (study) at the library after school today.
7. By the time we complete our volunteer hours at the park, we ________________ (not spend) more than ten hours picking up litter.

7 **Complete the text with the correct form of these verbs.**

be finish hike melt plan visit welcome

Yosemite National Park is a beautiful site in northern California that has waterfalls, mountains, and amazing forests. In the year 2040, Yosemite (1) ________________ a national park for 150 years. The park is always extremely popular; in fact, by the end of this season, the rangers (2) ________________ more than three million visitors. I heard the other day that my friend Brian (3) ________________ a trip to Yosemite. Actually, he (4) ________________ last year but didn't have enough time. For this trip, though, Brian thought he (5) ________________ to Mirror Lake to take photos of Half Dome, one of Yosemite's most famous landmarks. I reminded him that Highway 120, which runs through the park, will remain closed until June or July, when the snow (6) ________________ from the road. He said he was planning to go in August and invited me. Perfect timing, actually, because I (7) ________________ my classes by then!

The Half Dome in Yosemite National Park

8 **Use the prompts to write sentences with the future in the past.**

1. I / thought / we / enjoy / new exhibit
   ____
2. By the time / you / take your Spanish exam / you / ready / go Costa Rica
   ____
3. We / finish decorating / house / by July
   ____
4. I / take drawing class / tomorrow / not enough time
   ____
5. Students / read the book / by Monday
   ____
6. I / hoped / the play / finish / earlier
   ____
7. He / say / ride bike / meet us / museum
   ____
8. We / had to leave early / because / he / arrive / 9:00
   ____

4D Building a Park in the Sky

TEDTALKS

AUTHENTIC LISTENING SKILLS

1 Listen to the extracts from the TED Talk and complete the sentences with these words. 32

a lot of	even though	going to	or for worse
right after	sort of	to try to	you know

1 I'm going to fast-forward through ______ lawsuits and a lot of sort of community engagement.
2 So we commissioned an economic feasibility study ______ make the case.
3 We opened the first section in 2009. It's been ______ successful beyond our dreams.
4 And this has been designed by Renzo Piano. And they're ______ break ground in May.
5 And the city has planned—for better ______—twelve million square-feet of development that the High Line is going to ring around.
6 And honestly, ______ I love the designs that we were building, I was always frightened that I wouldn't really love it.
7 Just one quick example is I realized ______ we opened that there were all these people holding hands on the High Line.
8 I think that's, ______, the power that public space can have to transform how people experience their city and interact with each other.

WATCH

2 Complete the sentences with one or two words.

1 But even with a cowboy, about one person a month was killed and ______.
2 But with the rise of interstate trucking, it was used less and ______.
3 It was a train loaded with frozen turkeys—they say, at Thanksgiving—from the meatpacking district. And then it was ______.
4 And what first attracted me, or interested me, was this . . . this view from the street—which is this, you know, steel structure, sort of rusty, this ______.
5 Mayor Bloomberg came in office, he was very supportive, but we still had to make the ______.
6 We opened the first section in 2009. It's been sort of successful beyond our ______.
7 The other thing, it's generated, obviously, a lot of economic value; it's also inspired, I think, a lot of great ______.

3 Choose the correct option to complete the sentences.

1 The railroad hoped that the "West Side Cowboy" *would / will* reduce the number of fatal accidents on the train tracks.
2 The city *would / was going to* demolish the High Line tracks before Hammond and his organization got involved.
3 Hammond thought it *would have been / would be* nice to incorporate wild flowers and plants into the park.
4 They commissioned a study and predicted that the project *will have / would* cost $100 million.
5 Hammond says that the Whitney *is moving / would move* downtown to build their new museum at the base of the High Line.
6 The final section of the High Line *would have gone / is going to go* around the rail yards.

VOCABULARY IN CONTEXT

4 Match the words and phrases (1–6) with the sentences where a synonym is used (a–f).

1 engagement ____
2 figure out ____
3 behind ____
4 run over ____
5 assumed ____
6 relic ____

a One of the major problems with the original rail line in the city was that people were frequently **hit by the trains** and killed.
b Many people simply **believed** that it would not make economic sense to turn the High Line into a park.
c Robert Hammond wanted to **try to understand** how to transform the High Line into a park that would improve the life of the city.
d One of the challenges Hammond faced was convincing people that the High Line could be part of the city's future, and wasn't simply an **object from the past**.
e Many citizens were interested in the fate of the High Line, and they held **several meetings** to debate what should be done with it.
f The community members who were **supportive** of the High Line Park were certain that it would provide great economic and social benefits.

4E What's the plan?

SPEAKING

Useful language

Making suggestions

Do you feel like going to…?

I was wondering if you'd like to go to…?

Rejecting suggestions

To be honest, it's not really my kind of thing.

Doesn't really sound like my kind of thing, I'm afraid.

Suggesting alternatives

OK. Well, in that case, how about going to…?

OK. Well, if you'd rather, we could always go to…

1 Read the two conversations. Decide which sentence (a–f) belongs in each gap (1–6). 33

a Doesn't really sound like my kind of thing, I'm afraid.
b OK. Well, in that case, how about going to the 90s party with a few of us on Friday?
c Do you feel like going to the zoo with me next Saturday?
d To be honest, it's not really my kind of thing. I'm more into pop music.
e I was wondering if you'd like to go to the Kamaal Williams gig that's on in town?
f Well, if you'd rather, we could always go to the sculpture park they've got there.

Conversation 1

A: Hey, what are you up to this weekend?
B: Well, I've got a project I was going to work on, but otherwise not too much, why?
A: (1) _____
B: Who's he? What kind of sound is it?
A: It's a kind of jazz funk music. He plays keyboard but he's got a band with him too.
B: (2) _____
A: (3) _____
B: You know, I'd like that. Thanks.
A: Great.
B: What time are you meeting?
A: I guess we'll head into town at about 8.

Conversation 2

A: (4) _____
B: What?
A: It's a big family trip. My cousins were coming but had to cancel, so my parents said I could bring a friend with me. What do you think?
B: (5) _____ There are all those animals and I really disagree with them being kept in captivity.
A: Oh, really? You know it's that sanctuary where they rescue them, so it's not that bad.
B: Hmm, sorry, I'm really not sure.
A: (6) _____ And there's also an animal art center. It's got some of those paintings done by horses and elephants and stuff.
B: Yeah, that sounds OK. Are you sure your parents won't mind us wandering off?
A: No, they'll be fine as long as I'm not on my own, and my little brother, Joe, won't let them take him anywhere near art.
B: Yeah, alright then.
A: Great!

2 Answer the questions about the conversations in Activity 1. You do not need to write complete sentences.

1 What style of music is the invitation for? _____
2 What instrument does the musician play? _____
3 Why does the invitation get rejected? _____
4 What do they arrange to do? _____
5 Are they going alone? _____
6 Why is Suzie invited to the zoo? _____
7 Does she want to go? Why? / Why not? _____
8 What's special about the zoo? _____
9 What part of the trip appeals to Suzie? _____
10 Why won't everyone be together on the trip? _____

3 Answer the following questions. Make notes and remember to include the useful language. Then, listen to the sample answers and compare your ideas. 34

- What do you enjoy doing in your free time?
- Do you listen to a lot of music in your free time?

WRITING *For* and *against* essay

4 Complete the steps for writing a *for* and *against* essay.

against	brief	conclusion	four
in favor of	introduction	personal	relevant
support	three		

A *for* and *against* essay is usually (1) ________ paragraphs long.

The opening paragraph is the (2) ________. It states the topic and tells the reader why it is currently (3) ________. It also gives a (4) ________ overview of the topic.

The main body of the essay is made up of paragraphs two and (5) ________. The second paragraph should offer a few points (6)________, or for, the topic. The third paragraph should supply two or three points opposing, or (7) ________, the topic. It is important to provide reasons and examples to (8) ________ these points.

The closing paragraph is the (9) ________. The writer sums up the essay and gives his or her (10) ________ opinion on the topic.

5 Read the *for* and *against* essay. Then match the underlined items (1–8) with their function (a–h).

Local artists who improve our community should be given free housing. Do you support or oppose this idea?

(1) There has been a significant increase in community art projects in the past year. Local artists have been working with residents to create public murals, installations, and various sculptures around our city. (2) By and large, these creations are warmly received by the community. It also bears mentioning that many of these artists are struggling financially.

One very convincing argument in favor of giving free housing to local artists is the value they bring to our city. (3) The work they do helps to establish a stronger sense of community. It is sometimes said that cities are unfriendly, lonely places, but these shared collaborations bring people together and give them an opportunity to express themselves creatively. (4) In addition, such meaningful creations give people greater pride in their neighborhoods. Providing free housing to the artists would be a worthy gesture of thanks from the city.

(5) However, many people strongly disagree with this proposal. First of all, it has been reported that some residents dislike the murals and sculptures in their areas. (6) Secondly, it is worth remembering that artists who collaborate in community projects are paid for their work. It is also important to point out that a career in art is a personal choice. Why should one profession be rewarded more generously than another? Finally, as our city has a high number of homeless people, many feel it would be better to give free housing to the needy rather than to artists.

(7) To sum up, (8) it seems to me that free housing should be reserved for those who need it the most. While it is true to say that local artists are doing excellent work in the community, giving them free housing does not seem to be a popular prospect.

a sequencing points in a list ____
b introducing the conclusion ____
c introducing a general statement ____
d introducing an opposing view ____
e adding a further point ____
f introducing a personal opinion ____
g supporting a main point with a reason ____
h establishing the recent relevance of the topic ____

6 Read the *for* and *against* essay in Activity 5 again. Then answer the questions. Write *yes* or *no*.

1 Is the essay about a definite plan to give free housing to local artists? ______
2 Does the writer show that local artists bring value to the community? ______
3 Can we infer that only a few people are opposed to giving artists free housing? ______
4 Do artists collaborate in community projects for free? ______
5 Overall, is the writer against artists being given free housing? ______

7 The local government is planning to fund a major arts festival in your town next year. Do you support or oppose this plan? Write a 300-word essay to respond to this question.

Review

1 Complete the sentences with a word from this unit.

1 The food festival has a big ________ on the city.
2 The sculpture creates a ________ of pride in the community.
3 There is wide ________ for a new football stadium; everyone wants it.
4 The museum ________ together people from across the city.
5 The comedy club ________ a lot of students.
6 The title "European Capital of Culture" ________ the local economy.
7 We hope the event will ________ a lot of income for the museum.
8 Thousands of people ________ the film festival last year.

2 Circle the item that is NOT a correct definition.

1 to have an impact on: *to influence / to not influence / to cause changes*
2 to generate: *to hold back / to produce / to stimulate*
3 to hold an event: *to cancel an event / to schedule an event / to have an event*
4 to raise money: *to find money / to earn money / to collect money*
5 to fade: *to become less important / to grow in importance / to get lighter in color*
6 an innovative scheme: *an idea or plan that's been done before / a new method / an unusual method*
7 mixed results: *good results / different types of results / both good and bad results*
8 driving ambition: *weak ambition / strong ambition / long-lasting ambition*

3 Complete the sentences with these verbs.

was going to	was starting	would make
would start	would take	wouldn't go
wouldn't sell		

1 Hana didn't rush because she knew the concert ________ late.
2 The painter said he ________ a presentation of his work to the art class.
3 The gallery owner promised he ________ the painting to anyone else but me.
4 She already said that she ________ to the music festival.
5 They always thought their son ________ be a writer.
6 Ivan said he ________ a lot of pictures at the art exhibit.
7 The play ________ so we had to take seats quickly at the back of the theater.

4 Match the two parts of the sentences.

1 By dinner time, ____
2 I'm looking forward to going to dinner because ____
3 I'll be eating dinner after ____
4 I'll eat dinner when ____
5 I told him I was ____
6 I'm going to eat dinner and then ____
7 Before I went to dinner, I ____
8 I'm about to eat dinner and ____
9 Before I went to dinner, ____

a going to eat dinner and then study.
b was planning to study.
c I thought I would study.
d I study.
e I'll have been studying for six hours.
f then I'll study.
g study.
h I've finished studying.
i I'll have finished studying by then.

5 Complete the sentences with the correct form of these verbs. Use one verb twice.

give	go	have	live	play	wait

1 I wondered if he ________ to hike all the way to the bottom of the Grand Canyon.
2 She ________ to come to the restaurant with us.
3 I thought I ________ until I got to the theater to buy my ticket.
4 He texted to say he ________ a presentation at our school next week.
5 I ________ in Buenos Aires for three months by the time you come to visit me.
6 I ________ three different art teachers by the time I go to college.
7 She ________ volleyball for eight years by the time she tries out for the national team.

5 It's Not Rocket Science

5A Steps in the Process

VOCABULARY Science in action

1 Review Choose the best options to complete the text.

Manuel Castillo is an experienced (1) ___, who has just been employed as a new member of the Help Team. Please contact him if you are having any problems with your computer (2) ___. Manuel can respond to your questions by email or he can come to your office and (3) ___ things face-to-face. He can also advise you on how to (4) ___ with other departments, (5) ___ for documents in the scientific library, and (6) ___ scientific research materials from other universities online.

1 **a** computing technician
b computer technician
c hacker
d software developer

2 **a** equip
b equipped
c equips
d equipment

3 **a** ask
b search
c explain
d find

4 **a** join
b connect
c access
d connection

5 **a** find
b search
c access
d get

6 **a** access
b invent
c connect
d ask

2 Review Complete the sentences with these words.

curious	data	discover	examine
proof	results	solution	technology

1 All the ________________ the scientists collected is still being examined.

2 The ________________ of the experiment were very disappointing. We did not learn anything new.

3 Many people still want to ________________ if there is life on other planets.

4 The ________________ to the problem still escapes us.

5 I won't believe you unless you give me ________________ of your statement.

6 Children ask so many questions because they are naturally ________________ about everything around them.

7 We will ________________ all the ancient statues we found on our trip.

8 The ________________ in computer science is changing every day.

3 Choose the correct option (a–d) to complete each sentence.

1 The first step is to ___ a hypothesis.
a release **b** record **c** track **d** form

2 I ___ the substance under the microscope.
a got rid **b** placed **c** recorded **d** formed

3 When did you carry ___ the experiment?
a off **b** in **c** over **d** out

4 The substance ___ in the water.
a released **b** got rid of **c** dissolved **d** added

5 The scientists ___ their eating habits over six months.
a tracked **b** proved **c** rewarded **d** submitted

6 We ___ an experiment to test the effects of heat.
a formed **b** designed **c** dissolved **d** placed

7 The action ___ a chemical reaction.
a did **b** added **c** proved **d** created

8 He ___ the results of the experiment.
a looked **b** carried out **c** analyzed **d** placed

4 Complete the sentences with these verbs.

analyze	carry	dissolve	form
heat	prove	submit	track

1 First, you need to __________ up the substance.
2 The team hopes to __________ the movement of the whales.
3 My goal is to __________ the hypothesis.
4 Doctors __________ the samples in a lab outside the hospital.
5 Make sure you __________ your report before the deadline.
6 I __________ out research as part of my job.
7 The salt didn't __________ in the cold water.
8 It's important to __________ an interesting hypothesis.

5 Number the steps of the research in order.

__ **a** Record the results of the experiment.
__ **b** Prove or discount your hypothesis.
__ **c** Carry out research.
__ **d** Design an experiment.
_1_ **e** Form a hypothesis.
__ **f** Analyze the data.

6 Cross out the mistake in each sentence and write the correct word.

1 The chemical reaction realized a gas.
____
2 You should add referees at the end of your research report. __________
3 Scientists are carrying in research into cancer.
____
4 We'll analysis the results at the end.
____
5 He heated out the chemicals. __________
6 We designed the test to get rid with a chemical.
____

7 Put the words in the correct order to make sentences.

1 researchers / demonstrate / their / experiment / to / designed / an / theory / .
____
2 the / energy / chemical / released / reaction / .
____
3 dissolved / the / heated up / substance / after / it / was / .
____
4 data / form / a / before / collecting / hypothesis / .
____
5 the / cell / placed / she / microscope / under / the / .
____
6 the / gorillas' / tracked / eating / scientists / habits / .
____

8 **Extension** Complete the table. Match these verbs with the noun they collocate with.

conduct disprove formulate perform set up test

Hypothesis	Experiment

9 **Extension** Complete the sentences with these words.

data	disprove	dissect	observation
performed	reacted	set	support

1 After the experiment, we analyzed the __________.
2 The chemicals __________ with each other.
3 She wanted to __________ her hypothesis and show it was false.
4 They __________ up the experiment in the laboratory.
5 We __________ the experiment over three days.
6 Students __________ animals as part of their biology course.
7 Biology is the study of the natural world through __________ and experimentation.
8 Does your data __________ your hypothesis?

PRONUNCIATION

10 **Listen to the sentences. Underline the verb that is stressed in the passive construction. Then practice saying the sentences.** 35

1 The heart was believed to be the center of intelligence until the Middle Ages.
2 It is claimed that computer training programs can limit the effects of aging on the brain.
3 Einstein's brain was said to be bigger than average, which explains his intelligence.
4 It's estimated that the human brain is about 75 percent water.
5 It's well known that most of the time we use only 10 percent of our brain capacity.
6 Doing exercise is thought to create chemicals that reduce your ability to think.
7 The part of the brain called the hippocampus is known to be connected to our sense of direction.
8 It has been generally accepted that creative people have a dominant right brain.

LISTENING

11 **Listen to a short talk about accents and perception. What would you say is the main finding of the researchers?** 36

a Looks and accent are the two traits that people perceive first.
b Good-looking people are generally perceived as more honest.
c The brain's response to different looks and accents is inconclusive.
d People with accents are sometimes perceived as outsiders.

12 **Listen again. Then complete the text with the words that you hear.** 36

When it comes to the way we speak, accents (1) ________________ more than where we come from. (2) ________________ at Germany's Friedrich Schiller University Jena found that speech wins out over looks when people (3) ________________ someone based on those two (4) ________________ alone. Accents may be key to social (5) ________________ because they can affect whether listeners (6) ________________ the speaker as being one of their own or part of a different group. Says Patricia Bestelmeyer, whose research at the University of Glasgow focuses on the brain's (7) ________________ to different accents: "They can (8) ________________ how much you prefer or trust someone."

A lion walks in the Okavango Delta.

13 **Listen to a story about being overly curious. What do you think would be the best title for the story?** 37

a The Curious Bayei
b Curiosity and a Cat
c A Curious Brother
d Curiosity Kills

14 **Listen again and answer the questions.** 37

1 How many lions are in the Okavango Delta?
a 10,000
b more than 2,000
c nearly 80,000
d around 20,000

2 What did the ancestors of the Bayei people hunt?
a crocodiles
b leopards
c lions
d hippopotamus

3 What raised the curiosity of the brothers?
a lions calling
b hippos swimming
c elephants running
d Bayei learning

4 After wandering from camp, how did the brothers feel?
a embarrassed
b defenseless
c curious
d ashamed

5 What did the brothers not want the lions to think of them as?
a naked
b curious
c inviting
d threatening

6 How did the brothers get the lions to relax?
a by staring at the lions
b by reasoning with them
c by focusing on some dung
d by running towards them

7 What lesson did the brothers learn?
a to be more cautious
b to take more risks
c to never be curious
d to forget consequences

GRAMMAR Passives 1

15 Read about important inventions of the 21st century. Then choose the correct options to complete the text.

It might be said that some of the most important advances of the 21st century have been the iPhone, the iPod, YouTube, and Skype. Today, they are a part of everyday life, but our lives (1) *has been changed / have been changed / have changed* by all of them.

Music players existed before Apple's iPod, but the iPod changed people's relationship with music—especially how it (2) *was enjoyed / was to enjoy / enjoy*.

The iPod and Apple's music store, iTunes, (3) *was develop / were developing / were developed* in 2001. The iPod's modern design and its large storage capacity made it very popular. And because of iTunes, digital music has become normal.

YouTube (4) *founded / was being founded / was founded* in 2005 and is now the world's most popular video-sharing website. Videos (5) *can shared / can be shared / can share* by anyone from anywhere. Millions of hours (6) *spent / is spent / are spent* each month watching music videos, clips from TV programs and films, how-to tutorials, and even cat videos!

How people communicate (7) *also been changed / has also been changed / is also changing* because of Skype. Before this, telephone calls to friends abroad were expensive, but that changed with Skype's free, internet-based calls. Now anyone with an internet connection can (8) *been "called" / is "called" / be "called"* for free! What's more, they (9) *can be seen / can see / have seen* thanks to the video chat!

Apple's iPhone was the first user-friendly smartphone with a large touchscreen. It came out in 2007 and took over the cell phone market, and a new industry (10) *created / was creating / was created*—app development. To date, nearly 900 million iPhones (11) *has been sold / have been sold / are sold*.

The 21st century is still young. Who knows how our lives (12) *improved / will improved / will be improved* by other inventions in the next few years!

16 Complete the sentences with the passive forms of these verbs and the tenses in parentheses below.

cause	conduct	confirm	question	select
submit	track	transform	win	

1. We were told that more research ________________ if there's enough funding. (modal + passive)
2. The other team's hypothesis ________________ by the teacher. (past perfect passive)
3. The smoke ________________ by escaping gas. (past continuous passive)
4. The results of the experiment ________________ by the surprised researchers. (simple past passive)
5. The raw materials ________________ into a unique substance. (present perfect passive)
6. Temperature changes ________________ by the scientists. (future passive)
7. The winner of the competition ________________ by the committee. (present perfect passive)
8. The innovation prizes ________________ right now. (present continuous passive)
9. The teacher was happy that our homework ________________ on time. (simple past passive)

17 Rewrite the passive sentences in active form and the active sentences in passive form.

1. An experiment was designed by the scientists to test the quality of the gold.
   ____
2. The fish had been released into the stream by the biologist.
   ____
3. The wire was attached to the battery, which started the experiment.
   ____
4. The powder is being dissolved in the liquid.
   ____
5. They used the smartphone to make a video of our experiment.
   ____
6. You can find the winners on our website or in our magazine.
   ____
7. The high cost has discouraged me from building a supercomputer.
   ____
8. Experts consider scientists from your country to be among the best in the world.
   ____

5B Playing to Learn

VOCABULARY BUILDING Adjective endings

1 **Complete the table with the adjectives that go with these nouns.**

adaptation	beauty	curiosity	effect	help
hope	imagination	innovation	~~treatment~~	

-able	-ful
treatable	
-ive	**-ous**

READING

2 **Read the article and choose the best headings for paragraphs 1–6 from the list of headings below. You will not use all the headings.**

Paragraph 1 ___
Paragraph 2 ___
Paragraph 3 ___
Paragraph 4 ___
Paragraph 5 ___
Paragraph 6 ___

a Guided play for learning
b Guided play for discovery
c How education is changing
d How children learn best
e Why rats play
f The problem with play
g Why animals play
h Playing for the future
i Play and the brain

3 **Read the article again. Choose the answer that you think fits best according to the article.**

1 In paragraph 2, what is the author's main point about animal play?
a Play makes rats more social and less stressed.
b Play is extremely important for animals to survive and succeed.
c Playful animals live longer than animals who are not playful.
d Rats, squirrels and bears are healthy animals because they play a lot.

2 The author gives examples of animals that play because
a it is interesting information for the reader.
b it is important information for teachers to understand.
c it helps explain why play is important for human children.
d scientists are focused on animal play.

3 In paragraph 4, what does the author suggest about guided play?
a It is better for learning than many traditional teaching methods.
b It should be used mainly to teach vocabulary.
c It should be directed by teachers, not children.
d It should be focused on fun more than on specific learning goals.

4 In paragraph 5, what is the author's purpose in describing the teacher's interaction with students about shapes?
a to prove that this is a good teacher
b to prove that guided play is important for children
c to suggest that teachers should never talk more than children
d to give an example of how guided play works

5 In the last paragraph, "this" refers to
a research.
b children.
c guided play.
d scientists.

4 **Complete each sentence with the correct ending based on information from the article.**

1 Rats that play regularly ___
2 Students in the past ___
3 The purpose of guided play is to ___
4 A teacher using guided play well will ___
5 Children learn best when they ___
6 Worksheets and flashcards ___

a have strong social skills.
b spend a lot of time listening.
c help students achieve learning goals.
d make connections to their own lives.
e do not always help students remember information.
f spent less time playing than they do now.

Playing to Learn 38

1 When most people think of school, we think of sitting in desks or at tables, listening to teachers, and taking exams. But today, especially in classrooms for young children, learning looks quite different. One of the biggest trends in early childhood education is for play-based learning. Instead of seeing children sitting at a desk, you might find them playing in a model kitchen or building towers of blocks. Rather than watching a teacher who stands at the front of the room, these students will be playing with their teacher in the park. What is play-based learning, and why do children need it?

2 To find some answers, we can look to the animal kingdom. Many species of animals have been observed playing, and scientists have begun to understand why. Animals play for a variety of reasons: to learn social skills, to master survival skills and to relieve stress. Rats are some of the most playful animals, and research shows that rats who play have better developed brains, are able to pay attention longer, and have better memories than rats who don't. Rats who play are also better in social situations with other rats; they get in fewer fights and have much lower stress levels. Squirrels are also playful animals. Scientists have found that squirrels who play have better coordination and even have more babies than those who don't. Brown bears who play as cubs are more likely to survive into adulthood than those who do not experience play. Play is crucial for animals to learn important social and survival skills, and might even create healthier brains.

3 It's not surprising, then, that human children also benefit from playing to learn. Educational researchers have found that children learn best when they are mentally active, interested, socially interactive, and able to make connections between what they are learning and their own lives. Teachers build on this research by practicing guided play in their classrooms.

4 Play is flexible, fun, and directed by children; guided play helps children focus their play to achieve a learning goal. For example, a teacher using guided play to teach farm animal vocabulary might read a book with the children and then let them play with toy horses, cows, and chickens. Studies show that this type of guided play helps children remember words better than regular school activities like worksheets or flashcards.

5 With guided play, teachers watch and listen more than they talk. If children are playing with toys of different shapes, a teacher might ask questions about the shape. This allows the child to learn about different shapes through discovery rather than instruction. They are able to form hypotheses of their own, test them, and become little scientists.

6 Research is showing that children learn better from playing, especially from guided play. Scientists are trying to learn more about what effects this has on the brain, but it is clear that play is an important part of development. Guided play helps prepare children to become curious, creative thinkers, and caring members of society. Many teacher training programs are now focusing on the importance of guided play so that the next generation gets the best education possible.

5C Mind-Blowing!

GRAMMAR Passives 2

1 Read the sentences. Are they active (A) or passive (P)?

1 My sister Roberta claims to be too busy to help me study. ___
2 It's well known that Beijing Capital International Airport is one of the busiest airports in the world. ___
3 I believe Barbara McClintock won the Nobel Prize in Physiology or Medicine in 1983 for her work in genetics. ___
4 The estimate the scientists made for how long it takes certain bacteria to multiply was accurate. ___
5 Louis Armstrong was said to be one of the most innovative jazz trumpeters. ___
6 Exercising every day is thought to lead to better sleep. ___
7 They said getting humans to the moon couldn't be done. ___
8 It's estimated that the world's population will be 9.7 billion by 2050. ___
9 Thoughts on the nature of the universe have changed throughout time. ___
10 Ella Fitzgerald was a well-known jazz singer. ___
11 Marie Curie was believed by many people to be one of the greatest scientists working in the early 20th century. ___

2 Choose the correct option to complete the sentences.

1 It ___ that human actions are increasing the negative effects of climate change.
a is claimed
b claimed
c is known to be
d is thought to

2 In the 1950s, it ___ by some people that women should not play sports.
a believe
b were believed
c has been believed
d was believed

3 The Space Launch System ___ a major step along the road to putting people in space to explore Mars as well as other aspects of deep space.
a it's expected to be
b is expecting to be
c is expected to be
d expecting

4 Rewriting your notes after class ___ help you learn the material better.
a is thought to
b known to be
c thought to
d knowing to

5 ___ that students who study every day get better grades.
a Thought
b It's considered
c It's thinking
d It's well known

6 British archaeologist Howard Carter ___ as the person who, in 1922, discovered Tutankhamun's tomb in Egypt.
a seems
b is said
c considered
d is known

7 In the 1400s, many people ___ India's spices were the best in the world.
a were said
b said
c have generally accepted
d have been said

3 Choose the correct option to complete the sentences about brain myths.

1 *It's said / It says* we use only 10 percent of our brain capacity.
2 Our brain *doesn't / is believed to be* work as well after we turn 50.
3 Brains *claim / are claimed* to be like computers.
4 It *generally accepts / is generally accepted* that we have only five senses.
5 *It's assumed / It assumes* that you have to speak one language well before you learn a new language.
6 Men's brains *were believed to / are* different in many ways from women's brains.
7 *It is thought / Thoughts* that adults can't grow new brain cells.

4 Which sentence, a or b, is closer in meaning to the original sentence?

1 Gabriel Garcia Marquez is said to be one of the greatest authors of the 20th century.
a I think Gabriel Garcia Marquez is one of the greatest authors of the 20th century.
b Many people think Gabriel Garcia Marquez is one of the greatest authors of the 20th century.

2 It's well known that tennis players who take extra lessons do better in competitions.
a Tennis players know to take extra lessons and do well in competitions.
b If tennis players take extra lessons, they generally do better in competitions.

3 Persuasive advertisements are thought to make customers buy more.
  a People generally think that customers buy more when they see persuasive advertisements.
  b Customers buy more items and like persuasive advertisements.
4 Lewis Hamilton is known to be one of the best Formula One drivers of all time.
  a Lewis Hamilton knows he is one of the best Formula One drivers of all time.
  b Many people think Lewis Hamilton is one of the best Formula One drivers of all time.
5 It's been generally accepted that science has made life better.
  a Though not everyone agrees, a lot of people think science has made our lives better.
  b Science making our lives better is accepted to be a general thought.
6 It's widely believed that teachers should encourage curiosity in their students.
  a Teachers generally want to encourage their students to be curious.
  b Most people think it's important for teachers to encourage their students to be curious.

5 **Use *have* or *get* + *something* + past participle to write a new sentence in the passive that is related to the first sentence.**

1 Someone took my photo for my new ID. (get)
  I got my photo taken for my new ID.
2 They displayed my research project at the science fair. (have)
  ____
3 They printed my aunt's favorite recipe in the newspaper. (get)
  ____
4 They took my temperature at the clinic. (have)
  ____
5 Some classmates finished Jamie's experiment for him. (get)
  ____

6 **Use the prompts to write present simple sentences with the impersonal *it*.**

1 well / know / people / like / ice cream
  It is well known (that) people like ice cream.
2 think / recording lectures / help / students / learn
  ______________________________.
3 assume / most students / need / study / regularly
  ______________________________.
4 think / exercise / good for / brain
  ______________________________.
5 claim / world / get / hotter / every decade
  ______________________________.
6 assume / scientific advances / help / people / live longer
  ______________________________.
7 well know / Mrs. Liu / be / best teacher / our school
  ______________________________.

7 **Rewrite each passive sentence so that it does not use the impersonal *it*.**

1 It is thought that studying abroad helps students become more curious about the world.
  ______________________________.
2 It's estimated that 37 percent of the people in our country have university degrees.
  ______________________________.
3 It was said that our experiment was doomed to failure since we didn't take into account the temperature.
  ______________________________.
4 It is claimed that brushing your teeth twice a day keeps your mouth healthy.
  ______________________________.
5 It's believed that fish such as salmon are good for the health of your brain.
  ______________________________.
6 It's thought that getting at least eight hours of sleep every night helps your brain work better.
  ______________________________.

5D Science is for everyone, kids included.

TEDTALKS

AUTHENTIC LISTENING SKILLS

1 **Listen to the extract from Beau Lotto's TED Talk, and choose the filler words where he uses them. If he does not use a filler word, choose X.** 39

Now, I want to tell you a story about seeing differently, and all new perceptions begin in the same way.
(1) *Right? / X* They begin with a question. The problem with questions is they create uncertainty. Now, uncertainty is a very bad thing. It's evolutionarily a bad thing. If you're not sure that's a predator, it's too late. (2) *OK? / X* Even seasickness is a consequence of uncertainty. (3) *Right? / X* If you go down below on a boat, your inner ears are telling you you're moving. Your eyes, because it's moving in register with the boat, say I'm standing still. (4) *OK? / X* Your brain cannot deal with the uncertainty of that information, and it gets ill. The question "why?" is one of the most dangerous things you can do, because it takes you into uncertainty. (5) *You know? / X* And yet, the irony is, the only way we can ever do anything new is to step into that space. So how can we ever do anything new? Well fortunately, evolution has given us an answer,
(6) *right? / X* And it enables us to address even the most difficult of questions. (7) *Yeah. / X* The best questions are the ones that create the most uncertainty. They're the ones that question the things we think to be true already. (8) *Right? / X* It's easy to ask questions about how did life begin, or what extends beyond the universe, but to question what you think to be true already is really stepping into that space.

WATCH ▶

2 **Do Beau (B) or Amy (A) make each of these statements?**

1. The brain takes meaningless information and makes meaning out of it, which means we never see what's there. ___
2. Science is not defined by the method section of a paper. It's actually a way of being, which is here, and this is true for anything that is creative. ___
3. We thought that it was easy to see the link between humans and apes in the way that we think, because we look alike. ___
4. Really, we wanted to know if bees can also adapt themselves to new situations using previously learned rules and conditions. ___
5. We asked the bees to learn not just to go to a certain color, but to a certain color flower only when it's in a certain pattern. ___
6. So the kids give me the words, right? I put it into a narrative, which means that this paper is written in kid speak. ___
7. It took four months to do the science, two years to get it published. ___
8. This project was really exciting for me, because it brought the process of discovery to life, and it showed me that anyone, and I mean anyone, has the potential to discover something new. ___

VOCABULARY IN CONTEXT

3 **Match the words 1–6 with the sentences that show their meaning (a–f).**

1. adapt ___
2. a voice ___
3. reward ___
4. surrounded ___
5. bother ___
6. link ___

a Joaquin's mother always told him that knowledge would be the **benefit he received** for his effort in school.
b Sometimes adults don't **make the effort** to take children's questions seriously, even though they can provide valuable insights.
c Amy and her classmates wanted to study the **connection** between the way humans solve problems and the way bees do.
d The students wondered whether the bees would **change** their behavior based on the experiments that they designed.
e When I go into the city, I have people and buildings **all around me**.
f Beau Lotto thinks that it is important for children to have **the opportunity to contribute** to scientific discussions.

5E Conducting Experiments

SPEAKING

Useful language

Staging

The first thing we'd need to do is…
We'd also need to make sure that we (didn't)…
I suppose then we'd probably be best… -ing…

Preparing research questions

I wonder if / how / why…
It'd be good to know what / whether…
We'd need to try and work out…

Hypothesizing

I'd expect the results to show… I'd imagine that the data would probably reveal…
I would / wouldn't have thought it'd be possible to prove that…

1 Match each useful language phrase with its function: Talking about Staging (S), Preparing research questions (Q), or Hypothesizing (H).

1 I wonder if / how / why ___
2 We'd also need to make sure that we (didn't) ___
3 I would / wouldn't have thought it'd be possible to prove that ___
4 We'd need to try and work out ___
5 I guess then we'd probably be best…-ing ___
6 I'd expect the results to show ___
7 It'd be good to know what / whether ___
8 I'd imagine that the data would probably reveal ___
9 The first thing we'd need to do is ___

2 Listen to the conversation and decide what the experiment will be about. 40

a commerce **b** science **c** technology

3 Complete the conversation with phrases from the useful language box. Then listen again and check your answers. 40

A: So, how are we going to plan our science project together?
B: Well, I think (1) ________________ design the experiment.
A: That's a good idea. So, if we're investigating the gas released in the chemical reaction with different metals, we need to use sound research methods.
C: (2) ________________ we can measure the rate of gas produced.
B: (3) ________________ measured and recorded the results accurately.
A: Yeah, and (4) ________________ how the reaction occurs.
C: (5) ________________ doing some research, forming a hypothesis about the reaction, and then proving it in our experiment.
B: Also, (6) ________________ the quantity varies at different temperatures.
C: (7) ________________ the speed of the reaction changes at different temperatures.
A: Yeah, (8) ________________ an increase in volume at higher temperatures.
B: What about the different metals? Are they all going to be the same?
C: (9) ________________ that one of the metals was the most reactive.
A: Right, let's decide how we're going to research this then.

4 Think about how you and some classmates would work together to plan one of the experiments from the list below (or an example of your own). Apply the research methods you learned in the unit to plan your task. Use the useful language to make notes. Then compare your ideas with the conversation in Activity 3.

- How do different building designs react in an earthquake?
- Frozen substances—expansion or contraction?
- How can we produce light without electricity (or fire)?
- The effectiveness of different materials to filter dirty water

5 Listen to part of a lecture from a biology course and answer the question below. 41

Using the information from the talk, describe the two main consequences of global warming and how the examples illustrate the concept.

Make notes and remember to use the useful language. Then listen to the sample answer. 42

WRITING A scientific method

6 Match the two parts of the sentences.

1 The experiment aimed to measure ___
2 The purpose of the experiment ___
3 Pavlov played the same sound ___
4 The reactions among the gases were studied in order to ___
5 During the experiment, the scientists ___
6 After the experiment, the properties ___

a determine their volumes.
b of radioactivity were described.
c was to demonstrate superconductivity.
d reproduced certain types of bacteria.
e so that the dogs knew they would be given food.
f the force of gravity in a laboratory.

7 Match each sentence with its function: Introducing the process (I), Linking the steps (L), or Explaining the steps (E).

1 The purpose of the experiment was to show the effects of gravity. ___
2 Next, the psychologist showed the child the choice of rewards. ___
3 A microscope was provided so that the cells could be seen. ___
4 The diagram illustrates the process used to complete the experiment. ___
5 The experiment aimed to prove that light travels faster than sound. ___

8 Complete the process for this scientific experiment using these words and phrases. Two items are not used.

after the experiment,	aim	before the experiment,
carried out	conform	discover
during the experiment,	finally	in order to
incorrect	once	then

The Asch conformity experiment

The (1) ______________ of this 1950s experiment was to (2) ______________ whether social pressure would make individual people conform. In other words, it tested whether individuals would (3) ______________, that is, agree, with an answer given by a majority of others even though they knew this answer was (4) ______________. The experiment was (5) ______________ with 50 male students from a college in the United States.

(6) ______________ seven participants were told what answer to give about a comparison between the length of lines on two different cards. One participant was not aware of this, and was not given any instruction.
(7) ______________ this person was deliberately placed last in the line of participants, who were all required to answer the question aloud.
(8) ______________ prove the theory, the first seven people were instructed to give the same incorrect answer.
(9) ______________ these seven had answered, the final participant (10) ______________ had to decide whether to conform and give the answer everyone else had given, or the one they personally knew to be correct.

9 Read the process in Activity 8 again. Then put the points (a–h) in the correct order (1–8).

a Before the experiment, seven of the eight people were told what answer to give. ___
b The plan was to ask the group to answer an obvious question. ___
c After hearing all seven answers, the eighth person had to decide whether to conform. ___
d Groups of eight people were formed to participate in this experiment. ___
e The eighth person didn't know the others had been told how to answer. ___
f The purpose was to find out whether people would conform to what others said. ___
g These seven people were all instructed to give the same incorrect answer. ___
h They had to answer aloud, so everyone in the group could hear their answer. ___

10 In your English class, you have been talking about robots. Now your English teacher has asked you to write an essay. Write 140–190 words in an appropriate style.

Today, scientists are developing more advanced robots that will carry out many functions for human beings in the future. Some people feel this is a bad idea. Do you agree?

Notes

Write about:

1 convenience
2 jobs
3 ______________ (your own idea)

Review

1 **Choose the correct option to complete the sentences.**

1. She *recorded / formed* the results of the experiment on her tablet.
2. In a *reference / hypothesis* you try to explain an observation.
3. The scientists *carried out / tracked* the progress of the athletes.
4. The chemicals *dissolved / released* a gas.
5. Can you *add / place* it under the microscope, please?
6. The team *designed / formed* a hypothesis.

2 **Complete the words to make the phrases.**

1. s _ _ _ _ _ an assignment before the deadline
2. c _ _ _ _ _ _ a chemical reaction
3. a _ _ references at the end of a report
4. d _ _ _ _ _ _ an experiment
5. c _ _ _ _ _ o _ _ research
6. a _ _ _ _ _ _ _ the results of an experiment
7. p _ _ _ _ _ a hypothesis
8. g _ _ r _ _ o _ a chemical

3 **Cross out the mistake in each sentence and write the correct word.**

1. Music streaming being used by more and more people these days. ________________
2. The electric car been developed to decrease our dependence on petroleum. ________________
3. The driverless car has been dream of for many years, but now it is a reality. ________________
4. Smartphones is now carried by the majority of adults. ________________
5. Before I left school, tablet computers had introduced into most lessons. ________________
6. The internet was using for research for the science project. ________________
7. Wearables (small computer devices that you wear) being advertised as the latest tech gadget. ________________
8. Her files stored in the cloud so she can access them from any computer with an internet connection. ________________

4 **Complete the sentences using the verbs in parentheses in the passive voice.**

1. It ________________ (generally agree) that travel sparks curiosity.
2. Certain senses and functions of the body ________________ (control) by the brain.
3. In the 15th century, it ________________ (say) that the world was flat.
4. The Copley Medal ________________ (award) annually by the Royal Society, London, to persons in any field of science who show outstanding achievement.
5. The report ________________ (write) after the students completed the experiment.
6. In the 16th century, the Earth ________________ (believe) to be at the center of the universe.
7. In many circles, it ________________ (claim) that scientific innovation depends on a solid secondary school education.

5 **Read the questions. Choose the correct answer.**

1. Who do you think the best soccer player is?
   - **a** It's claimed that either Lionel Messi or Ronaldo is the best soccer player in the world.
   - **b** I claims that either Ronaldo or Lionel Messi is the best soccer player.
2. Do I really have to study every day?
   - **a** You'll got better grades if you study more.
   - **b** Well, it's been generally accepted that the more you study, the better grades you'll get.
3. Name one of the happiest countries in the world.
   - **a** Denmark says to be one of the happiest country in the world.
   - **b** Denmark is said to be one of the happiest countries in the world.
4. How many people were in the world in the 1600s?
   - **a** It's estimated that the population then was around 500 million.
   - **b** The population in the 1600s it's estimated that it was around 500 million.
5. What can I do to stay healthy?
   - **a** If you wash your hands frequently, I think you'll get sick less often.
   - **b** It's well know washing your hands frequently leads to fewer illnesses.
6. Do you think I should join the drama club?
   - **a** If you do join, I think you'll have got better grades and you had liked it.
   - **b** Yes, I do! Participating in activities such as drama club is thought to help you get better grades. And I think you'll like it, too.
7. Didn't your hair use to be longer?
   - **a** Yes, I have it cut last Monday.
   - **b** Yes, I got it cut on Monday.

VOCABULARY LIST

UNIT 1

Review

a bike ride (n) /ə baɪk raɪd/
backpacking (n) /'bækˌpækɪŋ/
commute (v) /kəm'jut/
cruise (n) /kruz/
destination (n) /ˌdɛstə'neɪʃən/
flight (n) /flaɪt/
ride (v) /raɪd/
route (n) /rut /
taxi (n) /'tæksi/
train (n) /treɪn/

Unit Vocabulary

accessible (adj) /æk'sɛsəbəl/
B&B (n) /'bi ən 'bi/
ban (v) /bæn/
basically (adv) /'beɪsɪkli/
be up for (phr v) /bi 'ʌp ˌfɔr/
budget (n) /'bʌdʒɪt/
cause (v) /kɔz/
come across (phr v) /'kʌm ə'krɔs/
community (n) /kə'mjunɪti/
culture shock (n) /'kʌltʃər ˌʃɒk/
date back (phr v) /'deɪt 'bæk/
deal (n) /dil/
decline (n) /dɪ'klaɪn/
established (adj) /ɪ'stæblɪʃt/
evaluate (v) /ɪ'vælјuˌeɪt/
extensive (adj) /ɪk'stɛnsɪv/
fluent (adj) /'fluənt/
food poisoning (n) /'fud ˌpɔɪzənɪŋ/
genuinely (adv) /'dʒɛnjuɪnli/
get a real feel for (phr v) /ˌgɛt ə 'rɪəl 'fil fɔr/
get used to (the food) (phr v) /ˌgɛt 'juzd tu/
grand (adj) /grænd/
hiking (n) /'haɪkɪŋ/
honesty (n) /'ɒnɪsti/
host family (n) /'hoʊst 'fæməli/
ideal (adj) /aɪ'dɪəl/
incredibly (adv) /ɪn'krɛdəbli/
independence (n) /ˌɪndɪ'pɛndəns/
individual (n) /ˌɪndɪ'vɪdʒuəl/
influence (v) /'ɪnfluəns/
investment (n) /ɪn'vɛstmənt/
left to (your) own devices (idiom) /'lɛft tu (yər) 'oʊn dɪ'vaɪsɪz/
legal (adj) /'ligəl/
lie around (phr v) /'laɪ ə'raʊnd/
look back (phr v) /'lʊk 'bæk/
major (adj) /'meɪdʒər/
media (n) /'midiə/
move on (phr v) /'muv 'ɒn/
necessarily (adv) /ˌnɛsə'sɛrəli/
negotiate (v) /nɪ'goʊʃiˌeɪt/
opt (v) /ɒpt/
overseas (adv) /'oʊvər'siz/
participant (n) /pɑr'tɪsəpənt/
perspective (n) /pər'spɛktɪv/
reinforce (v) /ˌriɪn'fɔrs/
reliability (n) /rɪˌlaɪə'bɪlɪti/
reputation (n) /ˌrɛpjə'teɪʃən/
resource (n) /'risɔrs/
restriction (n) /rɪ'strɪkʃən/
revolution (n) /ˌrɛvə'luʃən/
ridiculous (adj) /rɪ'dɪkjələs/
robbery (n) /'rɒbəri/
roots (n) /ruts/
servant (n) /'sɜrvənt/
sights (n) /saɪts/
simply (adv) /'sɪmpli/
spread (v) /sprɛd/
standard (n) /'stændərd/
stare (v) /stɛər/
step out (phr v) /'stɛp 'aʊt/
strongly (adv) /'strɔŋli/
turn out (phr v) /'tɜrn 'aʊt/
tutor (n) /'tutər/
upgrade (n)(v) /'ʌpˌgreɪd/
vice versa (adv) /'vaɪsə 'vɜrsə/
voyage (n) /'vɔɪəʤ/
wealth (n) /wɛlθ/
welcoming (adj) /'wɛlkəmɪŋ/
worry (n) /'wɜri/

Extension

amenities (n) /ə'mɛnətiz/
availability (n) /əˌveɪlə'bɪləti/
downtime (n) /'daʊnˌtaɪm/
excursion (n) /ɪk'skɜrʒən/
overbooked (adj) /'oʊvərˌbʊkt/
secluded (adj) /sɪ'kludɪd/
tourist trap (n) /'tʊrəst træp/
wander (v) /'wɑndər/

Vocabulary Building

break down (phr v) /'breɪk 'daʊn/
come down to (phr v) /ˌkʌm 'daʊn tu/
hang out (phr v) /'hæŋ 'aʊt/
line up (v) /laɪn ʌp/
look after (phr v) /'lʊk 'æftər/
pick up (phr v) /'pɪk 'ʌp/
pull over (v) /pʊl 'oʊvər/

Vocabulary in Context

anxiety (n) /æŋ'zaɪəti/
broke (n) /broʊk/
keep in touch (idiom) /'kip ɪn 'tʌʧ/
rush (v) /rʌʃ/
trip up (phr v) /'trɪp 'ʌp/
up for it (idiom) /ʌp fɔr ɪt/

UNIT 2

Review

career prospects (phr) /kə'rɪr 'prɑspɛkts/
flexible (adj) /'flɛksəbəl/
full-time (adj) /fʊl-taɪm/
in charge of (phr v) /ɪn ʧɑrʤ ʌv/
industry (n) /'ɪndəstri/
job market (n) /ʤɑb 'mɑrkət/
long hours (phr) /lɔŋ 'aʊərz/
part-time (adj) /'pɑrt'taɪm/
physically demanding (phr) /'fɪzɪkəli dɪ'mændɪŋ/
poorly paid (phr) /'purli peɪd/
responsible (adj) /ri'spɑnsəbəl/
stressful (adj) /'strɛsfəl/
well-paid (adj) /wɛl-peɪd/
work on (phr v) /wɜrk ɑn/

Unit Vocabulary

(a) matter (of) (idiom) /ə'mætər ʌv/
adapt (v) /ə'dæpt/
aspect (n) /'æspɛkt/
assume (v) /ə'sum/
attach (v) /ə'tætʃ/
automatically (adv) /ˌɔtə'mætɪkli/
backup (n) /'bækˌʌp/
banking (n) /'bæŋkɪŋ/
bargain (n) /'bɑrgɪn/
barrier (n) /'bæriər/
be based (phr v) /bi 'beɪst/
beg (v) /bɛg/
businessperson (n) /'bɪznɪsˌpɜrsən/
campaign (n) /kæm'peɪn/
capable (adj) /'keɪpəbəl/
climate change (n) /'klaɪmɪt ˌʧeɪnʤ/
code (n) /koʊd/
confirm (v) /kən'fɜrm/
corporate (adj) /'kɔrpərɪt/
cut down (phr v) /'kʌt 'daʊn/
data (n) /'deɪtə/
demonstrate (v) /'dɛmənˌstreɪt/
detect (v) /dɪ'tɛkt/
discourage (v) /dɪs'kɜrɪdʒ/
distant (adj) /'dɪstənt/
distribute (v) /dɪ'strɪbjut/
distribution (n) /ˌdɪstrə'bjuʃən/
diverse (adj) /dɪ'vɜrs/
edit (v) /'ɛdɪt/
email (n) /'iˌmeɪl/
entrepreneur (n) /ˌɒntrəprə'nʊər/
executive (adj) /ɪg'zɛkjətɪv/
expand (v) /ɪk'spænd/
export (v) /'ɛkspɔrt/
failure (n) /'feɪljər/
filter (n) /'fɪltər/
fund (n) /fʌnd/
fund (v) /fʌnd/
gender (n) /'dʒɛndər/
guarantee (n) /ˌgærən'ti/
handle (v) /'hændl/
harvest (v) /'hɑrvɪst/
illegal (adj) /ɪ'ligəl/
impressive (adj) /ɪm'prɛsɪv/
inbox (n) /'ɪnˌbɒks/
infect (v) /ɪn'fɛkt/
invent (v) /ɪn'vɛnt/
investor (n) /ɪn'vɛstər/
leadership (n) /'lidərˌʃɪp/
market (v) /'mɑrkɪt/
network (v) /'nɛtˌwɜrk/
origin (n) /'ɔrɪdʒɪn/
post (v) /poʊst/
potential (n) /pə'tɛnʃəl/
pressure (n) /'prɛʃər/
profile (n) /'proʊfaɪl/
profit (n) /'prɒfɪt/
publisher (n) /'pʌblɪʃər/
put together (phr v) /'pʊt tə'gɛðər/
raise money (phr v) /'reɪz 'mʌni/
reality (n) /ri'ælɪti/
recover (v) /rɪ'kʌvər/
risk (n) /rɪsk/
scam (n) /skæm/
social media (n) /'soʊʃəl 'midiə/
solar (adj) /'soʊlər/
source (n) /sɔrs/
spam (n) /spæm/
statement (n) /'steɪtmənt/
store (v) /stɔr/
strategy (n) /'strætɪdʒi/
summarize (v) /'sʌməˌraɪz/
supplier (n) /sə'plaɪər/
tribe (n) /traɪb/
victim (n) /'vɪktɪm/
wealthy (adj) /'wɛlθi/

Extension

chair (n) /ʧɛr/
delicate (adj) /'dɛləkət/
founder (n) /'faʊndər/
outsource (v) /ˌaʊt'sɔrs/
proactive (adj) /'proʊ'æktɪv/
self-starter (n) /sɛlf-'stɑrtər/
systematic (adj) /ˌsɪstə'mætɪk/
team player (n) /tim 'pleɪər/

Vocabulary Building

distant relatives (col) /'dɪstənt 'rɛlətɪvz/
luxury hotel (col) /'lʌgʒəri hoʊ'tɛl/
normal price (col) /'nɔrməl praɪs/
personal details (col) /'pɜrsɪnɪl dɪ'teɪlz/
well-paid job (col) /wɛl-peɪd ʤɑb/

Vocabulary in Context

go too far (idiom) /'goʊ ˌtu 'fɑr/
intrigue (v) /ɪn'trig/
knock on the head (idiom) /'nɒk ɒn ðə 'hɛd/
matter (n) /'mætər/
out of hand (idiom) /'aʊt əv 'hænd/
turn up (phr v) /'tɜrn 'ʌp/

UNIT 3

Review

achieve (v) /ə'ʧiv/
bounce (v) /baʊns/

coach (n)	/koʊʧ/
do yoga (phrase)	/du ˈjoʊgə/
encourage (v)	/ɛnˈkɜrɪʤ/
go cycling (phrase)	/goʊ ˈsaɪkəlɪŋ/
kick (v)	/kɪk/
net (n)	/nɛt/
play a role (phrase)	/pleɪ ə roʊ/
referee (n)	/ˌrɛfəˈri/
represent (v)	/ˌrɛprəˈzɛnt/
rink (n)	/rɪŋk/
spectator (n)	/ˈspɛkteɪtər/
swing (v)	/swɪŋ/
throw (v)	/θroʊ/
track (n)	/træk/
train (v)	/treɪn/

Unit Vocabulary

accelerate (v)	/ækˈsɛləˌreɪt/
advance (n)	/ædˈvæns/
agree with (phr v)	/əˈgri ˌwɪð/
amount (n)	/əˈmaʊnt/
anticipate (v)	/ænˈtɪsəˌpeɪt/
athletic (adj)	/æθˈlɛtɪk/
attitude (n)	/ˈætɪˌtud/
awareness (n)	/əˈwɛərnɪs/
billion (n)	/ˈbɪljən/
brand (n)	/brænd/
bronze (adj)	/brɒnz/
captain (v)	/ˈkæptən/
championship (n)	/ˈtʃæmpiənˌʃɪp/
change the face of (idiom)	/ˈʧeɪnʤ ðə ˈfeɪs əv/
closely (adv)	/ˈkloʊsli/
compete (v)	/kəmˈpit/
conquer (v)	/ˈkɒŋkər/
debt (n)	/dɛt/
determine (v)	/dɪˈtɜrmɪn/
elite (adj)	/ɪˈlit/
energetic (adj)	/ˌɛnərˈdʒɛtɪk/
entire (adj)	/ɛnˈtaɪər/
essentially (adv)	/ɪˈsɛnʃəli/
establish (v)	/ɪˈstæblɪʃ/
evolution (n)	/ˌɛvəˈluʃən/
evolve (v)	/ɪˈvɒlv/
expense (n)	/ɪkˈspɛns/
fade away (v)	/ˈfeɪd əˈweɪ/
fame (n)	/feɪm/
formal (adj)	/ˈfɔrməl/
forward (n)	/ˈfɔrwərd/
funding (n)	/ˈfʌndɪŋ/
gardening (adj)	/ˈgɑrdnɪŋ/
glory (n)	/ˈglɔri/
goal (n)	/goʊl/
greatly (adv)	/ˈgreɪtli/
hold (a record) (v)	/hoʊld/
host (v)	/hoʊst/
injury (n)	/ˈɪndʒəri/
instantly (adv)	/ˈɪnstəntli/
intensively (adv)	/ɪnˈtɛnsɪvli/
junk food (n)	/ˈdʒʌŋk ˌfud/
largely (adv)	/ˈlɑrdʒli/
long-term (adj)	/ˈlɔŋˌtɜrm/
marathon (n)	/ˈmærəˌθɒn/
medal (n)	/ˈmɛdl/
muscle (n)	/ˈmʌsəl/
nation (n)	/ˈneɪʃən/
participate (v)	/pɑrˈtɪsəˌpeɪt/
pay off (phr v)	/ˈpeɪ ˈɔf/
percentage (n)	/pərˈsɛntɪdʒ/
personality (n)	/ˌpɜrsəˈnælɪti/
popularity (n)	/ˌpɒpjəˈlærɪti/
positive role model (phrase)	/ˈpɒzɪtɪv ˈroʊlˌmɒdl/
preferably (adv)	/ˈprɛfərəbli/
principle (n)	/ˈprɪnsəpəl/
psychological (adj)	/ˌsaɪkəˈlɒdʒɪkəl/
quote (n)	/kwoʊt/
ranking (n)	/ˈræŋkɪŋ/
real passion (phrase)	/ˈrɪəl ˈpæʃən/
recreation (n)	/ˌrɛkriˈeɪʃən/
represent (v)	/ˌrɛprɪˈzɛnt/
role model (n)	/ˈroʊl ˌmɒdl/
roughly (adv)	/ˈrʌfli/
schedule (n)	/ˈskɛdjul/
season (n)	/ˈsizən/
select (v)	/sɪˈlɛkt/
set (a new record) (v)	/sɛt/
set up (v)	/ˈsɛt ˈʌp/
shrink (v)	/ʃrɪŋk/
slightly (adv)	/ˈslaɪtli/
slow down (phr v)	/ˈsloʊ ˈdaʊn/
smash (v)	/smæʃ/
specialize (v)	/ˈspɛʃəˌlaɪz/
specific (adj)	/spəˈsɪfɪk/
spirit (n)	/ˈspɪrɪt/
stamina (n)	/ˈstæmɪnə/
status (n)	/ˈsteɪtəs/
subsequently (adv)	/ˈsʌbsɪkwəntli/
subway (n)	/ˈsʌbˌweɪ/
suit (v)	/sut/
sum (n)	/sʌm/
surface (n)	/ˈsɜrfɪs/
tackle (v)	/ˈtækəl/
target (n)	/ˈtɑrgɪt/
technique (n)	/tɛkˈnik/
technological (adj)	/ˌtɛknəˈlɒdʒɪkəl/
tend to (phr v)	/ˈtɛnd tu/
terminal (n)	/ˈtɜrmɪnl/
throughout (prep)	/θruˈaʊt/
top (adj)	/tɒp/
vast (adj)	/væst/

Extension

aware (adj)	/əˈwɛr/
awareness (n)	/awareness/
competition (n)	/ˌkɑmpəˈtɪʃən/
competitive (adj)	/kəmˈpɛtətɪv/
energy (n)	/ˈɛnərʤi/
energetic (adj)	/ˌɛnərˈʤɛtɪk/
passion (n)	/ˈpæʃən/
passionate (adj)	/ˈpæʃənət/
positive (adj)	/ˈpɑzətɪv/
skill (n)	/skɪl/
skillful (adj)	/ˈskɪlfəl/

Vocabulary Building

amount (n)	/əˈmaʊnt/
elite (adj)	/ɪˈlit/
establish (v)	/ɪˈstæblɪʃ/
money (n)	/ˈmʌni/
selected (adj)	/səˈlɛktəd/
talent (n)	/ˈtælənt/

Vocabulary in Context

but (conj)	/bʌt/
conversely (adv)	/ˈkɑnvərsli/
rather than (phr)	/ˈræðər ðæn/

UNIT 4

Review

art gallery (n)	/ɑrt ˈgæləri/
broadcast (n)	/ˈbrɔdˌkæst/
concert hall (n)	/ˈkɑnsɜrt hɔl/
listener (n)	/ˈlɪsənər/
lyrics (n)	/ˈlɪrɪks/
mural (n)	/ˈmjʊrəl/
painting (n)	/ˈpeɪntɪŋ/
portrait (n)	/ˈpɔrtrət/
production (n)	/prəˈdʌkʃən/
sculpture (n)	/ˈskʌlpʧər/
verse (n)	/vɜrs/

Unit Vocabulary

actual (adj)	/ˈæktʃuəl/
authority (n)	/ əˈθɔrɪti/
behind (prep)	/bɪˈhaɪnd/
boost (v)	/bust/
carnival (n)	/ˈkɑrnɪvəl/
choir (n)	/kwaɪər/
claim (v)	/kleɪm/
comedy club (n)	/ˈkɒmɪdi ˌklʌb/
commitment (n)	/kəˈmɪtmənt/
confidence (n)	/ˈkɒnfɪdəns
construction (n)	/kənˈstrʌkʃən/
costume (n)	/ˈkɒstum/
creation (n)	/kriˈeɪʃən/
creativity (n)	/ˌkrieɪˈtɪvɪti/
demolish (v)	/dɪˈmɒlɪʃ/
desperate (adj)	/ˈdɛspərɪt/
discipline (n)	/ˈdɪsəplɪn/
dramatic (adj)	/drəˈmætɪk/
duration (n)	/dʊˈreɪʃən/
economist (n)	/ɪˈkɒnəmɪst/
economy (n)	/ɪˈkɒnəmi/
emphasize (v)	/ˈɛmfəˌsaɪz/
engagement (n)	/ɛnˈgeɪdʒmənt/
expression (n)	/ɪkˈsprɛʃən/
factor (n)	/ˈfæktər/
fatal (adj)	/ˈfeɪtəl/
festival (n)	/ˈfɛstɪvəl/
figure out (phr v)	/ˈfɪgjər ˈaʊt/
found (v)	/faʊnd/
foundation (n)	/faʊnˈdeɪʃən/
fulfill (v)	/fʊlˈfɪl/
gallery (n)	/ˈgæləri/
gang (n)	/gæŋ/
generate (v)	/ˈdʒɛnəˌreɪt/
impact (n)	/ˈɪmpækt/
income (n)	/ˈɪnkʌm/
industrial (adj)	/ɪnˈdʌstriəl/
initially (adv)	/ɪˈnɪʃəli/
inspiration (n)	/ˌɪnspəˈreɪʃən/
lead to (phr v)	/ˈlid tu/
literally (adv)	/ˈlɪtərəli/
mayor (n)	/meɪər/
minister (n)	/ˈmɪnɪstər/
minority (n)	/mɪˈnɔrɪti/
museum (n)	/mjuˈziəm/
official (adj)	/əˈfɪʃəl/
organizer (n)	/ˈɔrgəˌnaɪzər/
parade (n)	/pəˈreɪd/
physical (adj)	/ˈfɪzɪkəl/
poverty (n)	/ˈpɒvərti/
pride (n)	/praɪd/
private company (n)	/ˈpraɪvɪt ˈkʌmpəni/
process (n)	/ˈprɒsɛs/
professional (n)	/prəˈfɛʃənl/
public art (n)	/ˈpʌblɪk ˈɑrt/
redevelopment (n)	/ˌridɪˈvɛləpmənt/
rehearse (v)	/rɪˈhɜrs/
reject (v)	/rɪˈdʒɛkt/
relic (n)	/ˈrɛlɪk/
remarkable (adj)	/rɪˈmɑrkəbəl/
rhythm (n)	/ˈrɪðəm/
run over (phr v)	/ˈrʌn ˈoʊvər/
sell out (phr v)	/ˈsɛl ˈaʊt/
signal (v)	/ˈsɪgnl/
skilled (adj)	/skɪld/
stand for (phr v)	/ˈstænd fɔr/
straightforward process (phrase)	/ˌstreɪtˈfɔrwərd ˈprɒsɛs/
struggling (adj)	/ˈstrʌgəlɪŋ/
supposedly (adv)	/səˈpoʊzɪdli/
take charge (phr v)	/ˈteɪk ˈʧɑrʤ/
theater (n)	/ˈθiətər/
venue (n)	/ˈvɛnju/
violence (n)	/ˈvaɪələns/
vital (adj)	/ˈvaɪtl/
viewer (n)	/ˈvjuər/
volunteer (n)	/ˌvɒlənˈtɪər/
widely (adv)	/ˈwaɪdli/

Extension

arrangement (n)	/əˈreɪnʤmənt/
book launch (n)	/bʊk lɔnʧ/
composer (n)	/kəmˈpoʊzər/
conductor (n)	/kənˈdʌktər/
conservatory (n)	/kənˈsɜrvətɔri/
exhibition hall (n)	/ˌɛksəˈbɪʃən hɔl/
gig (n)	/gɪg/
independent cinema (n)	/ˌɪndɪˈpɛndənt ˈsɪnəmə/
jazz (n)	/ʤæz/
musical (n)	/ˈmjuzɪkəl/
open mic (n)	/ˈoʊpən maɪk/
poetry reading (n)	/ˈpoʊətri ˈrɛdɪŋ/
recital (n)	/rəˈsaɪtəl/
stand-up comedy (n)	/stænd ʌp ˈkɑmədi/
street performance (n)	/strit pərˈfɔrməns/

Vocabulary Building

diverse social background (col)	/dɪˈvɜrs ˈsoʊʃəl ˈbækˌgraʊnd/
driving ambition (col)	/ˈdraɪvɪŋ æmˈbɪʃən/
hard work (col)	/ˈhɑrd ˈwɜrk/
innovative program (col)	/ɪnəˌveɪtɪv ˈproʊˌgræm/
leading orchestra (col)	/ˈlidɪŋ ˈɔrkɪstrə/
low income (col)	/ˈloʊ ˈɪnkʌm/
mixed results (col)	/ˈmɪkst rɪˈzʌlts/
strict set (col)	/ˈstrɪkt ˈsɛt/

Vocabulary in Context

assume (v)	/əˈsum /
behind (prep)	/bɪˈhaɪnd/
engagement (n)	/ɛnˈgeɪʤmənt/

figure out (phr v)	/ˈfɪgjər aʊt/
relic (n)	/ˈrɛlɪk /
run over (v)	/rʌn ˈoʊvər /

UNIT 5

Review

access (v)	/ˈæk,sɛs/
connect (v)	/kəˈnɛkt/
curious (adj)	/ˈkjʊriəs/
data (n)	/ˈdeɪtə/
discover (v)	/dɪˈskʌvər/
equip (v)	/ɪˈkwɪp/
equipment (n)	/ɪˈkwɪpmənt/
examine (v)	/ɪgˈzæmɪn/
explain (v)	/ɪkˈspleɪn/
hacker (n)	/ˈhækər/
proof (n)	/pruf/
results (n)	/rɪˈzʌlts/
search (v)	/sɜrʧ/
software developer (n)	/ˈsɔf,twɛr dɪˈvɛləpər/
solution (n)	/səˈluʃən/
technology (n)	/tɛkˈnɑləʤi/

Unit Vocabulary

alter (v)	/ˈɔltər/
arm (v)	/ɑrm/
assignment (n)	/əˈsaɪnmənt/
beautiful (adj)	/ˈbjutəfəl/
belief (n)	/bɪˈlif/
bother (v)	/ˈbɒðər/
browser (n)	/ˈbraʊzər/
bubble (n)	/ˈbʌbəl/
bulb (n)	/bʌlb/
capacity (n)	/kəˈpæsɪti/
chemical (n)	/ˈkɛmɪkəl/
circumstance (n)	/ˈsɜrkəm,stæns/
conduct (v)	/kənˈdʌkt/
consume (v)	/kənˈsum/
cooperation (n)	/koʊ,ɒpəˈreɪʃən/
cooperative (adj)	/koʊˈɒpərətɪv/
curiosity (n)	/,kjʊəriˈɒsɪti/
deadline (n)	/ˈdɛd,laɪn/
determining (adv)	/dɪˈtɜrmɪnɪŋ/
discovery (n)	/dɪˈskʌvəri/
dissolve (v)	/dɪˈzɒlv/
dominant (adj)	/ˈdɒmɪnənt/
downwards (adv)	/ˈdaʊnwərdz/
effective (adj)	/ɪˈfɛktɪv/
electrical (adj)	/iˈlɛktrɪkəl/
embrace (v)	/ɛmˈbreɪs/
engage (v)	/ɛnˈgeɪdʒ/
evidence (n)	/ˈɛvɪdəns/
function (n)	/ˈfʌŋkʃən/
genius (n)	/ˈdʒiniəs/
grasp (n)	/græsp/
helpful (adj)	/ˈhɛlpfəl/
hopeful (adj)	/ˈhoʊpfəl/
identify (v)	/aɪˈdɛntə,faɪ/
imaginative (adj)	/ɪˈmædʒənətɪv/
increasingly (adv)	/ɪnˈkrisɪŋli/
innovation (n)	/,ɪnəˈveɪʃən/
innovative (adj)	/ˈɪnə,veɪtɪv/
intelligence (n)	/ɪnˈtɛlɪdʒəns/
journal (n)	/ˈdʒɜrnl/
labor (n)	/ˈleɪbər/
lid (n)	/lɪd/
link (n)	/lɪŋk/
listener (n)	/ˈlɪsənər/
make matters worse (phrase)	/ˈmeɪk ˈmætərz ˈwɜrs/
mark (v)	/mɑrk/
mature (v)	/məˈtʃʊər/
mechanical (adj)	/mɪˈkænɪkəl/
medical (adj)	/ˈmɛdɪkəl/
mode (n)	/moʊd/
movement (n)	/ˈmuvmənt/
myth (n)	/mɪθ/
network (n)	/ˈnɛt,wɜrk/
place (v)	/pleɪs/
pleasurable (adj)	/ˈplɛʒərəbəl/
pleasure (n)	/ˈplɛʒər/
practical (adj)	/ˈpræktɪkəl/
previously (adv)	/ˈpriviəsli/
ray (n)	/reɪ/
reaction (n)	/riˈækʃən/
reference (n)	/ˈrɛfərəns/
release (v)	/rɪˈlis/
researcher (n)	/rɪˈsɜrtʃər/
return (v)	/rɪˈtɜrn/
reward (n)	/rɪˈwɔrd/
sample (n)	/ˈsæmpəl/
scan (n)	/skæn/
social (adj)	/ˈsoʊʃəl/
society (n)	/səˈsaɪəti/
sophisticated (adj)	/səˈfɪstɪ,keɪtɪd/
submit (v)	/səbˈmɪt/
substance (n)	/ˈsʌbstəns/
surgeon (n)	/ˈsɜrdʒən/
surgery (n)	/ˈsɜrdʒəri/
surround (v)	/səˈraʊnd/
survey (n)	/ˈsɜrveɪ/
theory (n)	/ˈθɪəri/
threat (n)	/θrɛt/
transform (v)	/trænsˈfɔrm/
transparent (adj)	/trænsˈpærənt/
tremendous (adj)	/trəˈmɛndəs/
ultimate (adj)	/ˈʌltəmɪt/
uncertainty (n)	/ʌnˈsɜrtənti/
use (n)	/jus/
useful (adj)	/ˈjusfəl/
voice (n)	/vɔɪs/

Extension

conduct (v)	/ˈkɑndʌkt/
disprove (v)	/dɪˈspruv/
experiment (n)	/ɪkˈspɛrəmənt/
formulate (v)	/ˈfɔrmjə,leɪt/
hypothesis (n)	/haɪˈpɑθəsəs/
perform (v)	/pərˈfɔrm/
set up (v)	/sɛt ʌp/
test (v)	/tɛst/

Vocabulary Building

adaptive (adj)	/əˈdæptɪv/
beautiful (adj)	/ˈbjutəfəl/
curious (adj)	/ˈkjʊriəs/
effective (adj)	/ɪˈfɛktɪv/
helpful (adj)	/ˈhɛlpfəl/
hopeful (adj)	/ˈhoʊpfəl/
imaginative (adj)	/ɪˈmæʤənətɪv/
innovative (adj)	/ˈɪnə,veɪtɪv/
treatable (adj)	/ˈtritəbəl/

Vocabulary in Context

a voice (n)	/ə vɔɪs/
adapt (v)	/əˈdæpt/
bother (v)	/ˈbɑðər/
link (n)	/lɪŋk/
reward (n)	/rɪˈwɔrd/
surrounded (v)	/səˈraʊndəd/